# TURNING THE TIDE:
# ACCESS AND EDUCATIONAL
# DISADVANTAGE

*The Social Purposes of Higher Education*

David Davies

# Contents

Access and widening participation: the promise of learning
for diversity, creativity and transformation.

# Acknowledgements

A lifetime's thanks are due to Professor Sheila Allen of Bradford University who mentored generations of social science students. Access and social justice was in in her DNA. Stuart Bentley was a close friend and comrade to many of us in a remarkable social science department which provided a challenging 'university education' for the 68 generation.

In Northern Ireland: Joanna McMinn, Paul and Marie Nolan, Mick and Fiona Cox, Gordon McIntyre, Liam and Brigid McAnoy, Tom Lovett, Gill Kay, Jean Barr.

In Liverpool and Manchester: Emer Clarke-Davies, Deborah Thornton, Jane Cowell, Aubrey Black, David Moore, Alan and Lesley Fowler, Gus John, Roger Armstrong, Noel Boaden, Graham Davies, Keith Robinson, Gideon Ben Tovim, Gerry Cordon, Fredericke Hayes, Dave Robertson, John Moores junior, Baroness Seear, Waltraud and Mike Boxall, and the Liverpool Access Course tutors and students.

In Cambridge: Vanessa Nedderman, Mike Richardson, Dick Wheeler, Shelley Lockwood, Sue Osthuizen, Sarah Ormrod, Gaie Davidson and Frank Burnett, Colin Greenhalgh, Peter Jarvis, Gina and Alistair Wisker.

In Wales and the Lake District: the marvellous Sandra Sherwood, Keith Evans, Keith McDonagh, Clayton Heycock, Lord Frank Judd and Chris Judd and the indomitable Jack Rice who taught me more about education than he knew.

In Leicester, Birmingham and Derby: Fran Dooher, Sir Christopher Ball, Roger Waterhouse, David Jary, Stuart Watson, Jim Nyland, David Gray, Deborah Outhwaite, Lynn Basford, Chris Howard, Michael Kreindler, Reem Shamshoom, Maysoon Khalaily, Sister Teresa Kennedy.

Special thanks are due for more than half a lifetime's friendship and support from Irene Dooher, Dave and Chris Broadbent, Richard and Rachel Teare, Lee Solomon, Stuart Martin, Ulrike and Reinhard Poeschl; to my brother Tom and Marion, my cousins Carole, Hazel and Paula and families, and the Murphy and Browne families which I joined some 35 years ago. It would be remiss not to mention my family readers, so thank you Alan, Finola, James, Philip, Nick, Jacky, Brigid, Josie, Claire, Paul, Ellie and Nicky.

Thank you to the indefatigable Hans and Jutta Tuschar in the lovely Bodental Valley in Austria for friendship and guidance up mountains and to new horizons- Gluckauf, and to Sisse Rausch for talks and shared books; to Elli Laussegger and family and Guy and Patrycja Dessoy for being our good neighbours and friends. And in memory of our friend Maureen Newrick who also knew the mountains of Carinthia and for Ian and Jane Copeland, friends and mentors to us both.

And most of all to Emer who lovingly helped me through thick and thin in all the challenges we met together, from Liverpool Access courses to the places far beyond. This book is for you.

**David Davies – Chichester and Bodental 2023**

# Introduction

This book is about Access to higher education and learning and pivots between two separate but connected eras- the 1970/80s and the 2000s. The best part of 50 years- almost the length of my working life and career in education. The focus is mainly on Britain but examples from other societies and cultures are relevant to its themes, especially those of the USA and Australia. This was the time when mass higher education became the norm. Higher education went from an exclusive club of elite university institutions with medieval practices and outlooks, answerable mainly to themselves and serving a self-selecting elite from the upper classes of British society, to being a visible presence in towns and cities across the land and accessible for a majority of the people.

The focus of the book is analytical rather than descriptive and it relies on the social analysis of Access as a movement of learners and teachers rather than on a detailed narrative or history of specific institutions or type of access course. To signal this distinction Access is written in the higher case with apologies given for the elision and combining of so many different types of learning which contributed to this sense of a movement for educational change.

Access was the name given to courses which aimed to improve the learning and lives of ordinary working people and groups who had been excluded for no good reason from the opportunities to learn at higher levels. There had been a long history of struggles for knowledge and learning in Britain and many innovative and inspiring examples had emerged over time in each of the nation regions of the United Kingdom of Great Britain and Northern Ireland. However, it is the contention of this book that what appeared to be a fundamental *transformation* in the educational and life chances of ordinary British people, was in fact a *reconstruction* of forms of privilege, inequality and educational disadvantage. Yet there can be no doubt that Access signalled change and gave expression to a widely perceived need for higher education to be made available to a widening population. Following the Second World War social change and reform impacted across much of British society. Core industries and public services were nationalised, a National Health Service was set up, publicly-funded social housing was expanded and education came to be viewed as a means of social mobility and opportunity. Compulsory secondary schooling up to the age of 16 and an expansion of grammar schools and universities had taken place by the 1970s and there was popular support for comprehensive schooling. These trends in British social and cultural life became apparent as the post-war economic expansion appeared to be coming to an end and we entered a transitional era of economic decline and social disruption in the 1970s and 1980s. This was a time of change and transition for the whole society as deindustrialisation took firm hold of economic life and Britain's population became ever more mixed and multicultural. The stresses and tensions of life in post- industrial *and* post-colonialist Britain were becoming ever more apparent and society appeared to be taking a destructive path with social-industrial strife and racial tensions erupting periodically. Yet it was also a time of rising expectations when social inequality was mitigated by policies designed to increase opportunities and spread wealth, such as the increase in home ownership when social housing was privatised and sold to its tenants. It was a time of social and cultural change also when new ways of behaving, of sexual freedoms and of the possibilities of new identities for some were realised. Education was a crucial part of this mixture as a discourse emerged around the need to remove 'barriers to access'. A more egalitarian higher education was viewed as part of a rising tide of social equality and change. Access courses played an important part in 'Turning the Tide' on educational disadvantage. It was known that accessing knowledge was both a survival strategy and a means for changing a dysfunctional and highly unequal society into something better.

What was not known, as the 1970s came to its end, was the impending impact of globalisation and an era of neoliberalism in economic and geo-political life across the industrialised world. Change was accelerated as nations competed in this new world order which coincided with the invention of digital economies and surveillance capitalism along with the rise of China as the major world manufacturer of consumer goods. Britain became attached to the notion of being a 'service economy' where finance capital and services would be paramount. From having been the workshop of the world, Britain became 'cool Britannia', the purveyor of soft power and cultural experiences to anyone who would pay attention and buy such services. This was not without some success as by 2020 it was widely claimed (in Britain) that the UK was the world's fifth largest economy. By the mid-1980s the conservatives in Britain were benefitting from a global upswing and were constructing a new economic model based on cheap credit replacing high wages, mass home ownership and share ownership. Those who owned assets and property benefitted the most with asset price inflation built in. Eventually the financial elite would be able to cut themselves off from the fate of ordinary people, socially and educationally.

The Access movement occurred at precisely the time globalisation and cosmopolitanism was taking off though the *systemic* change that was about to impact was less easily discerned. At the point of *felt* and *lived* experience for its students and teachers Access was an engagement for a democratising public higher education. Its curriculum, generally if not universally, contested systemic discrimination based on racism, on sexism and on social class. It was a recognition that individuals lived and worked in communities and had collective interests which could not be met by simple self-advancement for talented individuals for whom 'meritocracy' might offer a route up and out of their circumstances. Access was a route to a better social outcome. It was a demand for change whilst accepting that those demands were within an elitist and relatively closed system. It was a countervailing movement to a dominant belief in the power of meritocracy and simultaneously it was incorporated within an expanding further and higher education system which offered enhanced opportunities to an increasingly diverse population.

The pivot in this book concerns the nature of Access some 50 years after the foundation period when it was faced with, albeit unrecognised, the on-coming neoliberal and globalising era. In the third decade of the 21st century we are facing another era with grave problems and challenges. The failures in globalism, the existential issues of climate change and global warming, the persistently embedded racism and social inequalities and injustices in our communities, the move to the digital world of communication and control, the presence of devastating global health pandemics and the threat of war and nuclear destruction all challenge us to find a better way of knowing and an improved way of learning. We need an education system and culture which is fit for purpose to meet the challenge of change. In other words, we are confronted with the dire need to find an education and curriculum to meet this overwhelming sense of systemic change and its threats to our sheer existence. If the original concept of Access was concerned with democratising higher education and producing critical thinking, then how much more relevant is that concern now that we are faced with the possible extinction of our planet as a viable place for humans to live. Access in its past guise implicitly challenged the existence of elitism and social division in our society as a necessary step towards social progress, equity and social justice. If education is to make its contribution to a new and progressive social contract which fits us to deal with the issues facing us today, then it must make its public purpose clear. The Access agenda for social transformation is still necessary and never more needed than in the third decade of the 21$^{st}$ century and beyond.

Chapters 1, 2 and 3 outline the social and historical background of Access, especially in its concern for social justice issues for black and ethnic minority communities and the removal of barriers to access for many working class people, including women. Access like mass higher education, of which it was a part, transcended social class and offered opportunities to study to all. However, as with earlier generations of adult learners, aspiring and middle class people were often able to benefit most. This provided a tension between the potentially contrasting purposes of Access- whether to place people within a competitive system so they can compete on equal terms or to transform the system to a fairer and more just basis? The book argues that Access should be seen as an attempt to find and construct alternative knowledge around the themes and issues that bedevilled communities of disadvantage. It was more than just another type of provision or course; it was in fact an incipient *movement,* capable of turning the tide on educational disadvantage. New and different methods of learning and pedagogy were needed for this enterprise and an engagement with the pervasive ideas of individual upward social mobility through education was required. In the wider and conservative social and political reality of the period, social mobility through meritocracy (for the very bright) was substituted for widening participation *as a social purpose* and the 'free market' was designated as the means of achieving this. A changing world meanwhile was being forged by the processes of globalisation and digitalisation. Between 1983 and 1986 the banking and finance industries in Britain experienced a massive round of deregulation which transformed Britain into an international financial centre and , 20 years later, the epicentre of the world's financial and banking crash and crisis. Chapters 4, 5 and 6 explore respectively the impact of neoliberalism as a social philosophy impacting on education, the significance of race and racism in Access provision and the role of new institutions- the short-lived open colleges - in sponsoring educational opportunity. The pivot from the historical Access movement to the present appears again at Chapter 7 which assesses the idea of critical thinking for the educational challenges facing us whilst chapter 8 outlines some potential ideas for 'frameworks' to provide points of departure for our future thinking. The final two chapters draw some conclusions about the changes we have seen across the period of the Access movement and the changed prospects for the future in which education can be transformative. However, attention is drawn to the co-existence of mass higher education and the continuing privileges of elite selection which do so much to distort and disfigure social justice and equality in our society.

Access is explored here as a movement for change and as an example of what have been called 'threads through time' which suggests there are interconnections between what we were when Access became a movement for educational change and what we are still seeking to become. The connections can be discovered in the methods, the ideas and the concepts we use to learn, to know, to assess and to judge the problems and issues facing us. These issues have become ever more *existential* as we face (potentially) extinction events through ecological and human-made disasters such as nuclear war and climate change. A different education with different learning was never more direly needed. Access can teach us something critically relevant to our need to change ourselves and the world in which we must live.

In a world still characterised by divisions and differences and still marked by forms of oppression and injustice, learning and education in general does not decline in importance. Access was an encounter with historic inequality which occurred at a particular time and place in British history. Inequality, injustice and oppression, which this book argues were ultimately in its sights, may in fact be the continuing threads through time which link the narratives of the 20th and 21st centuries. The terms of this encounter have changed over time, which nobody can seriously deny, however, the challenge remains and we need learning for progressive social change above all.

Accessing the ivory towers of the academy

# Chapter 1

# Access Education: an Agenda for Change

## What was Access?

In the world of education, the term 'Access' referred to courses and learning which had been specifically designed to get non-traditional students into universities and higher education colleges. From the 1970s through to the 1990s most of these courses were actually located in vocational further education colleges which were owned and controlled at that time by local education authorities. Many of these, though primarily starting out as technical and vocational colleges, saw themselves as part of their local and regional adult and community education provision. They were proud of their local civic connections and neighbourhoods (Davies 1997).

This was anyway a period of change and disruption in the UK's education systems: most secondary schools in Britain became comprehensives at this time. The British manufacturing industry and its apprenticeship system was beginning to breakdown as the country was transformed from a manufacturing economy into a neoliberal service economy under successive conservative governments; the nature and sheer availability of work came under scrutiny as unemployment rocketed in the 1980s and employment patterns shifted. Mining, heavy engineering, ship-building, motor manufacturing, textile manufacturing, locomotive engineering-the prime bases of Britain's industrial past were in severe decline. The 1980s saw industrial disputes between organised labour and governments reach new levels of internecine bitterness. The privatisation of nearly all the UK's public services was either underway or was being contemplated by the conservative governments of the time. The provision of gas, water, electricity, railways, local bus transport, social housing, social care of old and ill people and all manner of public services were included as well as that of post-school education. Inequality surged in the 1980s and Britain's Gini coefficient as its measure rose from 25 to 35 per cent and has remained there ever since (Mason 2022). In the meanwhile Britain had joined the European Union most of which had adopted a rather different approach to what they called a social-market economy which stressed the need for consensus and co-option of different interests so as to ensure long term growth and an integrated social result within a single market for goods, services and labour.

In education the Open University (OU) made a notable exception to the rule that higher education was only for those who had made a success of their school careers. From the early 1970s the OU demonstrated that thousands benefitted from a university education who had no entry qualifications except their desire to learn and their motivation to achieve a degree. There was a clear focus here on objectives for learning, a definitive curriculum, a highly organised study and assessment regime and student support at a distance and face-to-face for adult learners the like of which had never been seen in Britain- or possibly anywhere (Weinbrenn 2014).

If the Open University showed what could be achieved for masses of unqualified adults at degree level, the sheer range and variety of adult education that was available below that level almost defies description. Since the 19th century and earlier many different types and strands of adult education had been successfully developed. Across the UK, university extra-mural education by the mid-1990s had accumulated over 120 years of provision since Cambridge had begun its courses in 1873. Working class and labour movements had struggled for generations to establish learning and really useful knowledge for working people (Johnson 1988; McIlroy 1996). Churches, cooperatives and charities had established schools and colleges to spread literacy and enlightenment to the common people alongside struggles for political enfranchisement. Community education had its own contested history (Fieldhouse 1996: 126-127) and was a major player in providing alternative learning opportunities for the marginalised. In 1984 the Educational Centres Association members catered for 400,000 students whilst some 100,000 students attended courses in residential adult education colleges and centres. Millions of people were involved in one way or another in learning and adult education, and it is fair to say that many had struggled to define their needs and to get access to learning opportunities beyond compulsory schooling. For three quarters of the 19th century in fact there was no compulsory schooling but there was always a demand for learning and greater knowledge from the common people (Roberts 1976). By the mid- 20th century a whole set of terms had been invented to embrace these forms of education, including community education, recurrent education, lifelong learning and continuing education. Many different types of learning 'institutions' were created some of which were voluntary associations whilst the State's role in post-school learning was to grow as the 20th century proceeded.

Access then was part of a burgeoning growth of learning that was both part of local authority and state provision of what was effectively second chance education for adults and an expression of a long suppressed desire for opportunities through learning leading to university qualifications. There was no single ideological purpose driving Access. There was an abundance of public and private schemes which were designed to serve a range of social, cultural and political objectives. Some were utilitarian such as schemes to open access to social work and nursing for ethnic groups. Access courses were originally established in the 1970s with the Inner London Education Authority playing a leading role. A significant concern was the wish to encourage more non-traditional mature students to become teachers, especially in the inner-city areas where black youth were viewed as being in rebellion against school. Some courses were focussed on personal and recreational development for individuals motivated to study in higher education, some were linked and cooperative ventures between FE colleges and adult centres and local universities and polytechnics. Liverpool, for example, had a variety of access courses across its FE and Adult Education services including a Black Access to Business Course sponsored by the Littlewoods business empire and the local Chamber of Commerce with close links to two major Liverpool universities. This diversity was accompanied by no less a variety of approaches to teaching and learning and course content, though most stressed the need for high degrees of literacy and numeracy. There were day courses, part-time and full-time courses, evening classes, correspondence classes, distance learning schemes, study groups, week-end and longer term residential courses. The students on access courses were a heterogeneous group (QAA 2015; Busher and James 2018). All manner of people felt they had been excluded from further and higher education and from the 1970s onwards education and further learning was widely thought to be the key route to a better life and future. From this eclectic mixture of 'second chance' provision and the varied motivations and aspirations of its learners the features of an Access movement could be made out. It represented a desire for more opportunity and was a challenge to the existing educational order whose higher education had for generations been more concerned with selecting out and excluding the common people and producing a self-perpetuating elite, than widening access and opportunities for the many.

## How many Access students were there?

At the start of the twentieth century in the United Kingdom, there were 29,000 full-time students in higher education (HE) and by 1960 this had risen to 180,000 (Edwards 1984). Considerable growth occurred in the period between 1960 and 1970 and the number of full-time and full-time equivalent students in HE was 446,000 in 1970. In 1984, the number had risen to 677,000 (DES 1984). By 1979, 12.7 per cent of the 18 and 19 year old cohort were participating in higher education, and by 1986 this had risen to 13.7 per cent of the cohort (TES 22.8.1986).

In 1970-71, almost 21 per cent of the home (UK) initial entrants to HE were mature students and in 1983-84, this had risen to just over 23 per cent. A governmental DES (Department of Education and Science) report expected that the proportion of mature entry students would rise to 30 per cent by 1996-97 (DES Report 100 1984). In August 1984, the Council for National Academic Awards (CNAA) reported that of the mature entry students, 4.5 per cent were considered to be non-standard entry. Access students would presumably be considered as part of this group. However, the figure may not be accurate because there were definitional issues about what were non-standard entrants and data returns for HE institutions were not complete.

What was beyond all doubt was the fact that there was a large pent up demand for learning from adults in the last quarter of the 20th century. The younger generations were likewise demanding access to higher education as social and economic change removed traditional routes to jobs and occupations. Modernity was impacting on Britain in unanticipated ways and few people had predicted the massive expansion and exponential growth of education as the basis of an emerging knowledge economy. Together with the impact that computerisation and digitalisation was about to have on so many forms of work and employment there was an explosion into possibility that the revolution in information technology was bringing to everyday lives and work. As a result and at the same time, a profound shift took place in the public's perception of what was needed to succeed in the competition for skills, qualifications and ultimately the pathway to a decent life in British society. Education was of course a key, especially for those people who had little or no access to wealth or social and cultural capital. The growth of unprecedented further and higher education provision at low or no cost to the student was to prove crucial for current and future growth and prospects, as were the ever increasing demands from many varied sections of the population for the removal of the barriers to access to higher education (Edwards 1984; Eggins 1988).

The CNAA reported in October 1984 that there were 145 Access courses and 37,500 Access students. A DES sponsored evaluation of Access provision between 1979 and 1983 identified that 54 per cent of the students were from Caribbean backgrounds, 32 per cent were White British and 5 per cent Asian. In addition, 63 per cent of students were from skilled manual and non-manual classes (Millins 1984). An Inspectorate report in September1984 of ILEA (Inner London Education Authority) Access courses in London found that two-thirds of the students were women; 42 per cent of the total students were West Indian women; 11.8 per cent West Indian men; and 29.4 per cent White British. The great majority of these students came from the bottom three social classes. Access was serving the needs of black people, ethnic minorities and most certainly of many women regardless of ethnic origins who had found no other way to succeed in education. For many who came forward Access was not a second chance to learn but was in effect their *first* chance to study for entry to higher education.

Access was both a description of a type of course and a concept of learning. Many of the courses were focussed on generic learning skills and study in a range of subject knowledge areas including social sciences, arts and humanities and science and technology (QAA ibid). Some had vocational outcomes such as nursing, midwifery and social work. Learning on Access courses was intensive and most courses lasted an academic year. In the later phases of Access the courses led to an Access to Higher Education Diploma and these were awarded by regional award validating agencies for vocational education in England and Wales which were regulated by the QAA- the Quality Assurance Agency for Higher Education. By 2015 there were still over 40,000 students a year studying on Access courses, 60 per cent of whom were 'mature' that is over the age of 25. The majority of these, 74 per cent, were women, and 38 per cent came from deprived circumstances (QAA ibid: 1). Access, some 40 years after its inception as a distinctive entity, was still serving the needs of second chance learners many of whom had left school at 16 years of age to work or who had simply under-achieved in their school careers and failed to get qualifications necessary to enter higher education. As already noted levels of social and economic inequality from the 1980s into the 2020s remained high and the tide of educational disadvantage was running high though its forms and effects also mutated as Britain's population and class structure underwent change (Savage 2015).

By the mid-1980s a plethora of Access courses was available across the country. Barriers to learning and educational achievement were being removed as it became clear that there was a huge demand for higher education that the educational reforms of schooling and universities of the 1960s and 1970s had not met. The conservatism of the traditional universities was to be expected- their role had been to select and sort those deemed to be fit for higher education and to exclude those who had failed to achieve the entry requirements. However, the role of traditional adult education, some of it focussed on vocational or occupational concerns, some of it in the university extra-mural world focussed on liberal adult education for personal satisfaction and cultural enjoyment, was also 'conservative' and failed to address the emerging new learning needs of very large numbers of people who had had no possibility of university level learning. The Robbins Report in 1963 called for an expansion in higher education so that all those who were qualified by ability and attainment and wished to pursue higher education, should be able to do so (Fulton 1981: 5). The report admitted that over the three previous decades more than a million adults had qualified for university entry, thus acknowledging the immense pool of untapped ability in the nation. The greatest waste of talent was amongst the working classes whose access to learning opportunities had been severely restricted historically. The Robbins Committee reported that approximately six times as many children from non-manual homes gained places in higher education as compared with those from unskilled manual homes (Dean 1985: 16). A. H. Halsey, a notable sociologist of education, and his collaborators suggested in 1980 that for a student from a working class home to enter university he had to be on average 6.6 IQ points higher than someone from a service-class home. The desired increase in demand for higher education from working class children anticipating the introduction of comprehensive schools did not fully materialise. The majority of even grammar school 'successes' left school at the earliest possible date leaving only a small minority to complete A level GCEs and go on to university or college. However, Robbins had somehow opened Pandora's Box and the 1960s saw a significant expansion of higher education, though Robbins assumed that the vast majority of the new students would attend a university rather than any other type of HE institution. The key decision in the 1960s was to develop a substantial non-university sector of higher education from the existing local authority colleges. The polytechnic sector was born and by the middle of the 1980s the majority of higher education students were enrolled in non-university institutions (Fowler and Wyke 1993: 109). This sector was to be given a more explicit commercial and applied philosophy by successive Conservative governments and in 1992 the binary system was abolished as polytechnics became universities.

The 1970s and 1980s experienced the development of a new system of higher education which was totally different from that anticipated by Robbins. It was a mass HE system on a scale far greater than imagined by earlier generations. Within a single lifespan of say 60 years from 1960, more than 160 universities were established, ¾ of the total of UK universities (Scott 2021: 2). It was, however, a centralised system with financial power and control vested in controlling governmental agencies and after 1992 with no place for elected local authorities which had done so much to create many of the new institutions which were now universities (Fowler and Wyke ibid).This was not the system of relatively autonomous and independent universities intended by Robbins but it seemed to offer the possibility of a different system of higher education, accessible to the community and closer to the world of work and industry. The dangers at the time of merging two systems, the university model and the non-university colleges, was noted in 1965 when the education minister Anthony Crosland warned against creating a hierarchical system with universities at the top and the colleges as second-class institutions (Fowler and Wyke ibid: 113). The transmutation of the polytechnics into a 'separate but equal' sector of higher education (the binary system) was to last until 1992 when the unified university sector was decreed by the Conservative minister of education. But this new unified body had little unity of purpose or philosophy for the multiplying number of institutions that were now universities. It quickly became an hierarchical system with little sense of common purpose where social needs and social justice and social purposes were concerned. Nevertheless in the period of its existence the polytechnic sector greatly facilitated the Access movement in its development. The older local authority colleges and the new polytechnics were still far ahead of the old and new universities in addressing the educational needs of ordinary citizens.

## Access as an opportunity for adult learners

Most Access courses in the founding period of the late 1970s and 1980s were in fact partnerships between providers- including many further education (FE) colleges and adult learning centres– and 'receiving' institutions such as universities, polytechnics and colleges of higher education. Universities were notionally independent from direct government control as were teacher training colleges, though all were dependent on government finance. FE and adult education providers were generally speaking owned and controlled by local authorities and had at least an element of local democratic accountability in their makeup. Partnership meant joint involvement in course design, student selection, the assessment of standards and sometimes joint teaching and examining (Parry 1986: 45). Students offered a place on an Access course were usually offered at the same time a place on a linked higher education course, conditional on their successfully completing the Access course. The HE institution usually had a role in monitoring and evaluating the results of the course and later an 'open college' might have undertaken this role on a collaborative basis. Since students often had 'failed' in their earlier learning great care was taken to deliver success for these students. Careful diagnosis of potential, sensitive interviewing and systematic and sustained counselling and study support were provided in order to ensure that students' intentions and ambitions matched what was on offer.

## Adult education and Access

At the time Access courses were developing in the late 1970s and 1980s the links between further, higher and adult providers, though tenuous and uncoordinated beyond the local level, might have signalled the possibility of breaking the rigid and hierarchical divisions of status and reputation between continuing and second chance education for adults and the university sector. The Access movement indicated the possibility of a move towards a more formal relationship between sectors, but the Access courses were always marginal at this point for the higher level institutions. Though the expansion of mass public sector higher education was underway, the forces driving selection for entry to the elite universities in particular were powerful and were eventually to be responsible for the hierarchical structure of British higher education as it emerged in the 21st century (James 2018). The more 'elitist' the institution considered itself to be, the less likely it was to be involved in the Access movement.

This elitism was compounded in the larger scheme of things by the fact that the adult education movements which had been established for the purpose of assisting the working class in the nineteenth century had failed to reach the broad masses of those people for whom the movement was set up (Fieldhouse ibid: 391). Although adult education had allowed some workers to be incorporated into the middle classes and for some alleviated the impact of factory life and for others helped in their struggles for social justice, it very often was colonised by the middle class who were better able to take advantage of further education opportunities. The twentieth century saw an explosion of education possibilities with the development of both independent working class education and state funded and controlled provision eventually becoming predominant. In spite of the valiant attempts to get education courses and students to focus on radical and transformational change, there is little doubt that much of this educational provision has served in the long term to reconcile working class and educationally deprived people to their apparent fate of being near the bottom of the social hierarchies. For two hundred years, according to Fieldhouse (ibid: 399), 'the single most consistent purpose underpinning much of British adult education was to recruit working class students to its many forms. But in pursuit of this purpose, practice very frequently fell far short of intention'.

## Adult colleges

There had been for long enough special relationships between further and adult education and institutions of higher education. Ruskin College, Oxford may have been the best known with its connections to the trade union movement and its limited yet privileged status within Oxford University. Long-term residential colleges had existed since the end of the 19th century and had been influenced by the Adult School Movement, the Society of Friends (Quakers), the Danish folk high schools and by the Workers Education Association (Fieldhouse ibid: ch 9). Their aim had been broadly to provide opportunities for higher education and sustained study for adult learners whose full-time education had been cut short at an earlier age. Beyond the belief in the validity of learning and perhaps a belief in the idea of active citizenship, they had no real common philosophy or culture but reflected a wide variety of social and religious views and commitments to adult education. These residential colleges existed alongside extra-mural university departments and day colleges which specialised in adult students. The first university to open a department for adult students who were not required to matriculate at the university and therefore could not take degrees was Cambridge in 1873. Oxford and some other universities followed suit and were recognised and funded eventually as 'responsible bodies' through the government's education department. A world of 'extra-mural empires' (Marriott 1984) grew up with strong partnerships with the Workers Education Association (WEA) and many of the adult colleges and local education centres. For the mainstream of university life, however, this was marginal to what they considered to be their core mission- the furtherance of academic scholarship and research. Unqualified adults without formal degrees were unlikely to play a meaningful part in this enterprise.

By the 1960s the underlying purposes of the adult colleges had changed and there was now a focus on enabling working class students to enter higher education so that by the 1970s this was widely seen as the central purposes of these colleges. What the Robbins Report had identified for the wider society in 1963- the need to provide places generally for those qualified to enter HE- was being delivered for some working class people by the adult education colleges. Satisfying though this was, it represented only a small proportion of the potential market for students in the UK. In the universities after the Second World War there was a growth in extra- mural courses as a potentially more meritocratic society emerged. In 1973 the Russell Report (DES 1973) recommended the continuation of government funding for the adult residential colleges and the establishment of a further college in the north of England. As an outcome of the Report the 1975 Education Act introduced mandatory awards for adult college students so they were to be funded on the same basis as undergraduate students. The new Northern College near Barnsley was opened in 1978. The adult liberal education tradition of education for social and personal growth and change, and the challenge it represented to the elitist and exclusionary tradition of university entrance, was carried into the period of change and social transition in the 1970s and 1980s, though for limited numbers. Nevertheless, the adult colleges were in the vanguard of the Access and 'Second Chance' movements (Fieldhouse ibid: 240). These colleges and the extra mural university departments along with the Open University had created an important exception to the rule that only clever and exceptionally talented young people could benefit from the elitist university system. But this was precisely the point- they were the exceptions not the rule and were allowed to co-exist at the margins of the conventional educational system without challenging the central principles and assumptions of a profoundly conservative ruling elite. A vital component of this system was a selective and unfair set of educational institutions that seems to have been designed to polarise people and to stimulate greed and selfishness (Dorling 2018). As the 1980s drew to a close the adult education providers and the conventional universities and polytechnics were faced with a quite different challenge- the onset of *mass* demand for higher education.

## Marketisation and mainstreaming of university adult education

In 1989 the conservative government transferred financial and governance responsibility for university adult education to the newly created Universities Funding Council. This ended the 65 year-old, tripartite relationship between the 23 designated universities which received specific and ear-marked funds for adult education, and the DES and the government's Inspectorate. The result was to change the status of university adult education and to put it into competition with mainstream undergraduate provision with which it now shared a common funding methodology.

Throughout the 1980s the number of courses designed to prepare mature students of all kinds had grown rapidly and exponentially. The Open University expanded to become the largest single institution of higher education in the UK. Mass higher education became a reality for the nation and the transition of the polytechnics to universities, at the literal stroke of a pen by Conservative education minister Ken Clarke in 1992, marked the acceptance of a version of the 'learning society' in which the mass entrance of school leavers to university became the norm. The Tory government was bent on creating what they termed a 'market' for the provision of higher education where universities and colleges could compete for students who were envisaged as customers buying education as a type of commodity as they might any other consumer item. This was probably the point of maximum diversity for the higher education system in the UK. Encouraged by both government and an ideology of educational expansion, many colleges of further and higher education, art colleges, former teacher training colleges, former polytechnics and colleges of technology, specialist drama and music institutions, sought to enhance their status by becoming university institutions or amalgamating with existing ones. In abolishing the 'binary division' between public authority higher education and universities, the 1992 Further and Higher Education Act helped ensure the 'privatisation' of higher education within a unified funding system which differentially rewarded those elite institutions which emerged at the top of the hierarchy. This was no accident but was commensurate with the conservative government's view that a 'free market' in education could be created driven by consumer choice and that accredited learning was in essence a 'positional good' to be purchased by those who invested in it. The government's view was that higher education could become a market in which institutions competed for students and for financial support for research. The competition would be for reputation and on price which would be determined by student choice in a so-called free market for education. The problem with this was of course the market for education was neither a perfect nor a 'free' market. It was in fact a managed and very unequal arena of competition in which some players had massive advantages over others. Under the Act the long term residential colleges were placed in the further education sector and became dependent on the Further Education Funding Council for their public funding and so Access courses became firmly lodged in the FE system as feeders for the universities, which were at this point set on expansion.

The separation of FE-funded Access courses and adult education and students from the Universities themselves was later to have a significant impact on the character and development of mass participation higher education in Britain. The in-coming Labour Government of 1997/98 eventually set itself against the idea of 'mixed institutions' where FE and HE could be planned, taught and developed together within a single institutional setting. Several budding initiatives involving the amalgamation of local universities and FE colleges were abandoned or refused approval from Labour secretaries of state. Access courses had often been instrumental in bringing together FE and HE providers and there was a will to explore different models of higher education in some of the post-1992 new universities (Robertson 1994, 1995; Davies 1997 ibid, 1998; Davies and Davies 2021: ch 8). North American models of community-based 2 year plus 4 year Colleges served as examples of what might be possible in breaking down barriers to access and participation. But this was not to be. Hierarchies of separate status and prestige were to be erected on the frameworks of the old elitist systems and the successive New Labour administrations gave up the chance to introduce a more democratic further and higher education model in favour of a divided FE and HE system which proceeded with privatising and marketising its courses and monetising its students as sources of income (Williams 2013; Vogel 2017). The corporate model of financial and business development became dominant in FE and HE as the supposedly 'free market' in education was developed and expanded. None of this prevented the elitism of private schooling and of selective grammar schools within the English class system from continuing to feed into the selection procedures of the ancient universities and those of the next 'top 20' who sought to emulate them.

The changes in the designation of courses and funding meant that adult education departments in universities nationwide achieved parity with 'normal' degree provision but within a context in which government and some substantial opinion within universities themselves, it must be said, undervalued the rich tradition of liberal adult education. There was concern at this time that the value being placed on vocational and 'continuing education' would mean resources would be directed away from disadvantaged sections of society to business-oriented courses. The notable defender of educational access and equality Labour Peer Lord Frank Judd warned in the House of Lords in February 1993 that adult education was becoming geared to vocationalism at the expense of other forms of education (Judd 1993; Fieldhouse ibid: 230; Davies 2022: 82-83). It was a prescient intervention as subsequent events proved when later in the decade university adult education as a separate entity declined and then ceased to exist as a distinctive education sector.

Innovations did of course not stop in the 1980s and somewhat paradoxically the Access movement continued to grow and prosper- mainly within the new FE sector which especially in the urban areas with high unemployment and challenging social issues responded with an expansion of second chance and issue-based courses. The universities however, tended to become receivers of Access students rather than providers of Access courses though some did become substantial providers linking their courses with four year programmes of study, and generating government funding in the process. The growth of adult learners was quite widely anticipated and for the old polytechnics which became universities after 1992 there was no such thing as extra-mural or adult education as a separate entity. Part-time provision for adults was regarded as part of their mainstream undergraduate and postgraduate teaching. This was a major cultural difference between the new, post-1992 universities and the older extra-mural, liberal education traditions embedded in the designated 'responsible body' sector which came from the ancient and civic universities. Continuing education in universities in general was now fundable only if students were studying for a university award or for credits toward an award (Davies 1996).

The accreditation of university adult education programmes and courses proceeded apace as universities sought to protect their funding income. There was, however, resistance to the change from some teachers who thought it might inhibit critical thought and be less responsive to the variety of motives and purposes of adult learners. Some students simply wanted to continue to study extramurally for their own satisfaction and knowledge, as they had done for generations. It may be the case that accreditation helped universities eliminate sub-standard provision (Fieldhouse ibid: 236) and attract new younger age students who were less well educated than many of the older adult students. A criticism of extra mural courses was that they had historically failed to attract poorly educated working class people including members of ethnic communities. The newly accredited courses could now offer access to degree level study leading to degrees which were a tangible asset in the search for jobs and careers. Such access and opportunities had been closed to those lacking entry qualifications.

## The working class in the USA goes to college

The growth of mass education outside and beyond schooling in the UK almost certainly owed something to developments in the United States of America where vast numbers of people were involved in continuing education (House 1991). The 'community college movement' set up in the USA between 1951 and 1961 for working students recruited millions of adults who would not otherwise have had the opportunity for higher education (Fulton 1981; Shor 1980). Ira Shor argued that the evolving need for lifelong learning and higher education for ALL was, however, not a result of the discovery that learning was a benefit to humankind. The concept of greater access and the provision of available access to higher qualifications was a response to the problem of surplus labour (Shor ibid: 5). His analysis led him to believe that problems of over-production and under-employment in the American economy allowed education to be used to absorb the unemployed workers through the building and construction of colleges, employment within the colleges and by turning workers into students. College gave workers the opportunity to prepare for new careers in a rapidly changing job market. Higher education responded and changed as a result of the influx of working people into the system. It became more flexible and geared towards the needs of the people it served- both potential students and local businesses and government. Courses were modularised and classes arranged on a part-time and full-time basis during the day and in the evening. As a consequence many of those who would not otherwise have received higher education had their expectations raised. This was not to be without its problems though, as Shor argued … 'The job market used to reward college graduates with the best work, prior to the mass arrival of working people into higher education. The occupational hierarchy simply cannot now accommodate the demands of all those who successfully complete college' (ibid: 17). The growth of mass higher education in Britain from the 1980s onwards brought about similar challenges to the status and role of university qualifications which had been developed for the interests of a small minority but now were forced to address the needs of a near majority of every generation that was seeking higher education (Cantwell et al 2018).

For some of those whose aspirations had been raised by higher education there were feelings of frustration, disappointment and alienation. For some social groups in society who were previously under-represented in colleges and universities- especially women and minority ethnic groups- the widening educational franchise helped them to strengthen their identities and consciousness and perhaps contributed to their developing sense of autonomy. The development of lifelong learning and higher education opportunities in the USA was undoubtedly a momentous movement for social progress but it did not succeed, according to Shor, in equalising opportunities for working people with those of the upper classes. It was, undoubtedly, an important factor in helping women and minority groups become more equal with their white male peers.

## On the home front- a conservative social revolution

In the United Kingdom the 1980s saw rising unemployment, especially marked for young working class people and for black youth in the urban centres. Changes in the employment and labour markets as a consequence of neoliberal market reforms and the closure of many industrial concerns brought uncertainty to many working class communities in these years. The reality was that British society and economy was undergoing a transformation. The old industrial economy was being transformed under Thatcherite rules and policies into a service economy; what had been fixed and certain for generations was becoming fluid and insecure. Whole industries across the United Kingdom became redundant seemingly almost overnight and many towns became hollowed out as their traditional employment disappeared. The industrial market economy was being rapidly re-shaped as globalisation and the rapidly developing digital and communications industries expanded, especially in the metropolitan cities. But this was a conservative revolution where change was constant but the underlying realities in respect of its class system, its racial and ethnic distinctions and its discrimination against gender inequalities remained on very familiar terrain. Education was viewed as the key to unlocking the barriers to social mobility and if working class children could get a university place was that not testimony to the new egalitarianism?

The realities were that underneath the radical and rapid transformation of British economy and society in the 1980s and 1990s there was also a great continuity. The unequal and unfair distribution of power and privilege, the spread of poverty and inequality, the maintenance of socially unjust treatment of racial and ethnic minorities and the continued marginalisation of women- all persisted. These were the wicked issues from yester-year which stubbornly refused to disappear. Yes, the number of professional positions and careers was expanding and people from the working class were moving up, especially in the expanding public sector of health and education. However, the number and proportion of skilled and manual jobs was declining and youth unemployment became a scourge, especially in the old industrial and mainly northern towns and cities where adapting to the new 'service economy' was likely to be difficult if not impossible.

The new currency for buying your way to a better future was education and many more people were intent on acquiring it. The key was in expansion and growth and the rhetoric used was of increasing social mobility and the importance of equal opportunities for everyone who could benefit. This was the unexamined message and meaning of 'meritocracy' in which working class people, and their children in particular, could move up the social scale into the managerial and professional classes. And there is no doubt that the social class system in Britain had changed over time with new groups emerging, based on newer occupational and educational achievements (Savage ibid). But the deeper story was of the remarkable successes of the middle classes and the older elite upper class in taking the greatest advantage of the expanding education system, especially in the take up of places in the expanding and ever more stratified and 'unequal' hierarchy of universities. A rising tide floated all boats and working class children and adults got to access the newer universities in greater numbers than could possibly have been imagined a generation earlier. A cluster of universities declared themselves to be the 'Russell Group' of research intensive universities and thereby created a format for the new elitism. These so-called leading universities were in fact, mostly an old elite of established and well- endowed rich institutions. This was an example of what George Orwell (1941) once called the 'graded snobberies of the English' and its talent for creating a hierarchy out of a diversity. The mechanisms for allocating individuals to places in the elite universities ensured that the social groups and families that had enjoyed privileged positions in the old class structure secured comparable positions in the new one. They were able to do this by convincing large numbers of the population that they deserved their privileges and that success in the world of learning and beyond was down to the workings of a meritocratic society (Wooldridge 2021).

Outside of the selective university system, education and training began to be available where traditional work was disappearing. Young workers were being turned into trainees and students. Paradoxically, population forecasts showed that traditional recruits for higher education- the qualified 18 year olds- would decline after 1985, however student numbers continued to grow and record numbers took up higher education (TES 22.8.1986). Substantial numbers of these students were not school leavers but were older and drawn from amongst those who were suitably qualified but did not take up higher education places when they were under twenty one years of age (DES Report No 99). Many of the Access students were, however, unqualified for conventional university entrance by virtue of traditional examinations. It was the deeply held belief of their tutors that they were able to benefit from higher education if they were given the opportunity. The prevailing ideology held that education was the way forward for those whom a generation earlier would have had no hope of being a university student.

It is worth noting here that the concern for the under-achievement of the working classes in education even in the relatively enlightened 1980s concentrated on the inequalities impacting on boys. Gender inequalities were not considered in major works on this subject (Halsey et al 1980) and there is little doubt that class and ethnic inequalities were and still are accompanied by dramatic inequalities rooted in girls' and women's lives as was noted at the time (Allen 1982).

## Access as a movement for change?

Access courses bridged the artificial divide that had long bedevilled vocational and non-vocational adult education (Fieldhouse ibid: 399) since they appealed to those second chance learners who wanted to enter university education and they gave hope of entry to graduate employment. They were publically funded but the early phases of Access provision drew on the voluntary adult education and adult basic education traditions, often rooted in local communities and funded through LEAs and voluntary groups. They were arguably in many cases the means by which 'really useful knowledge' (Johnson 1988 ibid) could be put to good use in social action programmes- certainly where women's education and ethnicity were driving the need for change and the opening up of opportunities for further study. The importance of the liberal adult education emphasis on personal self-development was often inscribed into tutors' understanding of the value of learning beyond school.

What Access courses did not and could not accomplish was a radical transformation of educational opportunity within the wider and extensive education system that was developing in response to the ideologies of modernism, post-modernism, globalisation and the digitalisation of social and educational life in Britain and across the world (Zuboff 2019). In the 19th century and for a good deal of the 20th century, adult education can be understood as operating within contested views of the oppressions and inequalities of a class bound society which denied the broad masses of people access to education and opportunity. In the 21st century the paradigm in which Access has developed has stressed the individual nature of choice and education as a consumer choice. The emphasis has been on personalisation and the deficiencies of 'self' rather than on the nature of society and community which might be rectified or reformed through critical thinking and social action. Much the same could be said about the nature and organisation of schools where the provision of democratic schools was thought to require the reconstruction of schools attended by **all** the children in the communities they served: a vision commensurate with comprehensive schooling (Riddell 2016).

For much of 200 years of adult education in Britain the single most consistent purpose of adult learning was to recruit members of the working class and to raise their awareness and consciousness of the need for social improvement. The realities proved difficult to budge and these aims were historically unfulfilled by a combination of two sets of factors: first, many of the opportunities opened up through these educational struggles and reforms were taken up by the educated middle classes who prized the options available through wider social and educational reforms; and second the disadvantaged and working class were never convinced enough to demand post-school education as a fundamental 'right' and then to 'own' it as an expression of their own needs for really useful knowledge. The widespread apathy on these matters and the growth of the state's control and ownership of education at all levels is a narrative in which the people generally have yet to fully speak. It has been argued that leaving aside the trades union movement and its educational functions, the institutionalisation of post-school learning has proved to be a barrier rather than a facilitator to the involvement of social movements (Fieldhouse ibid: 400). There are echoes here of the idea of 'gentling of the masses' that some thought lay behind the middle class desire for the extension of mass primary education for the children of the working classes and which accompanied the 1870 Education Act and introduced young children into compulsory schooling. The idea that schooling might be a form of social control as well as a means of potential liberation has also had currency over a long period (Davis 1976; Freire 1972). Whether change through a more democratic schooling is illusory has remained a vital question for educators and the wider society over successive generations (Barber 1996; Porter 1999; Riddell 2010, 2016).

## Evolving Access and the principles of democratic learning

Access courses were at the most basic level a substitute for a failed GCE O and A level system that had relegated a majority of each generation to a lesser level of success and opportunity in the wider world of work, and ultimately in social life itself to a subordinate position. They were a compensation for a system that had failed to provide a variety of routes to higher learning. The need and desire for something better and more just signalled the failure of the meritocratic ideology to deliver better futures for generations who were less likely to settle for what was on offer. Motivation and ability asserted itself through the aspirations of ordinary people who saw education as the most likely route to a better life, if not for themselves, definitely for their children.

If this was the general background for the evolution of the Access movement and its appeal to actual and potential students, within the educational institutions and the classrooms there were notable and progressive departure points for teachers and learners. Access drew on the values, traditions and teaching styles of adult education- as opposed to those of the conventional universities- and it gave support and expression to the idea of critical thinking and learning. Access courses were 'critical' because by their nature they set out to be alternative modes of learning and placed themselves deliberately in a different relationship to higher education providers than the conventional routes to higher education- the O and A level GCEs- which were the major routes for school and college leavers.

In providing a potential alternative to the dominant paradigm for entry to higher education, Access proposed both explicitly and implicitly a more adequate framework for adult and lifelong learning. Drawing on a range of thinkers and theories and on education practitioners in community contexts in particular, some key principles of the movement can be identified:

## *Valuing the learner*

Learning and education have been often driven by a narrow understanding of cognitive development where different forms of intelligence and emotional well-being have been ignored. The concepts of multiple intelligence and emotional development are sources of alternative thinking which can underpin and enhance conventional learning and give recognition to the significance of self and self-identity.

## *Active social and community involvement*

Formal education has been constructed around a narrow and restrictive conception of its purposes. These have ignored the needs of communities for active and engaged citizens who can use education in the places in which they live and work for socially progressive purposes and for collective well-being and social justice.

## *Active and flexible learning*

If educational institutions are to be the focus of change and transformation they must become centres of critical learning and of practice. Investigative and reflexive learning, problem solving and independent learning can play an enhanced role in the educational experience of the majority.

## *Family and community*

A more holistic perspective of the learner would involve the key institutional and identity frameworks of the people and the recognition of difference and diversity as positive elements for a progressive pedagogy. The issues of race, ethnicity, faith and identity must be addressed as key aspects of modernity which impact on experience and shape expectations for everyone.

## *Engagement matters*

Social responsibility can be at the core of an academic mission and this can allow institutions to be advocates of the political and policy issues that matter to communities. The social purposes of learning and education should drive provision and inform the curriculum. Education is part of what can be fundamental transformations of life-chances for working people and can contest unfair forms of privilege and inequality.

## *Critical thinking*

The long and varied traditions of 'thinking differently' can be mobilised to provide for improved outcomes for those whose needs are greatest. A critical curriculum would address the great and pressing issues of the day from a social justice position and encourage a reflexive and self-critique to understand globalising influences on the one hand and personal dispositions on the other.

These outline principles are a means of thinking about forms of learning, including lifelong learning (Ranson et al 2000), which lay behind the development of the Access movement. They were not always and everywhere articulated as such, and neither students nor teachers were constantly aware of their continuing impact on what was experienced in the classroom. Nevertheless they are relevant to our understanding of education as part of both the individual and social experience of Access. They helped create the conditions in which public discussion and critical thinking could take forward key issues and concerns for educators and learners and allowed working people's history and biographies to figure as part of public and academic knowledge (Rowbotham 1999).

## What was gained? What was changed?

In the dash for growth and expansion Access and second chance courses were valuable assets for recruitment and space was given for experiments with different modes and methods of teaching and learning. Relationships within the classroom of a non-authoritarian kind could be developed since the students were present voluntarily and different ideas of what constituted knowledge could be explored. In the adult education tradition knowledge and self-understanding were as important as the formal qualifications or certificates that were available through formal schooling. Access education drew explicitly on the adult education tradition by entering the debate that preceded mass schooling over a century before by asking of itself- what kind of society do we wish to create for ourselves and how can education help us achieve it?

The debate proceeded by way of a critique of traditional schooling which, even where comprehensive schools had been established, as David Hargreaves noted, had failed to bring about social change:

'... the persisting damage that school does to the dignity of many school pupils, especially those from working-class homes, the erosion of working-class culture and community; the preservation of and dominant emphasis given to the cognitive and intellectual domain in the school curriculum; the growth of the cult of individualism and the failure of the school to make its proper contribution to social solidarity in society. In all these matters comprehensive re-organisation has promoted little change for the better or has even made matters worse' (1982: 113).

If schools were failing to bring about curriculum change, could the same be said of learning outside the schools? The fact was that the 'styles' and practices associated with progressive education could be found right across Britain in the provision of adult basic education (ALBSU May 1984). Student-centred teaching, experiential learning, co-operative study, self-directed learning, student-centred review, profiling and the development of community-conscious and relevant knowledge were all present throughout the 1970s and 1980s in the localities and communities where basic education, literacy and numeracy were taught to adults. In the often maligned schools there were always teachers and leaders who practised a critical and transformative curriculum, even in the face of massive odds against fundamental reform of state schooling (Wolpe and Donald 1983; John 2006; Benn 2011). ALBSU (the Adult Literacy and Basic Skills Unit), founded in 1980, itself experienced a substantial expansion and transformation in the period of Access growth. The adult education tradition stressed the significance of personal and collective experience and insisted that all individuals had potential for learning which needed to be tapped by the appropriate strategy and at the correct stage of personal maturation within each student (Hutchinson and Hutchinson 1978).

As the 1980s progressed it became ever more clear that public demand for mass higher education would impact on all universities in Britain and that Access was a significant part of this change towards mass higher education and high levels of participation (Cantwell et al ibid 2018). It was Access that placed diversity and difference in the forefront of concern for education and social justice and it was Access that offered some amelioration of the social and economic exclusion of working class people from higher education opportunities. If the elite universities and the older 'civic' red bricks were off limits to most working people, the newer emerging 'metropolitan' and post-1992 institutions were very keen to recruit them and their late teenage children. The sheer expansive growth of university institutions in the 1980s and 1990s allowed for what was called 'mission diversity' among universities. Such differences as existed between them were said to be indicative of the individualised 'unique selling points' of the different institutions which was a notion entirely compatible with the belief that a 'market' for higher

21

education could be created. The rising tide of HE provision floated all boats and Access was given serious consideration by many of the new universities. By the mid-1990s it was clear that widening access to higher education had become a major concern of social and educational policy (Ball 1994).

The expansion in youth participation rates in higher education from around 15 per cent in the mid-1980s to around 50 per cent, was achieved by broadening the base of the undergraduate population (Waller et al 2018: xv). However, this broadening still left significant inequalities in place and much of this can be explained by the changing class composition of British society (Savage ibid) and the class based opportunism that competitively uses education to buy and sustain privilege (Tomlinson 2014: 120). Wider access and higher participation has not in the longer run led to the greater social mobility and increase in opportunities for the many which was promised by Robbins in the 1960s. When a university place for each person qualified and wishing it was available, a very different type of higher education system had come about. Who gains access to which university and to outcomes for graduates remains problematic and central to on-going questions of inequality and social justice (Waller et al ibid). Much was gained historically through the long-term impact of adult education on Access, but arguably much was lost as mass participation eventually undermined the relative 'monopoly' of adult and Access learners held by the adult colleges and university extra-mural departments departments.

## From diversity to market conformism

For its part the established and conventional adult education providers within and outside the universities did very little to challenge the trend towards mass participation in HE; they saw themselves as a progressive expression of adult learning which the socially and economically excluded groups needed (Gidley 1996, Fieldhouse ibid: 400). However, amongst adult educators there had long been debate about the true purposes of the adult learners' movement. Those who had wanted it to support a radical and transformative social purpose still existed, but the fundamental character of the movement had been decisively shaped by the compromises demanded by government when it agreed to fund provision. The key objective was now not the transformation of society to a more socially just system but rather the incorporation and integration of the marginalised and the excluded into that same system. Where once the emphasis had been on 'active citizenship' the focus was on entry to higher education as an aim in its own right (Fieldhouse ibid: 240). For some this represented a form of social control and incorporation into the system in which the traditions of autonomous working-class education were lost. The knowledge and learning acquired did not lead to working people taking control over their own lives. Rather, they were assimilated into a hierarchical and fundamentally unjust and unequal educational and cultural system designed to ensure the continuance of existing elites and hence social inequalities. The relationship of knowledge, power and action became attenuated and weakened as education was increasingly viewed as a 'positional good', bought and sold on a market as with other commodities rather than as a transformational experience capable of giving people and communities the power to control their futures.

By the mid-1990s universities had experienced fifteen years of constant change in the funding methodologies and in the standing of adult education. The balance between vocational continuing education and non-vocational learning, sometimes called 'liberal adult education', had shifted decisively in favour of vocational provision. Adult education had effectively been integrated and assimilated within the mainstream of higher education. What had not been anticipated by most of its practitioners was the loss of the idea that adult education was in fact more than a set of courses- that it was in fact a *movement* of teachers and learners (Benn and Fieldhouse 1991; 1994) that had been lost. Adult education had been an open and progressive tradition *within* what were in effect closed and elitist institutions. Its integration into the mainstream meant that many extra-mural departments did not survive as independent entities and continuing education evolved into modular, part-time education, again within the HE mainstream. The Robertson Report of 1994 as the harbinger of reform through credit accumulation and transfer and its attempt to normalise and integrate continuing education within the mainstream became, whatever its intentions, in effect the grave digger of university adult education as we had known it. The triumph of vocationalism, though not envisaged by the Access movement seemed at hand and the era of extra-mural empires and of independent adult colleges was about to end.

The growth of the Access movement from the 1980s onwards and its flourishing existence within the expansive and burgeoning higher education system in Britain as the new 21st century approached, was a paradox. On the one hand it signalled the presence of new learners within universities and colleges and a recognition of their learning needs. These were students from the broad masses and represented working people and social groups who had been excluded from educational opportunities in the past. The power of educational reform to change prospects seemed to have been demonstrated by their very presence inside the ivory towers, hallowed cloisters and concrete and glass palaces of the educational institutions. Furthermore, the rhetoric and ideology of social mobility and meritocracy was in the air. Prime Minister Tony Blair seemed to capture the mood as he took power in 1997 with his exhortation to the nation – Education, Education, Education! On the other hand, a distinctively different mass **and** elitist system of higher education was emerging from the confused and contradictory policies of successive governments. The lineaments of this were evolving pragmatically and included: the creation of a unified HE funding method for all providers which ensured the continued privileging of the oldest and richest elite universities; the emerging predominance of the 'vocational' model adapted from the polytechnic sector and applied to the new mass-universities; the marketisation and commercialisation of all degree-level study; the failure to adopt and extend the Robbins model of independent universities with distinctive missions; the failure of the adult education colleges to adapt to the pace and scale demanded by the new Access agenda, and perhaps the failure by the liberal adult education tradition itself to create an authentic and transformative curriculum- what Stuart Hall (1983) referred to as a 'universal literacy'.

It was the possibility of a different curriculum involving new approaches to knowledge, learning and teaching which might lead on to critical thinking and transformations which animated and enthused Access learners and teachers. As Access and widening participation more generally was rolled out in the last decade of the $20^{th}$ century, many held the view that education was the key to a fundamental transformation in the life chances of ordinary British people. For this to happen a transformation of the education system itself would be required. There can be little doubt that significant change took place and many commentators could be heard to state that the only constant now was change itself. However, whether this change was in any way a fundamental reconstruction of the system of privilege and inequality which preceded it, is doubtful. Turning the tide of social and educational disadvantage would prove a formidable challenge and one that continues in the present.

# References

ALBSU (1984 May) - Adult Literacy and Basic Skills Unit- *Developments in Adult Literacy and Basic Skills: An Interim Report,* London: ALBSU.

Allen, S. (1982) *Ethnic Disadvantage in Britain*, Unit 4 of the Open University Course E354, Ethnic Minorities and Community Relations, Milton Keynes: The Open University Press.

Ball, C. (1994) *Aim Higher, Widening Access to Higher Education 1990-1994*, Report to the RSA, London: RSA.

Barber, M. (1996) *The Learning Game: Arguments for an education revolution*, London: Victor Gollancz.

Benn, M. (2011) *School Wars: The Battle for Britain's Education,* London: Verso.

Benn, R. & Fieldhouse, R. (1991) 'Adult education to the rescue in Thatcherite Britain' in Poggler, F. & Kalman, Y. (eds) *Adult Education in Crisis Situations*, Jerusalem: Magnus Press.

Benn, R. & Fieldhouse, R. (1994) 'Raybouldism, Russel and the New Realism' in Armstrong, P., Bright , B. and Zukas, M. (eds) *Reflecting on Changing Practices, Contexts and Identities,* Hull: SCUTREA.

Busher, H. and James, N. (2018) 'Struggling for selfhood: Non-traditional mature students' critical perspectives on access to higher education courses in England' ch 2 in Waller, R., Ingram, N. and Ward, M.R.M. (2018) *Higher Education and Social Inequalities: University Admissions, Experiences, and Outcomes,* London and New York: Routledge.

Cantwell, B., Marginson, S. and Smolentseva, A. (2018) *High-Participation Systems of Higher education,* Oxford: Oxford University Press.

CNAA- Council for National Academic Awards (1984 August) Access to higher education: non-standard entry to CNAA first degree and Dip. HE. Courses. London: CNAA.

CNAA- Council for National Academic Awards (1984 October) Access / Preparatory Courses: some data collected by CNAA, London: CNAA.

Davies, D. (1996) *Credit Where It's Due*, University of Cambridge, Madingley Hall and UK Government Department of Education and Skills.

Davies, D. (1997) 'From the further education margins to the higher education centre? Innovation in continuing education', *Education and Training* Vol 39 No 1, 1997, MCB University Press.

Davies, D. (1998) Lifelong Learning Competency in the 21$^{st}$ Century, ch 4 in *The Virtual University* with Richard Teare and Eric Sandelands, London: Cassell.

Davies, D. (2022) 'The Meaning of Vocational and Academic Education' pp. 82-83 in Freedom Through Education: A Promise Postponed, ch 5 Nyland, J. and Davies, D. (2022) *Curriculum Challenges for Universities: Agenda for Change,* Singapore: Springer Press Ltd.

Davies, D. and Davies, E. (2021) 'We once built a University in Buxton', ch 8 in *A Fair Go: Learning in Critical Times and Places,* Amazon pub.

Davis, B. (1976) *Social Control and Education*, London: Methuen.

Dean, A. (1985) *Moving Up: an overview of transition between vocational further and higher education*, London: FEU- Further Education Unit (government agency).

DES (1973) – UK government Department of Education and Science- The Russell Report, London: HMSO.

DES- *Report No 99,* April 1983 *and Report No 100,* July 1984, London: HMSO.

Dorling, D. (2018) *Peak Inequality: Britain's Ticking Time Bomb*, University of Bristol: Policy Press.

Edwards, E.G. (1984) *Higher Education for Everyone*, Nottingham: Spokesman.

Eggins, H. (1988) *Restructuring Higher Education*, Milton Keynes: SRHE and Open University Press.

Fieldhouse, R. and Associates (1996) *A History of Modern British Adult Education*, Leicester: NIACE.

Fowler, A. and Wyke, T. (1993) *Many Arts Many Skills: The origins of the Manchester Metropolitan University,* Manchester: the Manchester Metropolitan University Press.

Freire, P. (1972) *Pedagogy of the Oppressed*, London: Sheed and Ward.

Fulton, O. (1981) 'Principles and Policies' in Fulton, O. (ed) (1981) *Access to Higher Education,* Guildford, Surrey: SRHE- Society for Research into Higher Education at the University of Surrey.

Gidley, N. (1996) 'Multicultural Perspectives on Adult Education: Putting Policy into Practice' Centre for research into Continuing Education, Occasional Paper 2, University of Exeter.

Hall, S. (1983) 'Education in crisis' Part one: The politics of education in Donald, J. and Wolpe, AnneMarie (eds) (1983) *Is there anyone here from education?* London: Pluto Press.

Halsey, A.H., Heath, A.F. and Ridge, J.H. (1980) *Origins and Destinations: Family, Class and Education in Modern Britain*, Oxford: Clarendon Press.

Hargreaves, D. (1982) *The Challenge for the Comprehensive School*, London: Routledge & Keegan Paul.

House, D.B. (1991) *Continuing Liberal Education*, New York: NUCEA- Macmillan.

Hutchinson, E. and Hutchinson, E. (1978) *Learning Later: Fresh Horizons in English Adult Education,* London: Routledge & Keegan Paul.

ILEA (1984 September) *Access to Higher Education: Report of a Review of Access Courses at the Authority's Maintained Colleges of Further and Higher Education*, London: ILEA Inspectorate, County Hall.

James, D. (2018) 'Social class, participation, and the marketised university', in Waller et al (eds) (2018) *Higher Education and Social Inequalities*, London and New York: Routledge.

John, G. (2006) *Taking a Stand: Gus John Speaks on education, race, social action and civil unrest 1980-2005,* Manchester: Gus John Partnership Ltd.

Johnson, R. (1988) 'Really useful knowledge 1790-1850: memories for education in the 1980s' in Lovett, T. (ed) (1988) *Radical Approaches to Adult education*, UK: Routledge.

Judd, F. Lord (1993) *House of Lords Debate, Adult Education Funding*, Hansard February 23, 1993, 176-214.

McIlroy, J. (1996) 'Independent Working Class Education and Trade Union Education and Training', ch 10 in Fieldhouse, R. and Associates (1996) *A history of Modern British Adult Education*, Leicester: NIACE.

Marriott, S. (1984) *Extramural Empires: Service & Self-Interest in English University Adult Education 1873-1983*, University of Nottingham.

Mason, P. (2022) 'This isn't Big Bang 2.0. It's a spivs' charter necessitated by Brexit', The New European, Issue 321 December 15-21, 2022.

Millins, P. K. C. (1984) *Access studies to Higher Education, September 1979-December 1983: A Report,* London: Roehampton Institute, Centre for Access Studies to Higher Education.

Orwell, G. (1941) 'England Your England', *in The Lion and the Unicorn: Socialism and the English Genius,* UK: Searchlight Books/Secker and Warburg.

Parry, G. (1986) 'From Patronage to Partnership', *Journal of Access Studies*, Vol 1 No 1, April 1986.

Porter, J. (1999*) Reschooling and the Global Future: Politics, Economics and the English Experience*, Oxford: Symposium Books.

QAA- Quality Assurance Agency for Higher Education- (2015) *The Access to Higher Education Diploma. Key Statistics 2013-2014,* Gloucester: QAA.

Ranson, S., Rikowski, G. and Strain, M. (2000) 'Life-long Learning for a Learning Democracy' for Chapman, J. and Aspin, D. (eds) *International Handbook on Lifelong learning:* Dordrecht: Kluwer.

Riddell, R. (2010) *Aspiration, Identity and Self-belief: snapshots of social structure at work,* Staffordshire: Trentham Books Ltd.

Riddell, R. (2016) *Equity, Trust and the Self-improving Schools System,* University College London: UCL Institute of Education Press.

Robbins Report (1963) *Report of the Committee on Higher education,* UK: Cmnd 2154 HMSO.

Roberts, R. (1976) *A Ragged Schooling: Growing up in the Classic Slum*, Manchester University Press.

Robertson Report (1994) *'Choosing to Change'*, compiled by Prof. David Robertson for the HEQC- Higher Education Quality Council, London: HEQC.

Robertson, D. (1995) 'The Reform of Higher education for Social Equity, Individual Choice and Mobility' ch 3 in Coffield, F. (ed) (1995) *Higher Education in a Learning Society,* University of Durham on behalf of DfEE, ESRC and HEFCE.

Rowbotham, S. (1999) *Threads through time: writings on history and autobiography,* UK: Penguin Books.

Savage, M. (2015) *Social Class in the 21st Century*, UK: Pelican Books.

Scott, P. (2021) *Retreat or Resolution/ Tackling the Crisis of Mass Higher Education,* University of Bristol: Policy Press.

Shor, I. (1980) *Critical Teaching and Everyday Life*, Boston: South End Press and 1987 University of Chicago Press.

Times Educational Supplement - TES 22.08.1986.

Tomlinson, S. (2014) *The politics of race, class, and special education: The selected works of Sally Tomlinson*, Routledge: London.

Vogel, J. (2017) *The Ascendancy of Finance*, Cambridge: Polity Press.

Waller R., Ingram, N. and Ward, M.R.M. (eds) (2018*) Higher Education and Social Inequalities: University Admissions, Experiences and Outcomes,* London and New York: Routledge.

Weinbrenn, D. (2014) *The Open University: a history*, Manchester University Press.

Williams, J. (2013) *Consuming Higher Education: Why Learning Cannot be Bought,* London: Bloomsbury.

Wolpe, AnneMarie and Donald, J. (1983) *Is there anyone here from education?* London: Pluto Press.

Wooldridge, A. (2021) *The Aristocracy of Talent: How Meritocracy Made the Modern World,* UK: Allen Lane/ Penguin Books.

Zuboff, S. (2019) *The Age of Surveillance Capitalism: The Fight for the Future at the New Frontier of Power,* London: Profile Books.

Threads through time: Mosterton School, Dorset - 1912
For generations education was viewed as the key to unlocking
the barriers to social mobility and change.

# Chapter 2

# Knowledge, Learning and Teaching for Access

## Learning and teaching- Access as a different approach

For its teachers and developers Access was much more than a response to a changing labour market and the need for vocationally relevant learning. It was an approach to learning and to study which questioned the nature and practices of higher education institutions in so far as they continued to exclude so many capable of benefitting from a university education. What was at issue at that time was summarised by the government agency responsible for further education development:

'The Access approach places a responsibility on institutions: to identify barriers which are placed in the way of non-traditional learners, to accept that the learning environment of many institutions has contributed to the disillusionment many adults feel with their education, and to create conditions which support non-traditional learners and enable them to develop their maximum potential' (FEU 1986: 3).

For several decades before the era of Access, adult education providers and further education colleges had offered remedial learning leading to higher education through the medium of evening classes, including options for 'O' and 'A' level GCEs. Special facilities and support for such learners were generally not available and in spite of successes and satisfaction with this route by some students (Butler 1981; Smithers and Griffin 1986) there was a very high drop out and failure rate (FEU ibid). The public sector part of higher education was at this time regulated by the CNAA (the Council for National Academic Awards) and it too had adopted a flexible admissions policy including entry to its Diploma of Higher Education, often viewed as equivalent to the first two years of an undergraduate degree. The Open University was simultaneously forging ahead with an open entry policy to become the largest provider of degree level study in the UK. As the HE system in the UK grew however, these developments had less than complete success in increasing substantially the proportion of working class students in the system (Rogers and Groombridge 1976: 126-127). Right up to and beyond the start of the 21st century social class continued to shape the outcomes and content of education at all levels and the keynote of this was the reality of unequal access and social inequality (Ball 2002 and 2006).

The new Access courses of the 1970s and 1980s not only aimed at changing institutional practice in how students were recruited but were also focussed on change at the level of the students' own experience, much of which took place in neighbourhoods and local communities. Access had its entry requirements related directly to the perceived needs of non-traditional university populations and this often necessitated an encounter with these communities. This made the courses and the students different from conventional courses and they placed different demands on the universities and HE institutions.

## Community perspectives and learning experience

Access courses typically claimed to serve and reflect the interests of local communities. The idea of community is, however, a conceptual minefield often full of hidden value judgements and covert assumptions which can prove to be uncertain. Zygmunt Bauman (2001) thought that the elusive community so many sought was a way of seeking safety in an insecure world; John Berger (1984) the great art and social critic wrote … 'We live not just our own lives, but the longings of our century' which was for a sense of belonging to a community and Norman Dennis claimed it is one of those words which is … 'uttered in solemnity, and as soon as they are pronounced an expression of respect is visible on every countenance, and all heads are bowed' (Dennis 1968: 74). In spite of the ambiguity of 'community' there is a connotative power and more than just emotional potency in the relation of Access and the communities from which the students came and to which, unlike many conventional students, they were destined to return.

Most Access courses asserted the significance of the neighbourhood and community and the support it might offer to a relevant type of adult education.

Steven Brookfield identified a 'locational' concept of community which was relevant to this … 'Three dimensions of the community practice of adult education can be identified: adult education for the community, adult education in the community and adult education of the community' (Brookfield 1983: 156). Whilst clearly not all Access courses could claim or sustain an involvement 'in, for and of' the communities in which they were located, there was often in the learning group and community a feeling that 'immersion' in the lives of students as they were lived in inner-city areas and on council estates was an essential component of the course. Some courses drew on the lessons from inner-city adult education interventions which had wanted to bring about social change and greater social justice through transformative adult learning projects (Lovett 1975; Fletcher 1980). Many acknowledged the inspirational work of Paulo Freire (1972) as foundational for their ideas and practice (Shor 1980; Mezirow 1981).

Though Access courses sought to employ community education ideologies and practices, they were also bound up with the realities of mixed and sometimes divided communities where no consensus was available for how education might bring about desired change and progress. Working class communities throughout the land were becoming less and less homogenous. Inequalities of class, race, gender and power intersected the communities from which non-traditional students came. The old communally-based social solidarities of working class life in Britain were disappearing and a more fragmented and fluid class structure was emerging (Savage 2015; Davies 2021: 257-260). There was also the question of whether Access was in fact recruiting substantial numbers of middle class students who had missed out on earlier opportunities to enter higher education. Their motivations and aspirations were not coterminous with those of working class adults nor with the experiences of ethnic communities and black populations in the cities. If community education was problematical and likely to expose disparate views on the ways forward for communities and community-based education (Rogers and Groombridge ibid: 71), Access shared these disparities and reflected the immediacy of their particular environments. No two Access courses could be the same!

Nevertheless, Access courses everywhere were significantly aware of the formal and informal community networks by which adult students were surrounded and which mediated the self-help networks and political organisations which helped shape community life and expectations. Community life and development was always likely to be contentious and this was true where education had held a central place in the activities of community groups attempting to overcome racial inequalities (Marland 1980; Ben Tovim et al 1981). Access courses began partially as a response to the government's Department of Education and Science initiative in the late 1970s (Millins 1984) as an attempt to offer black communities some space and increased representation in higher education and professional occupations. This was an important goal for black community groups but it may have stood arguably in conflict with some of the educational goals desired by the communities themselves (Clay 2020). Community groups were anxious to increase their skills and knowledge including their understanding of how racism had worked to alienate and distance black people from the dominant white institutions concerned with employment, housing, and education. This had served, as Gus John stated in 1978 … 'to confine them to a marginal existence within society' (John 1978: 194; see also John 2006). This tension initially led to demands on the curricula of Access courses themselves and later as students moved on, it led to criticism of higher education itself (see Tomlinson 2019: 219-222). Suspicion was fuelled for black communities by the evidence of lack of promotion and unemployment amongst qualified black teachers and professionals (John 1981: 186-187).

## Experience and learning through Access

Access was a wide ranging set of courses and learning programmes designed for non-traditional adults who were interested in returning to learn- usually following some sense of failure in earlier schooling. Access was at the same time a conceptual framework within which educators and community groups pressed for alternative educational values. Social justice outcomes were wanted by many of the students as was a greater commitment to fairness and opportunity which appeared to many to have been withheld over generations. Some traditional notions of what was really useful and appropriate knowledge for these learners were critically scrutinised (Johnson 1988). The idea that education should certificate and validate individually acquired knowledge, rather than any notion of achievement by a social group to which students belonged, came under scrutiny. The importance of collective and shared experience was acknowledged by many Access courses which stressed the significance of applying knowledge to practical issues and challenges within defined and bounded community concerns. Such views did not always find a positive response in the higher education institutions and most change took place in the providing colleges rather than the receiving universities and HE colleges. The process was helped in the further education sector by the widespread adoption of forms of assessment for experiential learning in the so-called 'New FE' (FEU 1980 and 1981). In the world of adult education, informal learning and self-directed learning which took place outside of the formal state-aided system of formal classes, often in voluntary settings, was thought to be important (Percy, Burton and Withnall 1994).

The freedom of the learner to determine to some degree the pace and the content of learning and to draw on experience as a learning method derives from a long tradition of humanistic philosophy. John Dewey was of the view that an educational aim must be founded on intrinsically valid activities and the needs of an individual to be educated. Education was ... 'A freeing of individual capacity in a progressive growth directed to social aims' (Dewey in Skillbeck 1970: 119). Each individual can be helped and educated to make sense of his/her world and the social purposes of education can be re-affirmed. This approach and aim was consistent with the general philosophy of Access courses and appeared to support the emphasis given to 'learning about learning' and 'openness to experience' that Carl Rogers (1969), another precursor of the thinking which informed the Access movement, had advocated. The keynote for Access in the 1980s became how to relate collective experience and the need for transformation of disadvantaged communities into a viable learning programme that could equip students to succeed in higher education. The controlling bodies for both public sector HE (NAB 1984 and 1986) and for the universities (UGC- Universities Grants Committee 1984) had accepted that experiential learning was of increasing significance, though their power to intervene to shape curricula was extremely limited.

In all of this we cannot forget that teachers and developers of learning programmes also had collective and professional interests to safeguard. Where community groups sought to extend their identity interests and effectiveness amongst community members, teachers and lecturers wished to ensure the continuity and standards of their courses when new varieties of students enrolled. Access placed the issues that arose from this connection on the agenda of those who taught adults whether they were in higher or further education. Within the universities and public sector HE institutions Access courses shifted the power to determine the preparation of non-standard students for higher education from those academics who dominated A level subject committees to the admissions tutors and course committees of specific institutions who dealt with the new kinds of students.

Although the vast majority of Access courses were located in further education colleges and supported through local networks and adult and community education providers and adult colleges, there were a few universities that created Access provision within their existing offer to students. They were mainly the post-1992 universities and colleges which had previously been publically owned and often showed a sense of community engagement. The older 'civic' and 'redbrick' universities were less keen to admit what they generally considered less well qualified students to their conventional courses and curricula. There were exceptions of course: Liverpool University's Vice Chancellor, Graham Davies, sponsored Access programmes on the campus and worked closely with the 'municipal' ex-polytechnic, John Moore's University and Hope University to open up opportunities for Access students. In the mid-1990s the University of Cambridge Extra-Mural Department ran a consortium for Access programmes and sponsored three local Access courses, though students found immense difficulties in negotiating the collegiate admissions system in Cambridge itself. Fortunately, local 'new' universities such as Anglia Ruskin, Hertfordshire and the Open University were more open to non-traditional applicants, as was in fairness Lucy Cavendish College which recruited adult women students within the University of Cambridge.

Meanwhile the vast majority of university candidates remained locked-in to the traditional A level GCE qualifications acquired at schools, sixth-form colleges and further education colleges. In the longer term these traditional entry qualifications and procedures were developed into ever more detailed and sophisticated systems for selecting and 'sorting out' students for the ever more differentiated hierarchies of universities within the evolving mass university system.

## Access as alternative routes to knowledge

The Access movement had its origins in the efforts of working people and educationalists to improve their social and working lives and in the efforts of ruling groups to 'gentle' the masses and ameliorate their conditions of life as modern capitalist states evolved in the late nineteenth and early twentieth centuries. Education became a fulcrum for social change and social mobility, though there were always struggles over its form and often over the content of the curriculum, as well as over who should control and own it (Simon 1965 and 1990). These struggles were especially intense during the political battles for comprehensive schooling in the 1960s and 1970s... 'The battle over how to organise our schools, and what to teach in them, has a long, bitter and tangled history'. (Benn 2011: xx). State education, however, had never commanded the same loyalty as the National Health Service and schooling in the public domain was never presented to the people by conservative politicians as an essential part of the democratic and communitarian project that could challenge injustice and inequality. Though the fate and future of the nation is in the hands of the educators, the decisions that drive policy and finance are often made politically by those committed to retaining selection as a key principle of social life in which education should offer choice and diversity within a privatised culture.

Out of this long historical setting emerged, arguably, the belief that education was crucial to modern state formation (Archer 2013) and was central to the post- Second World War social democratic settlement in the United Kingdom (Simon 1991). Universal secondary education and an expanded further and higher education system evolved to be the expectation of the many and of the majority by the 21st century. The Access movement, however, grew in the interstices of the educational and social welfare systems, identifying and meeting needs and desires for learning in a wide variety of informal and community-based contexts. The role of the local education authorities was also very significant and they catered for some two million adult students in more than 100,000 courses in England and Wales each year in the 1980s (Fieldhouse 1996:100). Access grew also in part due to the continuing failure of schools to meet the learning needs of many who left without qualifications and skills. It infiltrated by design the institutional base of adult education providers and of the universities and colleges which were mainly publically funded. In a sense it was an 'organic' growth without any central organisation of control. There was no single policy or programme for Access nationwide. In hindsight a kind of convivial anarchy was allowed to exist and in local places throughout the nation a culture of locally relevant and locally devised second chance and Access courses and programmes was established, very often with the material and political support of local councils and education authorities.

There was no single philosophical or educational rationale or set of cohesive principles in the Access movement, though it had definitive values and practices which were distinguishable from the dominant values and practices of the conservative universities. The prime difference between the two was around the question of who had the ability to benefit from higher education? Access followed the adult education tradition of asserting the fact that there was a large pool of talent in the working classes which had remained untapped. Education was a potent force for the liberation of people who had been denied their right to learning and opportunity and hence their social and economic liberties had been artificially restricted. For this to change, new learning and teaching methods were needed. Knowledge encoded in the traditional curriculums and 'valorised' by traditional gate-keeping educational institutions would therefore have to be challenged and changed. Traditional higher education institutions on the other hand had been engaged in selecting out and excluding people from higher learning and all the good things that flowed from it, such as access to the professions. The right and legitimacy of this process lay ultimately in the argument that only a limited number of people had the ability and capacity to benefit from higher education. The selection procedures came down ultimately to judgements about who had acquired the relevant knowledge and curriculum. The public schools and state-funded grammar schools worked on behalf of the universities to preserve this symbiotic relationship which privileged the wealthy elites and educationally aware middle classes, whilst simultaneously excluding the majority.

The kinds of knowledge(s) that emerged within the Access curriculum were by no means universal and neither were they uniform. Access courses were locally devised and validated and accepted in general that there could be different teaching and learning styles and practices appropriate for different purposes and different kinds of students. These perspectives were of course contested and debated everywhere such courses were offered to the public through public institutions. How Access courses could be accredited and validated whilst maintaining standards and quality was a recurring theme of all those involved in the Access movement (Davies 1987, 1995; Wilson 2010). What was at issue was not the standards of particular courses or students' performances but rather the question of whose curriculum it was and whose version of what constituted knowledge would prevail? This was of particular concern to the established universities with their practices and procedures for selecting students on the basis of their having mastered the conventional curriculum.

The rigid selection process and three year degree excluded the possibility of students learning at their own pace and of using their lived experience as part of their course. Academic performance was judged on the ability a student had to handle concepts without reference to immediate personal experience. The ability to use concepts learnt in action was tested, if at all, only in courses of professional training. Even where political radicalism could be detected in universities, courses with a heavier load of abstract theory tended to be far distant from knowledge relevant to the social needs of individuals and communities. There were of course exceptions to this as shown, for example, in the pioneering and inspirational work of Jerome Bruner (1966), Paulo Freire (1972), Ira Shor (1980) , Eric Midwinter (1982), Stuart Hall (1980,1982 and 1983) Jack Mezirow (1981), Malcolm Knowles (1970 and 1981), Gus John (1978, 1981 and 2006), Tom Lovett (1975, 1983) and Sally Tomlinson (1979, 1983 and 2019). There existed in this period, and long before, a cohort and community of critical educationalists whose work was matched by their different but complementary emphases on the necessary connections between theory and practice and the need to create new social knowledge. The full extent of this body of critical thinking is by no means exhausted by the above list (see Seidman 1998; Ashwin et al 2015). In general though, the dominant teaching and learning styles of schools and higher education were well adapted to helping 'normal' new under-graduates fresh from their sixth forms at school through their degree courses. They played to their strengths in developing a limited facility in handling abstract concepts in the unreal context of the academic test essay without challenging their weaknesses in understanding and applying concepts and critical analysis to their own lives. Equally this approach disadvantaged non-traditional, mature students by providing little or no space for them to express the insights gained from experience or even to demonstrate how their education had helped them cope with their everyday lives. Where 'academic' learning and teaching detached the students' understanding of social reality from their existential dilemmas, if they had any, Access made social reality problematical and thus the object of critical understanding.

Access used a range of alternative teaching and learning strategies which put personal competences and understanding centrally into the curriculum. Subject knowledge, as traditionally taught in schools and colleges, was thought to be less important than the capacity to be resilient when needing to overcome barriers and when facing new tasks. Informal learning methods were encouraged where everyday culture could be recognised and be absorbed within academic study (Percy et al ibid). Continuous assessment was considered to be more effective for adult learners and course content was selected for its relevance to adult life and aspirations. Student support was built into course delivery at every stage so as to ensure student progress and success. Flexible time-tabling was used and the personal and social obligations of older students such as the need for childcare and family responsibilities were recognised. Experience and research at the time appeared to show that such measures could allow non-traditional adult students to succeed (Parry 1986). Mature Access students were capable of competing at least equally well with the younger cohorts in higher education.

## Lifelong learning and andragogy: a basis for Access

Students and teachers who view adult learning as a distinct category of learning can be grouped under the rubric of 'andragogy', which refers to the learning principles and practices relevant to adult education. In particular the focus is on the idea of stages and phases of personal development which are experienced and developed in relation to social change. The concept of andragogy has been in use for over a century (NAG 1983) and it was central to Malcolm Knowles' influential work in the 1970s and 1980s. Knowles identified four major assumptions. First, adults have strong needs to be self-directing and as we get older the self-concept moves from dependency on others to self-direction and personal autonomy. Second, maturity brings with it experience which is a resource for learning. Third, as life proceeds readiness to learn becomes associated with a person's social roles. Learning becomes relevant to the need to know – not because we are told to learn. Fourth, as a person grows older and matures, problem or project-centred learning takes over from subject-centred learning.

If we assume that andragogy denotes a distinctive pattern or category of learning and that this evolves over the lifespan of an individual, then it can be argued there should be organising principles for how such adult learning should be included and embodied within the learning process. These might then include the need for motivation of individuals which must be maintained through the setting of learning objectives which are compatible with personal goals. This in itself requires the recognition of individual differences within any learning situation. Formal schooling and the formal higher education curriculum often does not take into account such differences. Neither do they therefore allow new learning to be assimilated and integrated within existing frameworks of knowledge and experience. Formal educational institutions find it difficult to acknowledge and give credit for experiences which fall outside their domain. Action learning and problem-centred learning (Lovett 1983; Teare 2018) may also struggle to find a place in conventional schools and colleges, especially where subject and academic discipline boundaries are rigidly upheld. Bernstein's (1974, 1977) ideas about the use of integrated and collection 'codes' (see diagram below) are helpful in showing us how different learning and teaching styles embody normative expectations of what should be taught and what makes an appropriate curriculum.

Traditional and conservative institutions tend to use academic disciplines as separate and discrete entities around which to construct learning, which has the effect of reinforcing traditional conceptions of knowledge and the hierarchies of status and prestige within the academy. The adult education tradition, on the other hand, tended to recognise the validity of a 'collection code' where different disciplines could be brought together in new combinations for a more radical and critical account of how knowledge could serve a social purpose. In societies characterised by massive structural inequalities, large scale unemployment, de-industrialisation, poverty, social inequality and exclusion, racism and crime there are certainly debates to be had about what might be the most fitting and best curriculum content and methods of learning and teaching. There are in fact very different and contested frameworks of understanding and knowledge in play here. Access was an expression of this form of contested knowledge; it presented an embryonic alternative to the hegemonic university-dominated system at the apex of the educational ladder of achievement, one of whose major functions had been the legitimisation of selection and exclusion of the common people from higher education. Paradoxically, Access was at the same moment the best hope for the assimilation of a proportion of the excluded into the very same system. What was clear, however, was the fact that Access students had not come through a linear and sequential process comprising easily identifiable stages which corresponded to predictable behavioural or social experiences. Lifelong learning for Access students was often disjointed and unpredictable where the posing of problems was as important as the search for answers. In some cases the pedagogical relationship was forced to undergo change so that the learner's self-concept became a determining factor in her/his progress rather than the instructions from the teacher within a pre-digested formal curriculum.

The concept of knowledge embodied in andragogy insists that thinking and understanding develop as people interact consciously and critically in their social lives and communities. It asserts that there is no fixed or final stage of development and that the teacher-learner relationship is changed within an 'adult learning' approach. This approach underpinned much of the Access movement's understanding of itself in its early phases (Millins 1984; Davies 1987) though the diversity and often experimental nature of Access itself precluded any attempt at a cohesive or uniform system of courses or curriculums. It was a test-bed of innovative approaches to non-traditional learning and learners; a significant departure point for critical thinking and practice about the relationship of further and higher education.

The diagram below shows two approaches to learning and teaching, one, on the left of the diagram which could be said to be commensurate with the Access approach to knowledge, is rooted in adult learning traditions. The other approach characterises most higher education as it developed into the 21st century, prior to the intervention of the digital revolution in education. The terms andragogy and pedagogy were sometimes used to illustrate the differences in approach to learning styles and strategies that were used to grasp the world of adult learning (Knowles 1983). The use of the term 'codes' derives from Basil Bernstein's attempts to describe and analyse the way different vocabularies and styles of language and knowledge are bound up with social class and cultural experience.

| Diagram- Contrasting Teaching Styles | |
|---|---|
| **Adult Education** | **Higher Education** |
| **Andragogy** | **Pedagogy** |
| Non-selective: assumption of limitless untapped potential for learning within individuals and communities | Selective: assumption of a limited pool of talent with ability to benefit from HE |
| **Teaching Style** | |
| Progressive: centred on individual student and experience-led learning Often radical, using political analysis for students to understand past failures and to improve current interaction with institutions or create self-help activities | Academic: centred on subject disciplines and ability to detach concepts from experience Often radical, including abstract models of society and its cultural practices within undergraduate teaching programmes |
| Integrated Code | Collection Code |
| **The 'Normal' Student** | |
| Mature, experienced and responsible for others in family and social life Internalised sense of failure from school experience Easily intimidated by new written tasks | Immature, inexperienced and free from immediate responsibility for others in family or social life Internalised sense of success derived from school experience Relatively comfortable with written tasks |
| Knowledge is concerned with ' subjective' personal development Lived experience as a basis for knowing and learning | Knowledge is mainly concerned with ' objective' standards of attainment and performance |

## Class, race and gender

In the 1970s and 1980s many Access movement teachers working within community education settings, especially those in inner-urban areas with minority ethnic groups were likely to be in favour of using non-traditional methods of teaching and learning. The significance of local attachments and of being part of an ethnic group were lived realities rather than abstract academic categories of life (John 1978, 1981; Hall 1983; Martin 1986). Students needed social and political explanations of their history and contemporary existence as a means of releasing them from the sense of failure and personal inadequacy that earlier failure had transmitted to them. The realities of day-today racism and discrimination were the constant foreground for succeeding generations of black and white people who lived and worked in the cities of Britain in the last quarter of the 20th century. Adult education in its contribution to the Access movement at least was part of a critique which tried to give expression to life experience around themes of class, ethnicity and gender and to define their collective interests as being worthy of recognition in and beyond the academy (John 2006; Tomlinson 2019; Davies and Nyland 2021). Neither should we forget the immense contribution to education made by the labour movement in Britain in its struggles for knowledge and 'enlightenment' connected to the needs of working people for political representation and as a social voice for collective and community life (Simon 1965, 1990).

Family life and personal circumstances were the other key contexts of experience which impacted on adult students in the Access movement. Childcare, for example, became a major issue for all Access providers. The lives of students had a direct impact on the knowledge and skills considered relevant to adult learners facing many personal as well as educational challenges. The daily struggles to manage a worthwhile personal existence and simultaneously create the right conditions to sustain educational aspirations were part of every Access curriculum. Learning and scholarship had to be done in the face of rising unemployment, social decay in the inner city neighbourhoods and the challenges of poverty and deprivation for people who desperately needed education.

## Women and access to learning

The story of the struggles for education and social progress is also the story of women as learners, teachers and organisers who had to combat patriarchy and sex discrimination in all its forms since time out of mind. The social and political history of Britain and Ireland is also that of the evolving position of women in education and society (Rowbotham 1973, 1999; Open University 1982; Ryan and Ward 2019; Lynch 2022). The unequal gender division of labour in both the workplace and in domestic life has historically impoverished women, especially working class women and enriched men of all classes so that men were able to take up public power in ways that exercised control over women and ensured their subordination and exclusion from civil society. The role of women, especially in their care and affective relations with others and in nurturing and socialising succeeding generations has been seen to be outside the mainstream and often ignored by male scholars (Lynch ibid:59). Social class and gender constructs have in particular shaped women's experience of education and this has varied over time and place. Class and social divisions as well as ethnicity and faith dimensions of life can continue to exercise decisive influence over women's education in multi-racial/ethnic/faith communities such as exist in Britain.

Patriarchal attitudes and structures in the 19th century ensured that women had to struggle to overcome barriers which allocated them to the private sphere of the home and domestic subservience (Purvis 1980). The adult education curriculum for women in the 19th century was rooted in domestic ideology, in spite of the fact that large numbers of women were also wage earners. Voluntary organisations and schools stressed the need for female literacy and learning to be around the needs of children, family and home. Even by 1870 women were without voting rights, property rights or educational entitlement let alone the right to organise a trade union.

As social reform proceeded the women's movement(s) militated for greater freedom and opportunity alongside voluntary and religious organisations. James Stuart at Cambridge University set up a lecture series which led to the foundation of the North of England Council for the Higher Education of Women, which led to the birth of University Extension work in England (Benn 1996: 379). It was not, however, until 1948 that Cambridge allowed women to graduate with their degrees from the University even though women only colleges had been founded!

At the start of the 20th century women's adult education was said to be 'invisible' and the social and economic needs of women within the world of education were often ignored (Benn ibid: 381). The first waves of women's liberation and fight for suffrage, two world wars and the massive social and economic disruptions accompanying them saw the role of women in public life decisively shift as they began to take their place in public life. Full, formal equality was still more than a generation away though and had to await the Sex Discrimination Act of 1975 in Britain. A similar delay can be said to characterise the introduction of an emancipatory form of adult education for women, as opposed to the 'domestic version' which had held sway for so long. Women remained in general within the domestic sphere and as far as adult education was concerned were often subsumed under the category of men. This is not to say that women's education did not exist: between the world wars the Adult School movement, the WEA, the Women's Co-operative Guild, university extension, the Women's Labour League, the Townswomen's Guild, Women's Institutes and local education authority classes attracted women as a high proportion of students, teachers and organisers (Benn ibid 382). By 1936-37 one third of all LEA adult education enrolments were in women's subjects and recreational areas and 56 per cent of students were women.

The 1944 Education Act contained a rhetoric of equality of access but overall women's secondary status was of near invisibility. Girls could of course attend grammar schools and formally enter university but they were still largely excluded from higher education after the Second World War. The ideology of 'motherhood' was used as a powerful deterrent against further education and working class girls in particular were educated for domesticity (Deem 1981). Yet by 1950 women had risen to be 60 per cent majority of all adult education students in evening institutes and major establishments (Benn ibid). The demand from women for education at all levels was insatiable and it could no longer be suppressed by patriarchal or deferential social attitudes and values. The changing post-war world labour market, economic growth and the liberalisation of attitudes all changed women's position in the home and in public life as the second wave of women's liberation occurred. In the home domestic labour saving devices such as washing machines, vacuum cleaners, fridges, and cooking utensils made women's lives easier, though men still did not take up their fair share of housework and child care. Many women benefitted from the availability of the birth control pill from the 1960s because they could now control their own fertility. Social experimentation was everywhere in the sixties as traditions and cultures of the older generations were questioned and abandoned. Women demanded a more equal division of labour, a greater sharing of power and control over family and domestic life and recognition of how women constructed their own sense of really useful knowledge and learning. Women's educational studies evolved (Open University1982; Thompson 1983) and feminism became a major strand of academic and social life (Appelrouth and Edles 2007). These developments linked a feminist curriculum to other social liberation movements (Allen 1982; Arnot 1995) and these social knowledges began to contest the separation of knowledge, values and politics from women's lives. Sexuality, race, gender and identity were all re-examined to include the politics of self, culture and knowledge (Seidman 1998).The women's movements developed and explored the ideas of a more personal, experiential, 'dialogic' and person-centred curriculum and the need to create spaces where gender biased criteria for what counted as knowledge could be challenged (Lynch 2022).

Not all women were educated for domesticity (Kibworth Grammar School 1935)

In the 1970s and 1980s the Women's Liberation Movement was a focus for adult learning (Thompson 1983) and women continued to make up a very large part of the student cohort. Second Chance and New Horizon courses for women sprang up everywhere in Britain and many were linked-in to the emerging Access courses and Open Colleges (Wilson 2010). The Access movement at this time included many women's initiatives focussed on learning that was appropriate to women returners and a curriculum that centred around confidence building, counselling, study skills and women's interests; many were purposively located in local communities where women lived out their lives rather than on educational campuses. The government's Manpower (sic) Services Commission and the local authorities offered wider opportunities for women in areas where women had been traditionally excluded such as electronics and computing. The Women's Technology Scheme set up in Liverpool in 1983 was one such course. Positive action courses such as 'women into management' and 'professional updating' for women returners to their careers proved popular. There were feminist women's studies programmes in universities and colleges which raised questions of what women's knowledge and a feminist curriculum might be. Feminism became a major strand of academic life and infused wider cultures in the workplace, the community and beyond. Some community-based courses emphasised student-centred participatory learning which was intended to be transformational in that it recognised women's own power to shape their experience and futures (McMinn 2000). By 1995 some two thirds of the over 30,000 students on over 1,000 Access courses were women (Benn ibid: 388).

The rapid growth in women's education coincided with the desire of the Conservative governments to cut education budgets in the 1980s and 1990s. Contraction and rationalisation became watchwords for the controlling Conservative Party in government. Combined with inadequate childcare provision women's education became constrained and subject to the same forces as other forms of adult education (McGivney 1994). In the wider political and cultural debate the ideologies of individualism and economic neoliberalism were combined with the belief in the sanctity of the family to limit access to women's education. This was part of a paradox where the needs of the labour market were evolving towards a more educated workforce and a massive increase in women's part-time work was taking place. Simultaneously welfare and childcare provision funded by the state and local government was decreasing, re-imposing domestic burdens on women.

The reality is that the growth and expansion of Access education in the 20th and 21st centuries is at one and the same time the story of women's education. The emphasis on their learning in the 19th century had been on a curriculum focussed on the domestic division of labour- one that positioned most women as subordinate to men and beyond that fashioned them for cheap labour in service industries or factories. For some women of the middle classes there existed greater opportunities, if not in work and the professions, in world of literature. Women writers were able to create their own spaces and meanings and gain public access and recognition through their own work and increasingly through the 19th century writing became an accepted profession for women. Despite all the possibilities of discrimination learning, reading and literature were paramount among the arts for women for the last 200 years. In the 20th century women were in the majority in much adult education and by the end of the century they had asserted their right to equality and fair treatment.

The norms, values and practices that underpin modern society, however, especially in its neoliberal and marketised forms nevertheless remain gendered, and women and men everywhere resist the definitions of themselves as merely economic actors and seek authentic learning for self-fulfilment and better social results. There is what Lynch (2022) refers to as a parallel world to the political-economic world- **an affective care-relational world**- in which women have played and continue to play the vital part. This world is the world of care and affective relations and its contribution to social justice and learning; a world Lynch states has been silenced in academic and other discourse. Women's voices within Access were perhaps one significant aspect within the wider feminist resistance to historic oppression and a means of demanding change and progress.

## Continuing growth of the learning society

By the 1980s the growth in demand for relevant adult education quickly outstripped what was on offer in conventional further and higher education. Routine qualifications such as O and A level GCEs could not satisfy an awakening demand for more relevant and useful knowledge. In response, teachers in further education who had adopted adult learning methods and styles undertook negotiations with higher education institutions locally. Diploma of higher education courses were encouraged by the Council for National Academic Awards (CNAA) to recruit mature adult students and exceptional entry requirements for polytechnics and colleges of higher education made it possible to admit significant numbers of non-standard (NS) entrants to validated courses. Informal arrangements between different institutions in further and higher education developed using the potential for credit transfer between degree and diploma studies. In London cooperation on course design, learning strategies, selection and assessment was endorsed within the ILEA (Inner London Education Authority), the largest local education authority in the land. These arrangements provided a model for all the new Access courses established within the authority (Millins ibid). Outside the capital the model was widely imitated and remained as the dominant model into the mid- 1980s.

These developments did not meet with universal approval. The government's Lindop Report (DES 1985) considered that standards were at risk if existing minimum entry requirements were lowered. Further, they thought there was a danger of lowering academic standards if too high a proportion of mature students were admitted to degree courses. The conventional universities with some notable exceptions (Edwards 1984) carried on regardless with their mission to sort and select those from each generation thought worthy of access to higher learning. A rising middle class and a small proportion of working class grammar school pupils were by now making their way to university through the expanding secondary school system. The battle for comprehensive schooling for the majority had been won by the late 1970s (Benn 2011) and higher education was about to expand for the masses. In the mean-time the elite, ancient universities continued to select the offspring of the wealthy elites through the well-trodden public school-university escalator with very little criticism of their academic standards and quality.

Access movement supporters meanwhile were able to demonstrate the direct involvement of higher education tutors in curriculum design and student assessment. Quality and reliability were protected by HE participation in the selection of students and in the external moderation of results and performance (FEU 1985, 1986). The refusal by some at this time to recognise the achievements of Access students may have had more to do with contrasting conceptions and values concerned with teaching and learning than with the objective assessment of standards and attainment (ILEA 1984; Millins ibid). Access courses continued to thrive as part of a movement towards greater equality whilst the wider society was moving into a new period with a surge in income and wealth inequality that defined it as one of market supremacy. This was the era of neoliberalism and globalisation which was to be most beneficial to people with the highest human capital and the highest financial capital and wealth (Picketty 2013). A struggle was about to develop between rival concerns and ideological shifts around the nature of a 'learning society' and the role of education within it.

# References

Allen, S. (1982) Ethnic Disadvantage in Britain, Unit 4 of Open University Course E354, *Ethnic Minorities and Community Relations*, Milton-Keynes: Open University Press.

Appelrouth, S. and Desfour Edles, L. (2007) Feminist Theory, ch 7, *Sociological Theory in the Contemporary Era: Text and Readings,* Thousand Oaks, Cal. Pine Forge Press/Sage Publications.

Archer, M. (2013) *Social Origins of Educational Systems*, Oxon: Routledge.

Arnot, M. (1995) 'Feminism, education and the New Right', in Dawtry, L. et al. (eds) *Equality and Inequality in Educational Policy*, Multilingual Matters/Open University, Clevedon.

Ashwin, P. et al (2015) *Reflective Teaching in Higher Education*, London: Bloomsbury Academic.

Ball, S. J. (2002) *Class Strategies and the Education Market: The Middle Classes and Social Advantage,* London: Routledge/Falmer.

Ball, S. J. (2006) *Education Policy and Social Class: The Selected Works of Stephen J. Ball,* Oxon: Routledge.

Bauman, Z. (2001) *Community: Seeking Safety in an Insecure World,* Cambridge: Polity Press.

Benn, R. (1996) Women and Adult Education, ch 15 in Fieldhouse, R. and associates, *A History of Modern British Adult Education,* Leicester: NIACE.

Benn, M. (2011) *School Wars: The Battle for Britain's Education*, London: Verso.

Ben-Tovim, G.S., Gabriel, G., Law, I. and Streddar, K. (1981) 'The Equal Opportunity Campaign in Liverpool' ch 6.4 in Cheetham, J., James, W., Loney, M., Mayer, B. and Prescott, W. (eds) (1981) *Social and Community Work in a Multi-Racial Society,* London: Harper and Row and the Open University.

Berger, J. (1984) *And our faces, my heart, brief as photos,* London Writers and Readers Publishing Cooperatives Society Ltd. See also Davies and Davies (2021) 'Learning and the ecology of community' 256-257.

Bernstein, B. (1974) *Class, Codes and Control,* Vol 1, London: Routledge & Keegan Paul.

Bernstein, B. (1977) 'On the classification and framing of educational knowledge', *Class, Codes and Control: Theoretical Studies Towards A Sociology of Language,* London: Routledge & Keegan Paul.

Brookfield, S. (1983) 'Community Adult Education: A Conceptual Analysis', *Adult Education Quarterly*, 1983, 33(3) 154-160, Washington: Adult Education Association of the USA.

Bruner, J. (1966) *Towards a Theory of Instruction*, New York: Norton.

Butler, L. (1981) 'GCE for Adults: a case of conflicting methodologies', *Adult Education*, 53(5).

Clay, D. (2020) *1919-2019 A Liverpool Black History 100 Years: A Liverpool Black Perspective,* 60-63 ISBN: 978 178645 469 0.

CNAA- Council for National Academic Awards (1984 August) Access to higher education: non-standard entry to CNAA first degree and Dip. HE. Courses. London: CNAA.

Davies, D. (1987) New Approaches to Access to Higher Education in England: Issues and Prospects, University of Liverpool M.Ed. thesis 1987.

Davies, D. (1995) *Credit Where It's Due*, University of Cambridge and Government Employment Department.

Davies, D. (2021) 'Working Class Community in Time and Space' in Davies, D. and Davies, E. (2021) *A Fair Go: Learning in Critical Times and Places: 257-260*, UK: Amazon.

Davies, D. and Nyland, J. (2021) 'Freedom Through Education: A promise postponed', ch 5 in Nyland, J. and Davies, D. (2021) *Engagement Matters: curriculum challenges for universities,* Adelaide, Australia: Engagement Australia/ Transform.

Deem, R. (1981) 'State policy and ideology in the education of women, 1944-1980', *British Journal of Sociology of Education*, 2, 2, pp. 131-43.

Dennis, N. (1968) 'Popularity of the neighbourhood community idea' in Pahl, R. (ed) (1968) *Readings in Urban Sociology*, Oxford: Pergamon Press.

DES (1985) The Lindop Report, Academic Validation in Public Sector Higher Education, London: HMSO.

Dewey, J. (1916) *Democracy in Education: an introduction to the philosophy of education,* New York: Macmillan- extracts in Skillbeck, M. (ed) (1970) *John Dewey*, London: Collier Macmillan.

Edwards, E.G. (1984) *Higher Education for Everyone*, Nottingham: Spokesman.

FEU (Further Education Unit of the government Department of Education and Science) (1980) *Active Learning: A register of experiential and participatory learning, parts 1 and 2,* London: FEU.

FEU (1981) *Active Learning: A guide to current practice in experiential and participatory learning,* London: FEU.

FEU (1985) *The Experience of Open learning,* London: FEU.

FEU (1986) Access to Further and Higher Education, management board paper 9 October 1986 (unpublished) and see also FEU (1986*) Response to the academic validation of degree courses for higher education* (the Lindop Report), London: FEU- (ISBN 0946469 54 Y).

Fieldhouse, R. and Associates (1996) *A History of Modern British Adult Education,* Leicester: NIACE.

Fletcher, C. I. (1980) 'Community Studies as practical adult education', *Adult Education,* 1980, 53.

Freire, P. (1972) *Pedagogy of the Oppressed,* London: Harmondsworth Penguin Books.

Hall, S. (1980) 'Teaching Race' in James, A. and Jeffcoate, R. (eds) (1981) *The School in the Multicultural Society,* London: Harper and Row/The Open University Press.

Hall, S. et al (eds) (1982) *The Empire Strikes Back,* Centre for Contemporary Cultural Studies, University of Birmingham.

Hall, S. (1983) 'Education in crisis' 'Part one: The politics of education' in Donald, J. and Wolpe, Anne Marie. (eds) (1983) *Is there anyone here from education?* London: Pluto Press.

ILEA (1984 September) *Access to Higher Education: Report of a Review of Access Courses at the Authority's Maintained Colleges of Further and Higher Education,* London: ILEA Inspectorate, County Hall.

John, G. (1978) 'Black Self-help Projects' ch 4 in Cheetham, J. et al (eds) (1981) *Social and Community Work in a Multi-Racial Society,* London: Harper and Row/ Open University Press.

John, G. (1981) 'Black Youth as an Ideology' ch 4.7 in Cheetham, J. et al (eds) (1981) *Social and Community Work in a Multi-Racial Society*, London: Harper & Row/Open University Press.

John, G. (2006) *Taking a Stand: Gus John Speaks on education, race, social action and civil unrest 1980-2005,* Manchester: Gus John Partnership Ltd.

Johnson, R. (1988) 'Really useful knowledge 1790-1850: memories for education in the 1980s' in Lovett, T. (ed) (1988) *Radical Approaches to Adult education*, UK: Routledge.

Knowles, M. (1970) *The Modern Practice of Adult Education*, New York: Associated Press.

Knowles, M. (1981) *The Adult Learner: A Neglected Species*, London: Houston Gulf, 2nd ed.

Knowles, M. (1983) 'An Andragogical Theory of Adult Learning' *in Learning about Learning: selected readings* (1983) Milton Keynes: Open University Press.

Lovett, T. (1975) *Adult Education, Community Development and the Working Class,* London: Ward Lock Educational.

Lovett, T. (1983) *Adult Education and Community Action*, (with Clarke, C. and Kilmurray, A.) London: Croom Helm.

Lynch, K. (2022) *Care and Capitalism: Why Affective Equality Matters for Social Justice*, Cambridge: Polity Press.

McGivney, V. (1994) 'Women, education and training: a research report', *Adults Learning*, 5, 5.

McMinn, J. (2000) *The changes and the changed: an analysis of women's community education in groups in the North and South of Ireland,* Ph.D. Thesis, 8102, University College Dublin, 2000.

Marland, M. (1980) 'A Programme for a Community of Schools' in Marland, M. (ed) (1980) *Education for the Inner City*, London: Heinemann Educational Books.

Martin, I. (1986) 'Education and community: reconstructing the relationship', *Journal of Community Education* 5.3 17-23.

Mezirow, J. (1981) A Critical Theory of Adult Learning and Education in Tight, M. (ed) (1983) *Adult Learning and Education* (reading 2.6) London: Croom Helm/ The Open University.

Midwinter, E. (1982) *Education in Later Life: A Bibliography*, Centre for Policy on Ageing, May 1981-May 1982.

Millins, P. K. C. (1984) *Access studies to Higher Education, September 1979-December 1983: A Report,* London: Roehampton Institute, Centre for Access Studies to Higher Education.

NAB- National Advisory Body (for public sector/ local education authority higher education) (1984), August, *Report of the Continuing Education Group*, London: NAB.

NAB (1986) *Transferable Personal Skills in Employment: The Contribution of Higher Education,* London: NAB.

NAG- Nottingham Andragogy Group (1983) *Towards a Developmental Theory of Andragogy,* University of Nottingham: Department of Adult Education.

Open University (1982) Course U221 *The Changing Experience of Women,* Milton Keynes: The Open University Press.

Parry, G. (1986) 'From Patronage to Partnership', *Journal of Access Studies*, Vol 1 No 1, April 1986.

Percy, K., Burton, D. and Withnall, A. (1994) *Self-directed learning among Adults: The Challenge for Continuing Education,* ALL: University of Lancaster.

Picketty, T. (2013) *Capital in the Twenty-First Century*, Cambridge, Mass/London, England: The Belknap Press of Harvard University.

Purvis, J. (1980) 'Working class women and adult education in nineteenth-century Britain', *History of Education*, 9,3. pp.193-212.

Rogers, C. R. (1969) *Freedom to Learn*, Columbus, Ohio: Charles E. Merrill.

Rogers, J. and Groombridge, B. (1976) *Right to Learn: The Case for Adult Equality*, London: Arrow Books.

Rowbotham, S. (1973) *Hidden from History: Three Hundred Years of Women's Oppression and the Fight Against It,* UK: Pluto Press.

Rowbotham, S. (1999) *Threads through time: writings on history and autobiography*, UK: Penguin Books.

Ryan, L. and Ward, M. (eds) (2019) *Irish Women and Nationalism,* Irish Academic Press.

Savage, M. et al (2015) *Social Class in the 21st Century*, UK: Pelican/Penguin Books.

Seidman, S. (1998) *Contested Knowledge: Social Theory in the Modern Era*, Oxford: Blackwell.

Shor, I. (1980) *Critical Teaching and Everyday Life*, Boston: South End Press and 1987 University of Chicago Press.

Simon, B. (1965) *Education and the Labour Movement 1870-1920*, London: Lawrence & Wishart.

Simon, B. (1990) *The Search for Enlightenment: The Working Class and Adult Education in the Twentieth Century*, Leicester: NIACE.

Simon, B. (ed) (1991) *Education and the Social Order 1940-1990,* London: Lawrence & Wishart.

Smithers, A. and Griffin, A. (1986) *The Progress of Mature Students*, Manchester: Joint Matriculation Board.

Teare, R. (2018) *Lifelong Action Learning: A journey of discovery and celebration at work and in the community*, Amazon: @Richard Teare.

Thompson, J. (1983*) Learning Liberation: Women's Response to Men's Education*, UK: Croom Helm.

Tomlinson, S. (with) Rex, J. (1979) *Colonial immigrants in a British City: A class analysis*, London: Routledge & Keegan Paul.

Tomlinson, S. (1983) *Ethnic minorities in British schools*, London: Heinemann.

Tomlinson, S. (2019) *Education and Race: From Empire to Brexit*, University of Bristol: Policy Press.

UGC- University Grants Committee (1984) *Higher Education and the Needs of Society,* London: UGC.

Wilson, P. (2010) *Big Idea, Small Steps: The Making of Credit-Based Qualifications,* Leicester: NIACE.

Women's education, knowledge, communication: the possibilities
of doing things differently through dialogue.

# Chapter 3

# A Learning Society or a Learning Market: Does the Race Still Go to the Swift?

## How much higher learning was there in the new 21st century?

The first two decades of the new century marked the later stages of a long 50 year transition from a planned elite system of higher education to a mass market in learning and qualifications. It saw a shift from education viewed as a social and public good to one where the consumer's perspective was paramount. Governments had indicated their preferences for a shift towards vocational learning but the massive investment in social and educational strategy and policy to bring this about was never undertaken. Individuals were encouraged to 'invest' in themselves and their own futures as a private and personalised choice, as if education was a commodity to be bought in the market-place. This was supposedly an act of free choice and the articulation of values that modern Britain had chosen to adopt, signalled by the election of conservative governments after 2010 dedicated to the 'free market economy' and neoliberal economic and social policies (Vogel 2017). This was at least the position in England which accounted for around 83 per cent of the UK's undergraduate population. The national systems of Scotland and Wales, however, diverged from England at least in terms of student financial support and other elements during this time though it is debatable whether the underlying philosophy and policy considerations which shaped their higher education were radically different from England.

# Lifelong learning for a learning age

At the end of the twentieth century it was clear that Britain and other industrial nations faced the challenges of economic regeneration and of the need to re-construct social cohesion. The globalising economy was at the same time re-shaping international trade and manufacturing and many of its dependent features such as how labour markets and human resources were organised. These transformations were re-shaping modernity and the nature of advanced capitalism both in local communities everywhere and across the world at large.

1996 was the European Year of Lifelong Learning and in Britain it became a central policy preoccupation which was used to justify any modest change to the status quo. Change was in the air as a long period of stagnant conservative government was about to end and education became a cynosure and focus for this sense of impending change impressed on the public by New Labour and its charismatic leader Tony Blair. Meanwhile, the values and philosophical bases of 'lifelong learning' continued to be contested and no long term consensus emerged as to exactly what it might mean for all of those who claimed its importance (Duke and Tobias 2001).

In Britain in 1997 the newly elected Labour government had declared that its priority vision for the future improvement of the nation was 'education, education, education'. The Dearing Review had pointed out earlier in the same year that there were very marked social divisions between those who participated in higher education. The working classes were suffering from inequalities and education was in the front line of attack, as it were. Learning was to be the foundation for an active citizenship and for greater well-being for both individuals whether at work or in their communities. *The Learning Age* (DfEE 1998) was declared and reforms to the divisive curriculums which separated knowledge-based learning from competency-based vocational qualifications, as well as those that separated adolescent from adult learners, were proposed. Remedies were suggested for the high levels of illiteracy and innumeracy and for the low participation of young people from semi-skilled and unskilled family backgrounds. Some of the barriers to learning were at last formally recognised and the consequences acknowledged for social exclusion and cohesion (Oppenheim 1998). In 1999 the government issued a framework for post-16 education, *Learning to Succeed* (DfEE 1999), in which the influence of the Access agenda could be detected. It stated…'too much learning provision is unsuited to the needs of learners. Many learners do not want to be tied to learning in a classroom. Many adults, in particular, are looking to learn in informal, self-directed and flexible ways- in the evenings, in their places of work, at week-ends and in their holidays. This flexibility will be essential if we are to attract into learning those for whom traditional learning methods have formed a barrier- including women returners and those turned off learning in a classroom by poor experiences at school.' It was recognised that formal education had failed many in its first phases and had furthermore delivered experiences of learning that had been emotionally and educationally disabling (Ranson et al 2000).

If Access had an influence on these policy developments it was as a shadow passing in the penumbra behind the full light of concern demonstrated by both Conservative and New Labour governments in this last decade of the 20th century- and beyond. This concern was for the development of lifelong learning to support a national policy for improved employability and competiveness in a global economy. The Conservatives stressed the need for individuals to take responsibility themselves for acquiring skills and knowledge and invest in themselves. Individuals had in this view to make themselves marketable in the competition for jobs. The labour government of the time did not fundamentally dissent from this viewpoint though it sponsored thinking and research around a more liberal and inclusive notion of lifelong learning.

The lifelong learning theme was taken up in the context of further education by the Kennedy Report, *Learning Works* which appeared in 1997. It evaluated widening participation in terms of how a strategy might promote a self-perpetuating learning society and it was critical of aspects of the marketisation of FE following the incorporation of colleges in 1993 when they were 'privatised' and released from local authority control and ownership (Ransom ibid: 4). Learning for work and learning for broader life purposes were regarded as inseparable in the report but one can see the wider, historical influence of the adult tradition coming through... 'Learning may also be undertaken for fun, for personal development or to achieve an appreciation of broader issues' (Kennedy 1997: 29). Kennedy's recommendations also supported the launch of a credit accumulation system and for new pathways of learning in further education, especially in relation to open college networks. For her work on widening participation Helena Kennedy QC was awarded an honorary degree by the University of Derby. *The Fryer Report* of 1997, issued by the incoming Labour government, went further and stressed the need to address social inequalities, highlighting the importance of involving local communities, and the need break down barriers to access in order to bring about cultural and social change through progressive education and learning. Tackling employability and social injustice called for support for learning cultures from a wide range of work, community and family contexts. A second Fryer Report was published in 1999 concerned with creating learning cultures for the much discussed 'learning age' that it was thought was about to be constructed.

The Kennedy and Fryer Reports had similar perspectives on credit frameworks and qualifications and were published within months of each other in 1997. However, they had significantly different emphases on the scope and meaning of education such that in Kennedy's view FE included *everything* outside schools and universities, whilst Fryer's report was perceived by government as a concept to replace the unfashionable idea of adult education (Wilson 2010: 100). *Lifelong Learning* was apparently a more acceptable concept and more in tune with the globalisation and human capital theories adopted by New Labour, which stressed the need for individuals to invest in their own skill development and employability in an ever more competitive global environment. Much responsibility for the further development of the progressive aspects of the Fryer and Kennedy Reports and the Learning Age went to a centralised government agency- the Qualifications and Curriculum Agency (QCA). This signalled the likely end of significant provider-led developments such as the idea of democratic and locally led credit frameworks for adult learning and learning experience. It also marked the impending demotion of the voluntary partnerships between providers which had been characteristic of the widening participation and Access movement. From now on centralised and government-funded agencies which were bent on implementing centralised strategic government policies would occupy the driving seat (Wilson ibid).

Much of this thinking about lifelong learning and the debate surrounding it found a point of condensation in the Labour government's Green Paper *The Learning Age* (DfEE ibid). The main thrust of this proposal was, however, to bring the focus back on to the question of improving 'human capital' in the context of globalisation and international competitiveness (Ranson ibid: 5). In the foreword of the Green Paper, David Blunkett the Minister for Education and Employment stated… 'Learning is the key to prosperity- for each of us as individuals, as well as for the nation as a whole. Investment in human capital will be the foundation of success in the knowledge-based global economy of the twenty-first century' (DfEE ibid: 7). Enhancing employability was clearly the main agenda for Blunkett and T*he Learning Age*. Worthy though this is, it was a long way away from the ambitious project of creating a *learning society*, let alone from the transformational power and potential of a mass learning movement, which might conceivably challenge entrenched privilege and militate for a more socially just and equal society. And though the Access movement may not have formulated such an aim for itself (it did not), it facilitated the critical thinking that allowed it to be considered and debated by the Access movement.

The needs of lifelong learning were now to be focussed primarily on human capital and the skills required throughout working life. New funding principles were produced which gave preferential treatment to students from lower social-economic groups and employment related concerns such as re-skilling of workers, job insecurity and the significance of guidance and counselling for employment applications. High quality vocational education and the creation of new vocational opportunities for learners of all ages became available, at least in theory. This was no longer an agenda that governments thought could be safely left in the hands of voluntary partnerships spread out across the local authority regions of the country.

As the old century moved inexorably into the new one it became clear that a substantial expansion of learning had taken place in the previous two decades. Some of this was in response to the historic deficits and 'wicked issues' which had deprived many of the opportunities that came with and through further and higher education. Adult educators had shown the way with a diverse and creative array of courses and ways of teaching which appealed to adult learners. The formal commitment though to the need for lifelong learning came about when governments and the wider public came to appreciate that education was for most people the only coping strategy to deal with social and economic regeneration. The threats this posed rather than the opportunities it presented was the unacknowledged motive force for change. However, the reforms that took place from the 1980s and into the 1990s were driven by governments whose grasp of the problems was shaped by a narrow focus on training and education for work and employment. The improvement of human capital was the fundamental concept that drove change rather than the need to re-examine the unequal and often unjust social relations of a society and what new conceptions of learning might improve them. What was becoming more clear to all concerned was the fact that work and the labour market cannot be separated from the need to re-think the relations between the sexes, races and the generations. Questions of how we organise work, of unemployment and the nature of work in the future were of great concern in the 1980s and of great interest to educationalists. These were some of the crucial issues and themes that preoccupied the Access movement but could not be resolved outside of the wider political framework of public policy and debate.

The Dearing Review of 1997, coinciding with the newly elected 'New Labour' government, was a key departure point for government thinking about education and Britain's future. The abolition of the 'binary' system of polytechnics and universities in 1992 had created the potential for a unified higher education sector and the possibility of educational reform was in the air. Tony Blair's striking election slogan of 'Education, Education, Education' signified the concern but it lacked a clear focus on exactly what the educational problem was and how it might be resolved. Dearing had concluded that there were marked differences in participation in HE between the different social groups in society and that this was no longer acceptable. The highest status occupational groups were six times as likely to participate in higher education as the lowest. The key lessons of the Robbins Report of some thirty years earlier had not been sufficiently learned but social awareness of some of the wicked issues was now very different from that earlier time. In particular it was noted, application rates for universities were notably lower from most black and minority ethnic (BAME) groups. All of this had been the common currency of Access providers for some thirty years who had been responding to grass roots concerns and independent movements, and sometimes revolts, rooted in their own communities and neighbourhoods (Martin 1996; John 2006). They knew full well that education was a vital component of much needed reform of opportunities and access just as they knew that issues of social injustice, historic racism and a profoundly divided society along racial, ethnic and cultural/class lines would not be resolved by schooling and universities alone (John 2006 ibid; Hall 2017; Tomlinson 2019).

The new direction was to continue the expansion started under the previous governments with an increased emphasis on 'widening participation' so the excluded and marginalised groups identified by Dearing could be brought into the mainstream and the social inequalities addressed. One policy aim was to ensure that 50 per cent of all young people should have 'an experience' of higher education by the age of 30. The then current participation rate was around 35 per cent which was perceived to be lower than some of Britain's competitors such as the USA and South Korea. The main policy instrument for this was the Aimhigher programme which in 2004, inheriting from previous programmes designed to enhance access and progression to HE, was funded to develop a wide range of activities with schools and colleges, universities and community organisations. The aim was to raise aspirations for higher education amongst groups that had been historically under-represented (Harrison 2018: 55). Aim Higher had been the title of Sir Christopher Ball's pioneering report on widening participation published in 1994 by the Royal Society of Arts.

The early years of the new Labour government after 1997 saw other significant developments. One of the first was the decision to introduce higher education tuition fees in Britain for the first time and to abolish student grants in favour of a single means-tested loan. This was to have seismic effects on the whole direction of higher education in the UK. New curricular reforms allowed the introduction of two year foundation degrees aimed primarily at workers who wanted to upgrade their skills and knowledge but who lacked entry qualifications for university. Some grants were re-introduced from 2004, limited to selected urban areas of deprivation. A continuing theme was the long-standing inequalities in elite universities' admissions practices- a topic which always generated great debate in the press and media outlets but which impacted only a tiny minority of disadvantaged students who were themselves an elite within their own cohorts.

Expanding higher education to address the inequalities and social injustices in the wider society was, however, held to be unaffordable by New Labour and student fees were tripled to £3,000 a year. Individual institutions could charge less in an attempt to conjure up a 'market' between competing providers but very few did. Grants and bursaries for low income students were expanded but most students now took out the student loan which had to be repaid on graduation. A governmental Office for Fair Access was created which required institutions to lay out their plans and commitments to widening participation but this had no real teeth to enforce compliance and there was no national policy for access or widening participation.

The predicted shockwaves from the introduction of student fees did not occur and they were to be raised again by successor governments to over £9,000 a year after 2012. Participation rates for disadvantaged groups did not rise greatly at first and this became the focus for policy development (HEFCE 2005, 2007). The HE system as a whole continued its inexorable expansion in spite of a scaling back of widening participation initiatives following the financial global crisis of 2008-09 (Harrison ibid: 57). The desired economic redistribution of wealth and opportunity envisaged at the start of the Labour governments did not happen. Social and economic inequality continued to grow throughout this period and accelerated after the conservatives were re-elected to office in 2010 (Wilkinson and Pickett 2010; Savage 2015; Dorling 2015, 2018; Toynbee and Walker 2020). What did happen, however, was the further development of the national obsession with representatives of disadvantaged groups attending elite universities (McCraig 2016). As Harrison (ibid: 57) states…'this group has become an ever-present, if ill-defined and misunderstood, focus for higher education policymaking since they were identified as being 'missing' (Sutton Trust 2004)'. Another major change was the abolition by 2014 of student numbers controls by government so that HE institutions could recruit as many students as they could handle. This was a signal to the elite universities to expand at the expense of the lower status institutions and to use their 'quality' provision to expand the market. From 2012 the government signalled its willingness to allow private providers to enter the higher education market. By 2016 the government had comprehensively rebranded the notion of widening participation as 'social mobility' (Waller et al 2015) as a government priority. The key aims were to double the proportion of people from disadvantaged backgrounds entering universities in 2020 compared to 2009 (Harrison ibid: 58) and to increase the number of BAME students in universities by 20 per cent by the same date.

It was the emphasis on elite universities and issues of high achieving young people, especially those from disadvantaged backgrounds, which dominated government thinking and served to distinguish this concern from the wider and deeper historical problems of an unequal class-ridden and socially unjust society that was Britain. Arguably, the earlier Access movement of the 1970s and 1980s had attempted to build a consciousness from the bottom up as it were by mobilising community awareness and the social solidarity generated by community development (Lovett 1975; Midwinter 1975; Kirkwood 1978). The 21$^{st}$ century developments including the later rhetoric of 'levelling up' served to highlight the mixed messages and confusion about the function of higher education in modern Britain … 'On the one hand, there has been a sustained objective to diversify institutions' intakes, especially among the elite universities who are deemed to offer the greatest opportunities for social mobility and access to high-status professions … On the other hand, the personal cost of higher education to students has increased from around £1,000 p.a. to £9,000 p.a.- a move which has restricted access from low income families and deprived communities, although evidence for this is slight.' (Harrison ibid: 59-60). There were also concerted attempts to persuade applicants deemed to be 'bright' from poor or deprived backgrounds to apply to elite institutions, regardless of their own priorities and engagements with local communities. These high status universities were of course more able to game the market to attract such students. The lower status institutions were financially far less well equipped to meet these challenges, yet they were historically and contemporaneously the ones that served the under-represented groups highlighted by the Dearing Report more than twenty years earlier.

## Who got to participate?

There are problems in analysing social class trends in participation in higher education since there is no single and reliable and valid and generally accepted measure. Harrison (ibid) assembles three distinct 'markers' using various sources: participation of young people at local governmental ward level; eligibility of young people to receive free school meals, means tested on their parents' income; and occupational data related to parental occupation if the student was under 25 or to the student's prior occupation if they were 25 and over.

Harrison analysed data on young (that is 18-19 year olds and under 21 year olds) full-time entrants to HE between 2000 and 2016. Reliable data for this cohort was available whereas a pool of reliable data for mature students was unavailable and there were great difficulties in allocating mature students to socio-economic groups for analysis.

The issue of unequal access and participation was not a new one and the question was whether the growth and expansion of HE would allow for and encourage a fairer and more equal opportunity culture to emerge. The trends in full-time participation in HE of young people between 2000 and 2016 showed a sustained growth in young people from lower socio-economic groups. However, there was no indication of a significant shift in the social mix of mature students across this same period. It remained broadly constant between 11.5 per cent and 12.5 per cent from areas with the lowest participation in HE. The growth in young people from lower socio-economic groups would appear in reality to be driven by improvements in GCSE attainment. In fact Crawford (2014) concludes that 95% of the difference in young people's participation in HE are captured within qualifications gained at age 16, rather than qualifications gained later (just before entry to HE). Furthermore the slowest improvement in GCSE attainment profiles were for the White British community. This community also had the lowest increase in its participation rate in HE from 2007 onwards, from 21.7 % to 27.8% whereas the Black group increased their participation rate in HE from 20.9% to 36.7%. In addition, many commentators had believed that students from low income families would be discouraged by the introduction of and increases in tuition fees. However, there was little evidence to support this view according to Harrison (ibid).

Between 2005 and 2014 improvement in participation rates for 18 and 19 year olds across all social groups were recorded with improvement rates being faster for the less affluent sectors. Some narrowing of the gap between the highest participation areas and the lower took place with demand reaching saturation levels for the affluent groups. Paradoxically when the tuition fee rises of 2006 and 2012 took place demand from lower status and income groups actually rose. Overall there was a long term improvement in the participation of disadvantaged young people as they took an increasing share of the higher education market. To some degree the increased tuition fees were offset by a variety of grants and bursaries for students from disadvantaged backgrounds but the vast majority of students were saddled with significant debt repayments for fees and maintenance loans once their working life had begun.

The strong stratification of the university sector, especially marked in England, is noteworthy and after 2012 the Russell Group of 'high tariff' and supposedly elite universities saw participation rise, reflecting the change in policies controlling student numbers that allowed these institutions to increase their enrolment of high achieving young people. However, the big improvement in participation for young people from the lower socio-economic groups in British society was concentrated in the 'lower tariff' institutions- those which did not normally figure as winners in the dubious league and performance tables. The growth in participation of lower socio-economic groups in elite institutions was a step in the right direction but as Harrison (ibid: 69) points out, it was modest and needs to be understood in the wider context of stronger growth and participation for more advantaged groups in the elite and elitist system (Croxford and Raffe 2015).

On the matter of ethnic categories and identities and participation, the period saw significant change. Whereas the Dearing Review in 1997 noted BAME communities had a lower rate of participation in higher education than the majority white community, Chinese and Indian populations had strong participation rates. By 2015 the position had been reached where the white majority community had the lowest participation rates, below those of BAME communities. Between 2007 and 2015 the Black population had the fastest growth in participation of all the ethnic groups.

The period was one in which participation increased very substantially as the whole HE system was set on expansion and rapid growth. Ethnic groupings and black populations benefitted and their participation rates improved though not all equally. Afro-Caribbean students did less well than students from Chinese and some south Asian backgrounds. White working class students appeared to perform comparatively poorly. The system as a whole became larger but simultaneously more stratified with 'high' and 'low' tariff institutions emerging. High tariff universities could recruit the best performing A Level students and claim to be of higher quality. Eventually a whole series of performance league tables were adopted in which the elite universities (the Russell Group) out-performed the others in an unequal and unfair competition and for which the playing fields were not level. The most successful institutions received more funding than those at the bottom of the scale and a self-generated and self-serving hierarchy of universities was created. The more homogenous, elitist and very much smaller internally egalitarian university system of the post-war world had, some 70 years later, morphed into a mass higher education system hoovering up more than 50 per cent of school leavers. In doing so it had also transformed itself into an economic generator of huge significance to the wider economy and for the scientific and research communities. It was a diversified yet highly differentiated, stratified and hierarchical system. Its importance for the social and economic state of the nation could not be denied though its contribution to social justice and the social purposes of higher education was open to question and controversy.

## Explaining the market model

The decade of the 1990s was a period of creative foment in higher education in Britain. The Thatcherite version of neoliberalism in the market economy was rampant and the government had made it clear that it wished to see a competitive market created in higher education in line with its dominant ideology that education was a positional good: something to be bought and sold on the market by those who either deserved it due to their meritocratic qualities, such as possessing greater intelligence or having the right educational values or rightly belonging to those who could afford to pay for it. Private schooling in the form of 'public schools' had after all provided for generations a model for successful learning and the social and economic placement in society that followed for the wealthy and privileged (Green and Kynaston 2019). State funding for both further and higher education in this period was radically disrupted first by Conservative governments and then by New Labour after 1997, so that money followed students who were seen as consumers of learning. In reality of course elite institutions continued to select their students and 'sorting them out' and legitimating the selection of students continued to be one of their major functions on behalf of a deeply unequal society. In justifying inequality through unfair but hidden selection, universities colluded then, as they do today, in subjugating the people they are supposed to liberate through learning.

It was obvious to many at the time that the marketised post-school system was dysfunctional (Scott 1997; Jary and Parker 1998). However, this was an era of globalisation, of the growth of multi-culturalism, the fragmentation of older identities and certainties, the fracturing of political affiliations and the demands of new cohorts of students coming out of multi-racial and multi-ethnic communities all over the UK. It was a time of change and disruption and the Thatcherite ideology of market-driven change was in its ascendancy. The only game in town for universities and colleges was that of growth. Institutions that grew survived whilst those that remained small were often amalgamated with more 'viable', that is bigger, institutions. The commitment to neoliberal economics did not prevent the Conservative governments from expanding the role of the state into the organisation, control and financing of further and higher education. The financial models adopted by the government funding councils for further education (FEFC) and higher education (HEFC) rewarded growth and drove demand from students. The operations and implementation around the country of this work were directed from a centralising London-based government. One outcome was to deprive local communities of the power and money to decide and control their own institutions (Waller et al 2015), a process that had been underway for at least a generation.

The time was also remarkable for the explosion of educational institutions and systems (Robertson 1994, 1995; Davies 1995, 1997). Open colleges and open college federations were at this point emerging nearly everywhere to find that their voluntary adult learning programmes were now fundable (Wilson 2010), as were accredited extra-mural classes in universities. The government had decreed that adult learning that was 'accredited' could be given funds, provided that qualifications and academic credits could be awarded for learning achievement. A whole new accreditation industry and related institutions came into being claiming to link all the various levels of learning right up to the apex of the system at the universities (Davies 1995 ibid). If the market for educational qualifications was part of the neoliberalism everywhere in society, progressive teachers and learners could compensate for its dysfunctional impacts through providing really attractive learning packages - smaller courses and units of learning which could be accumulated towards meaningful and useful qualifications. A progressive ethos seemed to pervade the air we breathed! What could possibly be better than growth? Opportunities through education might now be opened up for those long denied their chance to succeed. It was easy to overlook the fact that what can be given with one hand can be taken away with the other. Within two decades most of this expanded sector of learning had disappeared; gone with the onset of austerity politics which drove local and community provision of post-school education out of existence. But all that was for the future.

## New century: old inequalities

As the 20th century moved towards its end it was possible to see the contours of a new system of higher education emerging from out of the old. For most of the post-Second World War period, universities formed the pinnacle of the British education and training system. Their students had been mostly 18 year old male school leavers and were selected from elite public schools and grammar schools. The universities in theory selected their students but much of this work was done by proxy in the selective schools themselves. There was a fairly seamless transition from a relatively small number of providing schools to universities which formed a ladder of progression into the higher echelons of British society and economy. A well-known and well-trodden path upwards for the existing and aspiring upper social classes and elite groups was available for those whose values and wealth could be preserved across the generations through schooling. Universities set the standards for the rest of the education system and through their teaching and research defined what kind of knowledge and skill and understanding would be most highly valued in society.

By the mid-1990s as we have seen many of these things had changed, though many did not simply disappear but re-emerged and persisted as they adapted to change in the wider society. The private schools, for example, adapted their teaching and learning strategies to preserve their advantageous relationships with elite universities, and the universities themselves gave attention to the selection of what they thought were the most talented young people from black and ethnic groups. The growth of the mass education system had, however, opened up opportunities for study in general and it was not just the young that could benefit. In the middle of the decade there were almost as many mature undergraduate students who were aged over 21 as younger students (HESA 1995-96) and the proportion of women students of all ages had rapidly increased. The growth of new universities in the 1960s was followed by the expansion of polytechnics which all became universities overnight in 1992 by virtue of a decree by conservative education minister Ken Clarke. The Open University became the biggest university in the UK with open entry for most degree courses and fees liable for local government support. Adult learning in university extra-mural departments flourished as did adult colleges and evening classes all over the country. An explosion of open learning took place with the creation of 'open colleges' and open college federations all over the UK whose task was to provide and recognise through accreditation a whole raft of learning and skills which had never before been recognised.

The measure of the changes underway as the new 21st century approached can be gauged by the following sketch:

- in 1960 there were 22,426 people obtaining university degrees and by 2011 there were 350,800
- in 1967 full-time student numbers in universities were 197,000 and in 2018 there were 1.8 million undergraduates

- in 1960 there were 24 universities in the UK; in 2019/20 there were 282 higher education providers; major growth in the number of institutions took place in the 1960s (23 more) and in the 1990s (73 more)
- in 1950 participation in higher education was 3.4 % of the age cohort; in 1970 it was 8.4 %; in 1990 it was 19.3 % and in 2000 it was 33%; by 2015 the earlier target of 50% had been confirmed
- in the year 2000 there were more women obtaining degrees than men (University World News 2013).

Paradoxically, the explosion of learning opportunities was financed mostly by successive Conservative governments which saw advantages in the willingness of people to learn. The new learning kept some people off the dole and out of the unemployment statistics. What else were literally millions of displaced working people to do when their factories and workplaces had closed? The 'deconstruction' of swathes of British firms during the Thatcherite governments of the 1980s and 1990s saw post-war unemployment rates rocket. The dysfunctional impacts of neoliberal market fundamentalism were felt everywhere as young people became NEETS (not in education, employment or training), as child poverty rates rose to disgraceful levels unknown since the inauguration of the welfare state and as people appeared to reconcile themselves to a continuous increase in social inequality. Throughout this period- from 1979 to 1997- Conservative governments were elected. It was widely thought at the time that the somewhat unexpected bonuses accruing from the discovery and exploitation of North Sea oil throughout this period were squandered on paying for the Youth Training Scheme (YTS), which kept potentially rebellious and disruptive young people off the streets by forcing them into learning and training schemes with dubious prospects for their working futures (Raffe 1998). British society and culture as well as British education was being re-modelled at this time and education was perceived as offering new possibilities as well as rectifying older injustices as discussion and debate around 'modernity' took place (Giddens 1990, 1991; Hall and Gieben 1992; Harvey 1994). Both higher and further education were experiencing substantial change as mass higher education appeared to be the harbinger of increased diversity and increased educational opportunity (Davies 1998). More meant different, not worse, as we moved into a globalising and cosmopolitan future (Skrbis and Woodward 2013). The imagination needed to create *educational* change grew out of this wider maelstrom of social and economic change. The idea that something in British society was broken gained currency, whilst at the same time the wider and sometimes global social and economic disruption offered the possibility of radical change through education (Ranson et al 2000; Nyland and Davies 2022). Education was a key part of how society could be fixed and new possibilities opened up through a transformed education system. It is worth briefly reviewing the concerns of the time which shaped awareness and understanding of the social and cultural changes which were underway.

## A changing world

Among the many ways in which Britain was changing the following had a bearing on what was expected of an expanding mass higher education system in which access and widening participation was an expectation:

### An ageing and changing population

Whilst life expectancy was still rising at the turn of the century birth rates remained low. The opportunity to put further education and higher education together in creative packages and programmes was taken after careful evaluation of the future prospects of the labour market (Davies 1997 ibid). Developers also knew through experience gained in education and curriculum development that learning demand can be created where none apparently existed before.

### Changing structures of employment

The 1990s saw an increase in the number of part-time workers and casual and freelance work became more popular. This was partly driven by the needs of women wanting to work outside the home and the need for a second income in addition to a male bread-winner to sustain the family home and its ever-growing consumerism and unsustainable housing costs. In the longer term there was downward pressure on wages as British industry lost out to foreign competition and productivity fell. Immigrant labour became a more important factor in the British economy as manufacturing employment declined. The move to a service economy was being consolidated as the City of London increased its influence over government policy. Meanwhile, new forms of learning including work-based programmes and the accreditation of prior learning and experience were piloted throughout the country.

### Higher skills

The older industrial heartlands began to be referred to as 'left behind' as the knowledge-based industries expanded in the larger metropolitan centres. However, many areas had not benefitted from the rapid development of IT and information-based industries. It was clear that structures and fields of knowledge were changing rapidly as was computer and digital learning. It was widely thought that Britain was moving inexorably towards a 'knowledge economy' where education and qualifications would be commensurate with the burgeoning growth of science and technology based employment. The older manufacturing economy of Britain as the workshop of the world was being consigned finally to the dustbin or to history.

## Changing communities

Change may be said to be global but it is felt and experienced locally. The drive for qualifications and for vocational relevance in learning was felt in many communities throughout the country and this reflected the major changes taking place in the labour market and the British economy. The political and economic policies of the 1980s had signalled both the growth and importance of markets and the idea that these could be created to provide and deliver social and educational services. Many local communities could no longer sustain local labour markets for employment and young people and graduates in particular moved to the greater urban centres.

## Growth and change

Growth was a means of delivering change this since it could in theory incentivise people and organisations to be more flexible and entrepreneurial. If we had growth then, ran the argument, consumers and providers, in fact all the stakeholders in the system, could benefit. There was no need to redistribute opportunities or resources on the grounds of equity and fairness; instead the market mechanism would ensure this took place. This had a bearing on both further and higher education and for a period (which was not to last) the boundaries between providers - between colleges and universities - were dissolving. The previously different and antithetical worlds of higher education and further education were, however briefly, seen to be the beneficiaries of processes of change experienced as common. The market could provide the means of a beneficent convergence where the individualisation of choice, diversity of provision and the growth of a relevant vocationalism would ensure Britain's education was able to benefit from the inevitably globalised and competitive world we were entering. This was the providential or panglossian view that was assumed by those who wished to commercialise higher education and subject learning to the disciplines of the free market (Scott 1997; Williams 2013).

## Part-time students and extra-mural decline

Perhaps the most notable *negative* outcome of higher education development in the period was the collapse of part-time mature adult numbers which dropped dramatically after 2012 following growth from 2006 to 2010. The fall in 2012 was less dramatic than for younger part-time students but the recovery was slower than for younger students. From a high point of 247,375 in 2008, part-time mature students went down to 97,925 in 2014 (HESA 2016). No doubt the fees increases in 2012 and the global financial crisis in 2008-09 played a part, as did the abolition of funding for part-time students wanting to take a second degree. A more significant yet inevitably more speculative reason for the decline in 'adult learning' in universities may have been the pressures for financial control and the marketisation of education and learning which accompanied the 'globalising' of educational opportunities. Few universities resisted the lure of distance learning and the digitalisation and centralisation of the curriculum offer to students. Overseas and distance students could be recruited and brought with them lucrative fee income for cash-starved universities at relatively low costs. Full-time mature student numbers remained buoyant in the early decades of the century but the collapse of part-time numbers signalled the end of one version of the Access movement, as far as university participation was concerned. Extra-mural departments in Britain just about everywhere were eventually closed as flexible and distance learning expanded to encompass what was once considered a unique form of face-to-face adult education (Marriott 1984). The traditional part-time students in the traditional extramural departments of the universities could not afford the fees once effective subsidies were withdrawn. This was one example of the decline of the liberal adult education tradition which had flourished in the absence of a popular or mass higher education tradition. Adult education as a whole, however, since before the start of the 20th century, had included a wide range of traditions of learning and organisations dedicated to developing learning for the ordinary citizens and for the working classes in particular (Simon 1990; Kelly 1992; Fieldhouse 1996).

In 1953 R.H.Tawney gave a lecture to mark the half-centenary of the Workers' Education Association (WEA). His involvement with the WEA was part of a wider and dense web of adult education organisations which included the Women's Co-operative Guild, the residential colleges, the labour colleges, the educational activities of the labour movement organisations, the co-operative movement and the trades unions. Engagement with mass movements was a feature of adult learning and prominent intellectuals and social analysts such as Tawney, who had been president of the WEA, and G.D.H. Cole were leading figures who sought to share their learning with the emerging leaders of working class movements (Field 2013). The Plebs League and the National Council of Labour Colleges achieved a reputation for radical views on the how knowledge might transform social conditions for the betterment of working class people. In the post-Second World War period emancipatory and democratic literacy movements flourished in selected and influential pockets in the voluntary sector and in the metropolitan LEAs (Fieldhouse 1996: 161-162). In 1946 the WEA had 45, 000 members and 936 branches; it was a democratic organisation and the students controlled the class! Eventually the WEA was to face the issue of being incorporated and assimilated into the state funded mainstream where the space and capacity for radical education and social action was curtailed. Some saw this government investment as a political investment against extremism (Fieldhouse ibid: 169). G.D.H. Cole had earlier summed up the dilemma facing the WEA… '(it) cannot have it both ways. It cannot be a general adult education provider and at the same time the educational representative of the working-class movement' (Cole 1952: 6-9).

## Adult education as part of the state

After the Second World War education as a whole including adult learning, was seen as part of the mixed economy and welfare state provision that comprised the 'post-war settlement'. However, the early years of the 21st century saw ideologically driven attempts by governments to reverse the interventionist structures and thinking of the welfare state in order to create a more 'enterprise culture' and to combat state and welfare dependency. As Roger Fieldhouse (ibid: 391) pointed out, even long before these tendencies became fully dominant in educational discourse, adult education became caught up in these ideological shifts because it was expected to contribute to both social welfare and socially just outcomes and to the individualistic and self-help culture which drove much political choice.

The long term development of adult education saw it become incorporated in the state's funded provision and its transition from a 'movement' into an educational service. This meant it would lose much of its distinctive local character and mission and its local autonomy. By the time the Access movement itself was underway in the 1980s the local educational authorities (LEAs) were having their functions and funding progressively removed by central government. The 1988 Education Reform Act reduced the powers of the LEAs which contributed to a growing fragmentation and eventual destruction of a comprehensive adult education service. The 1992 Further and Higher Education Act further reduced the role of the LEAs leaving them with only residual adult education responsibilities unprotected by earmarked funding. One of the results of this was a decline in participation by the poorer and the older populations as the LEAs abandoned much direct provision which many had fostered in the previous half century. The new demands and the burgeoning provision for young adults would have to be met by central government policies which after 1992 were prepared to fund further and vocational education at the expense of the broader liberal adult learning which had encompassed in many places aspects of personal and social development for change, including 'community education'. University extra-mural provision similarly had been incorporated into mainstream university education fuelled by government incentives in the 1980s for vocationally relevant provision of continuing education. As with the incorporation of major parts of the previous LEA system and the voluntary but publically funded WEA provision within government funded programmes, these developments marked the end of a separate and distinctive social movement involving universities. It is worth noting that the same forces impacted on the long-term adult residential colleges which shared similar values and pedagogies and sometimes partnerships with university adult providers. Many of these colleges closed in the early 21$^{st}$ century along with short-term residential colleges, many of which had been supported by the LEAs. The rich variety of adult learning institutions and opportunities lost public funding and support as the uncertain world of full-cost fees and marketised provision became the norm.

The great paradox for adult educators and adult learners was that this undoubted loss of learning opportunities and the closure of adult education providers coincided with social and economic changes that were themselves the signal for an expanded mass participation system. In the long term the working class were going to college and in spite of obstacles in the way and abrupt policy switches by all types of government, there was an inevitability about widening participation and access to higher education. There was, however, no inevitable blue-print for the precise system that would emerge nor for the way in which students would be selected and sponsored as British society and culture came to terms with the 21$^{st}$ century and the challenge of change.

## The access students and widening participation: when everything was changing

The growth and expansion of education after the Second World War seemed unstoppable and right up to the late 1960s the staying on trend at schools beyond the compulsory age was rising at 5 per cent per year for boys and 7 per cent for girls. In 1969, however, it stopped nearly entirely for boys and reduced to 3 per cent for girls. The trend for school leavers at age 18-19 to go on to higher education of all kinds peaked at 14.2 per cent in 1972 and did not rise above that until the late 1980s (Mandler 2020). Widening participation seemed to have stalled, though it was a period of gestation for Access and second chance courses both in the adult education colleges and the local education authorities and the Open University was making great strides forward in distance learning and teaching and in reaching adult students who had been denied access to HE in their earlier lives.

The 'long 1970s' was a period of great social and political disruption. Changing labour markets, the collapse of great swathes of traditional British industry, changing social attitudes and popular cultures, new identities emerging, the impact of migration and acknowledgement of ethnic diversity and the disruption within and across the educational system as whole all contributed to the contested character of British society. There was little sense of general consensus on what contemporary life should be like and a great deal of strife and social conflict took place in the industrial heartlands and in the race relations of Britain's increasingly multi-racial and multi-cultural cities. This period also saw the onset of neoliberal economic and social policies within what was taken to be the globalisation of economic and increasingly of social life as the network society (Castells 1996, 2000) and its later digitalisation of communication and entertainment took off. Britain became a 'post-industrial' society and the 'service economy' was somehow declared to be paramount, leaving vast areas of previously industrialised Britain without investment in well paid jobs and only poor future prospects for young people. Both general and youth unemployment levels were high in the early 1980s and social and political life was extremely fractured. Under these conditions it was difficult to predict how educational expansion and democratisation could deliver opportunities and social mobility for the majority of aspiring parents and their children.

Some of the previous and widely held assumptions about the benefits of education were in question, not least by students themselves as they 'revolted' in the late 1960s and early 1970s against what they believed were the undemocratic and authoritarian controls used in the higher education institutions. The validity of education as a channel for social change and mobility was up for question as schools and universities became the sites of clashes between the generations and between social and ethnic groups who wanted a better life and future and saw education as a means to that end.

Part of the problem was that this was a period of general and pervasive change. The post-war social consensus on major social and political issues was in the process of being dismantled. The role of the welfare state, the extent of nationalised industries and public utilities, ownership and control of housing and transport and the responsibility for managing public investment in industrial development and renewal were put into question by the Conservative governments of the time. Much of the public sector infrastructure of Britain was in fact being privatised by the Thatcherite neoliberal project in this period. It was also a time where *everything* appeared to be changing, including British culture and social life.

The apparent decline in public confidence that education could produce a democratic and more egalitarian society did not mean that education was taken out of the front line of conflict and debate. Inner-city schools especially were freighted with ethnic and racial tensions, as we shall explore in chapter 5 below, and class issues regardless of other dimensions of inequality remained significant in determining outcomes and futures. Yet after the earlier expansion of the 1970s and1980s there was a relative stagnation in the growth of higher education and belief in social mobility through education was increasingly questioned. From the left this perception came from those who thought it was not happening and that increased social mobility could not fundamentally shift the embedded inequalities of unreformed capitalist social and economic structures. And from the right, social equality and equal opportunity policies were opposed by those who wished to re-assert the values of elite selection on the grounds that the brightest and best should be rewarded with life's prizes. From this perspective unequal outcomes demonstrated the rightness and fairness of competitive and meritocratic values. Those who succeeded in life clearly deserved to do so; so much was self-evident.

Many Conservatives supported the retention and re-introduction of grammar schools. Their rationale was that of *meritocracy and rewards for the brightest and best* but their target was the possibility of a more egalitarian school and university system which they opposed. They did not win the day and the Labour governments of the 1970s abolished direct grant grammar schools, instructed local education authorities to complete comprehensive reorganisation of secondary schools and tried to implement the Robbins principle of a university place for every qualified applicant (Mandler ibid). Demand for educational outcomes from below was continuing to grow. Everything was changing but not fast enough to meet contrasting and competing expectations of education; some for the best possible results for *all* children and students and others for 'parental choice' and the freedom to either purchase educational advantage through private schooling or to ensure geographical or cultural selection of the 'better schools' by middle class parents. Much debate was had around 'standards' as the key problem of what was wrong with education.

# The key question- what drove participation?

The slump in participation rates in the early 1970s could be ascribed to a wide range of factors but the causal relation between any one of them and decisions to engage in further and higher education by individuals and families is difficult to prove. We have already noted that after 1972 the participation rate for 18 and 19 year olds failed to rise until the late 1980s. A check to widening participation for young people took place which according to Mandler (ibid: 96) was unique in the history of the 20th century. Some argued that there had been a loss of confidence in public life and public institutions, whilst other points of view stressed the growth of self-assertion by different parts of the British population. The rise of popular individualism and the decline of deference were suggested as reasons for dissatisfaction with the status quo and popular cultural 'resistance', especially by young working class people and ethnic groups was explored by some sociological thinkers and researchers (CCCS 1975). At the same time others noted the existence of the sense of civic entitlement that the welfare state and post-war social settlement had brought about amongst the less privileged (Mandler ibid: 105-106). It was clear that the trend towards individualism and the aspirations for a better life and future were continuing to grow whilst traditional communities were losing their traditional identities and in many cases their actual reason for being as single-industry towns and villages lost their workplaces. In addition the school age population dropped in the 1980s as the post-war 'bulge' in population tapered off.

Nevertheless support for universal educational and health entitlements remained strong and neighbourhood comprehensive schools became the norm. The unsettling social and occupational changes of the 1970s and 1980s meant latent demand for higher education was growing, even though economic outcomes were uncertain and industrial employment was in very severe decline. Nobody could with certainty say what young people wanted or would get from life and anyway they were deciding their own futures and fates in many cases in ways that could never have been anticipated by earlier generations. For example, Punk rock and style was writing its own musical and cultural script without reference to what had gone before except to reject its overt commercialism, consumerism and social conformism (CCCS 1975; Hebdige 1979).

The question was then to focus on whether further and higher education was a consumer good, demand for which rose with generally rising living standards and expectations or whether it was an investment decision made by individuals who expected to gain income in the short term by leaving education. Mandler notes what he calls 'the Indian Summer of manual employment experienced by Britain in the first half of the 70s' (ibid : 111) which may help explain the low rates for staying on at school and consequently the lower rates of applications and demand for higher education by young people. This affected mainly boys and the longer term trend away from manual work and rising youth unemployment meant that by the late1980s more people wanted more education than ever before. In particular girls and women were participating in education and the labour market to a greater degree than ever. Whether this upsurge was as a result of consumer choice or as an investment decision is to pose a false dichotomy since the social and mass-psychological forces which shape individual choice are only known in the aggregated and collectively experienced outcomes. The trend was clear – more young people stayed on at school and further education colleges whilst age participation rates for **higher education** remained stagnant up to the late 1980s. For the young there was suppressed demand. On the other hand adult returners and learners were a burgeoning sector as shown in this volume in chapters 1 and 6.

From the late 1970s the Access movement and in particular the role and participation of women and members of black and ethnic groups drove many thousands into colleges and polytechnics as the harbingers of a new landscape of higher education, notwithstanding the fact that staying on rates for the young and their demand for higher learning were falling. The point about this is that education is unlike normal consumer durable goods. It is not simply a desirable commodity subject to supply and demand relationships within a market. Demand for education can be created through a range of social experiences and expectations. Learning and knowledge have transformative capacities and self-knowledge can be fostered and created so that the conditions of its existence can be re-created or extended or be entirely reformed. Education and really useful knowledge is about more than the private decisions taken by individuals about staying on at school and attending universities. The social mission of higher education and the role of Access within that was a factor in expanding opportunities and if possible increasing social mobility, though this mission was a contested one. By 1991 the colleges and the polytechnics were educating almost twice as many higher education students as universities (Pratt 1997: 28-31).

By the early 1980s the Conservative government was actively restricting access to higher education by cutting student allocation numbers and reducing unit costs. A version of the meritocratic principle was used to justify reductions in spending on higher education so that the elite students could continue to benefit whereas the mass take up of HE places was expected to decline. It did not happen. Higher education continued to grow and the polytechnics were prepared to accept lower unit costs traded against higher growth numbers. Meanwhile the Conservative government tried to resist democratic pressure for more university places by introducing meritocratic competition for a number of places decided by the government's view of what the national need was. It was argued that was necessary to maintain high standards in British higher education. This did not work either and there was a failure to cut numbers. A further attempt was made by Sir Keith Joseph, the far right education minister, to introduce student loans to replace the maintenance grants which failed in the teeth of furious opposition from just about all political quarters.

## The great turn-about

The great paradox then came about when Mrs Thatcher's government performed an almost complete U-turn of policy in 1986, after sacking Sir Keith Joseph and initiating Britain's greatest expansion of higher education into a mass participation system. The explanation for this much delayed about-turn was *not* the recognition of the value of learning and especially higher learning for the masses by those who had up to this point argued the need for elite selection. Rather, it was a retreat by populist Conservative party politics in the teeth of rising demand for a better life and fairer society. This demand had been building throughout the 1970s and 1980s, exemplified by the expressions of dissent and alienation from public life that accompanied de-industrialisation of swathes of British towns and cities and the neoliberal era initiated by the Thatcher governments. An untapped reservoir of demand from below was brought into play and the Access movement was able to tap into this as the waves of dissatisfaction were felt politically.

The mid-1980s to the early 2000s saw perhaps the most extraordinary and rapid growth of higher education in Britain. 'Nothing like it had ever been seen before or has been seen since, not only in British history, but practically in the history of any other country…' (Mandler ibid: 130). Social demand for change was effectively channelled into student demand for places. Access courses were at the margins of the formal system of further and higher education but nevertheless were a harbinger of what was to come as non-traditional students joined those staying on as the new mass entrants to higher education.

The wider concerns of politics continued throughout this upsurge in interest and engagement with higher education but there can be no doubt that post-school education was now a theme of broader political debate within the discourse of social change. The themes of who should pay for student fees, maintenance grants and loans, per capita grants to universities, capping of student numbers and who got access to which universities, all developed problematically out of the issues which student demand posed.

In 1996 the soon-to-be New Labour Prime Minister Tony Blair announced Education, Education, Education was his mantra for economic growth and the new government from 1997 duly continued the expansion of further and higher education already underway. Britain had developed a successful if eclectic pattern of non-traditional routes to higher education and was perhaps the leading European nation in this regard (David 2010). Perhaps some 10 per cent of university students in the 1980s were mature Access-type learners (Mandler ibid: 133) and large numbers, especially so in Scotland, were coming through conventional A levels and Highers *and* vocational courses, recognised by the polytechnics. All of this had implications for many people as members of social groups that had previously been excluded or marginalised by the education system. They were now participating in growing numbers: ethnic groups, people who identified as black or people of colour, women and the often mature children of working class parents- all began to achieve participation rates which were comparable to the 'mainstream'. There were, however, substantial exemptions to this picture which continued to bedevil British educational and social life. White British working class boys continued to be poor performers in education with lower participation rates than other comparable groups.

The debate over the nature and meaning of higher education did not end with this new reality of higher participation and mass education. In fact it can be argued that it stimulated dialogue and dispute over a range of issues which continue to divide opinion even as near-universal higher education participation becomes the new reality for the 21$^{st}$ century. These include the on-going issue of the attainment gap between social classes, social and inter-generational mobility, meritocratic ideology and the legitimation of social privilege, the marketization and privatisation of education, the continuing presence and reproduction of elites in society through selective schooling, the role of university engagement and the need for a universal literacy and a critical curriculum in universities. These are issues and themes that were raised by Access Education and the Access movement and continue to be relevant as an agenda for change and progress as the transition to mass education proceeds.

# What was driving the change?

What drove so many more people to stay on at school and in post-compulsory education, and also underpinned the Access movement, was, as Mandler points out (ibid: 135), demand from below. Supply in the form of government policy literally could not create the realisation that literally masses of people were being made aware that education might help them and their children achieve a better life. This awareness grew from within the daily lives and struggles of ordinary citizens whose aspirations could be met in no other way than through education. They bought into the prevailing beliefs that better and fairer schooling could lead to university-level education and a better future. The emerging knowledge economy and the learning society, it was perceived, had a pay-off for many whose backgrounds had not included a university education. This was not just a matter of economic incentives since there is no clear correlation between economic growth and incentives and participation rates (Mandler ibid: 136). It may be the case, however, that in certain circumstances education can create its own demand. There is an argument, for example, that the Open University in creating a new and dynamic system of open access in terms of entry qualifications, fees, study methods, open access study materials, teaching strategies, assessment techniques and student support, actually created its own demand for its products and learning experiences. There can be no doubt that black and ethnic group populations in the inner cities in the 1970s and 1980s also created their own learning cultures and opportunities, which were eventually recognised by the education authorities and institutions (see chapter 5 below; John 2006). At the same time a large number of jobs became 'graduate jobs' as the employment markets changed and these carried a graduate premium. The graduate premium was, however, itself a variable factor and was greater for some occupations than for others, yet the general trend towards graduate status was upwards regardless of specific jobs and their differential rewards.

Going to university became common if not the norm and progression from school to college was viewed as a more democratic and meritocratic experience, nomatter that access was sharply stratified by social class and in the elite universities in particular beset by ethnic exclusions. At a later stage women and ethnic minorities became over-represented in the universities as higher education itself became a normalised and near-universal aspiration for young people. This might not have been the knowledge economy but it was certainly a version of the learning society.

There can be little doubt that the new 'Learning Age' (DfEE 1998) had arrived by the turn of the 21st century. A fast globalising economy, flexible employment and rapidly changing labour markets put education firmly in the forefront of public policy for change. The demand for education was driven by the structural changes in economy and society impacting greatly on working class people, women, young people and the ethnic groups. These were and remain matters of social equity and social justice and these were the fundamental drivers from below, as it were; the realities of chronic inequality of opportunity. These were the actual content of the felt experience of masses of people who felt excluded and marginalised by the inadequate and divisive post-compulsory education system in Britain. Of course there were theories of human capital which explained why more education was needed (Ransom et al 2000) in the interests of the economy and competitiveness and undoubtedly these factors helped shape public policy towards widening participation. But they did not explain the deepening change that was occurring and the scale of the challenges that were facing British society. Dislocation, instability and insecurity characterised British society and the transitions to modernity were being made with ever greater social and employment insecurity and a continuing and highly unequal and socially divisive education system. This was the context for the Access movement as people sought more and different types of learning to overcome the disabling effects of their previous education which had for too many failed to enhance essential skills and create motivation to go further. Enhancing employability became the mantra and prime mission of the New Labour government after 1997 and education was seen as the best economic policy that the Labour Party had (Mandler ibid: 141; DfEE Learning to Succeed).

Following the years of Conservative government the Access movement might have expected more; a deeper understanding of the need for education which would re-engineer and re-think the relationship between work, education and wealth creation. This prospect was suggested within Labour Party policy documents (DfEE 1998, 1999) but no such social transformation occurred. Mass higher education and an expansion of further education was achieved more in spite of rather than because of conservative policies because it was unstoppable. America had shown the way and Europe was catching up fast with the notion that the working people could go to university and that graduate status was within the grasp of the many, not merely the selected few.

## Has educational inequality grown since the late 1980s?

If the driving force of educational change was not economic development and was **not** due to demand being driven by either a wish to personally invest in learning or by the perceived benefit of greater income returns from work (Mandler ibid), and if human capital theory does not adequately explain the growth of demand for education, then what does? Is the answer that attainment levels have simply risen across the board and that public investment in education was increased by successive governments, regardless of their political colouring? Is it no more than just a generic growth of sentiment that wider, pervasive economic changes alongside the wish for greater choice and diversity can be detected among modern populations? Is there an inevitable movement from the state providing education to the market doing so, and doing so more efficiently and better? Such reasoning questions the narrative that education was something struggled over within contested visions of what learning might be in a society characterised by precarious futures and uncertainty and a growing middle class which wanted what that class had always sought- privileges and protection for its own members and their children. Mandler states, for example, that … 'in any case educational inequality has not grown since the late 1980s' (ibid: 148).The reality of such an assertion depends upon how we understand and define educational inequality. If our concept of inequality is limited to participation rates and 'attainment gaps' between different social groups then it may be the case that inequality has not grown. There is more education available and more people wish to have it- so much is certain. In fact there is little chance of success in life without education in modern capitalistic society but that particular reality is far from being the whole story.

The realities are that income and wealth inequality in Britain has increased greatly since the 1980s and in some respects spectacularly since the Conservatives were returned to office in 2010 (Wilkinson and Pickett 2010; Toynbee and Walker 2020; Dorling 2018; Brewer 2019). As the 2020s approached, the United Kingdom had the second highest level of inequality among the countries with the seven largest economies, behind the United States (Brewer ibid: 148-149). In Europe only Lithuania was more unequal. If we go beyond the idea of equal opportunities and consider disparities of income and wealth as measures of unequal *outcomes,* we can observe massive social inequality and social injustice. But inequality is also about the nature and organisation of opportunities which shape those outcomes and this takes the argument beyond the fact that the third decade of the 21st century produced shocking levels of poverty in Britain, including extensive child poverty. The categories of the educationally disadvantaged continued to include black and Asian and minority learners, learners from deprived areas and low participation neighbourhoods, disabled learners, learners with mental health conditions, part-time learners, vocational learners, people with literacy and numeracy problems, refugees and socio-economically deprived learners (TASO 2022). There was, and remains, working class disadvantage all the way down the social ladder. Structural disadvantage, deeply embedded in British social, economic and cultural institutions, is diffused and extended by the ideologies of equality of opportunity, the supposed advantages of the 'free market' in education and the misconceptions of meritocracy (Lynch 2022).

The Access movement was a departure point for considering alternatives and as such it suggested that the elite universities might not be the only high point of intellectual development and that an alternative could be imagined which would serve the masses of the people better. However, in the imagined struggle for a better outcome the contestants were by no means equal and it was always fully known that wealth and power often wields the greater force, privileging choice and exacerbating inequality.

It has been argued in this book that within this growth of mass participation, the Access agenda brought into the debate the need to re-examine the relations between the social classes and groups, between the sexes and races and generations and the need to make sure that education serves the needs of equal and active citizens within a democratic culture. Access became a curriculum expression of what was needed to inform learning and teaching for an improved future for the many. Its departure points included the following: education must be relevant to people's lives; the recognition of the needs of all learners; development of a universal literacy and critical self-reflection; recognition of family and community life across all ages and stages and the need for a pedagogy which re-connects knowledge with the burning and wicked issues of our time. These were some of the crucial issues that lay behind the defining themes of educational equality and opportunity which were to shape the emerging mass education system in Britain. However, the ideas of meritocracy and freedom of choice within a market for education, which were to be paramount for governmental decisions and public policy, were to gain traction and credibility and to impact greatly on Britain's mass higher education system and the realities of access within it.

# References

Ball, Sir Christopher. (1994) *Aim Higher, Widening Access to Higher Education 1990-1994,* Report to the RSA, London: RSA.

Brewer, M. (2019) *Inequality: what do we know and what should we do about inequality,* Los Angeles/London: Sage.

Castells, M. (1996) *The Rise of the Network Society*, Oxford: Blackwell Publishers Ltd.

Castells, M. (2000) (2nd ed) *End of Millennium: Vol 111 The Information Age: Economy, Society and Culture*, Oxford: Blackwell Publishers ltd.

CCCS (1975) - Centre for Contemporary Cultural Studies, *Working Papers in Cultural Studies 7&8 resistance through rituals*, University of Birmingham.

Cole, G.D.H. (1952) 'What workers's education means', *The Highway*, 44.

Crawford, C. (2014) *The link between secondary school characteristics and university participation and outcomes,* London: DFE.

Croxford, L. and Raffe, D. (2015) 'The iron law of hierarchy? Institutional differentiation in UK higher education', *Studies in Higher Education*, 40 (9) 1625-1640.

David, M. (ed) (2010) *Improving Learning by Widening Participation in Higher Education*, UK: London.

Davies, D. (1995) *Credit Where It's Due,* University of Cambridge, Madingly Hall and Government Employment Department.

Davies, D. (1997) 'From the further education margins to the higher education centre? Innovation in continuing education', *Education and Training,* 39 (1) MCB University Press.

Davies, D. (1998) *The Virtual University:* London: Cassell- ch 4 *Lifelong Learning Competency in the 21st Century-* with Richard Teare and Eric Sandelands *-The Virtual University: An Action Paradigm and Process for Workplace Learning,* London: Cassell.

Dearing Review/Report (1997) *Higher education in the Learning Society,* NCIHE-National Committee of Inquiry into Higher Education, Norwich: HMSO.

DfEE (1998) *The Learning Age: a renaissance for a new Britain*, London: Department for Education and Employment.

DfEE (1999) *Learning to Succeed: A new framework for post-16 learning*, London: HMSO.

Dorling, D. (2015) *Injustice: Why Social Inequality Still Persists*, University of Bristol: Policy Press.

Dorling, D. (2018) *Peak Inequality: Britain's Ticking Time Bomb*, University of Bristol: Policy Press.

Duke, C. and Tobias, R. (2001) *Lifelong Learning and the University in the 21 st Century,* monograph, Centre for Continuing Education, University of Canterbury, New Zealand.

Field, J. (2013) 'Adult education as a social movement: inspiring change or fading dream?' *Adults Learning* Summer 2013.

Fieldhouse, R. and Associates (1996) *A History of Modern British Adult Education,* Leicester: NIACE.

Fryer, B. (1997) *Learning for the Twenty-First Century*, London/ Sheffield: NAGCELL- National Advisory Group for Continuing Education and Lifelong Learning.

Fryer. B. (1999*) Creating Learning Cultures: Next steps in achieving the learning age,* second report of the NAGCELL, Sheffield: Department of Education, Employment and Training.

Giddens, A. (1990) *The Consequences of Modernity,* Cambridge: Polity Press.

Giddens, A. (1991) *Modernity and Self-Identity: Self and Society in the Late Modern Age*, Cambridge: Polity Press.

Green, F. and Kynaston, D. (2019) *Engines of Privilege: Britain's Private School Problem,* London: Bloomsbury Publications and see Verkaik, R. (2019) *Posh Boys: How English Public Schools Ruin Britain*, London: Oneworld Publications.

Hall, S. (2017) *The Fateful Triangle: Race, Ethnicity, Nation*, Cambridge, Mass/ London, England: Harvard University Press.

Hall, S. and Gieben, B. (eds) (1992) *Formations of Modernity,* Cambridge: Polity Press and The Open University.

Harrison, N. (2018) 'Patterns of participation in a period of change: social trends in English higher education from 2000 to 2016', ch 4 in Waller, R., Ingram, N. and Ward, M.R.M. (eds) (2018) *Higher education and Social Inequalities: University Admissions, Experiences, and Outcomes,* London and New York: Routledge.

Harvey, D. (1994) *The Condition of Postmodernity*, Cambridge, Mass and Oxford, UK: Blackwell.

Hebdige, D. (1979) *Subculture: The Meaning of Style*, UK: Routledge.

HEFCE-Higher Education Funding Council for England (2005*) Young participation in higher education* (Report 2005/03), Bristol: HEFCE.

HEFCE (2007) *Higher education outreach: targeting disadvantaged learners* (Report 2007/12), Bristol: HEFCE.

HESA- Higher Education Statistics Agency (1995-96) UK- https://www.hesa. ac.uk.data-and-analysis/publications/higher-education-1995-96.

HESA- Higher Education Statistics Agency (2016) UK.

Jary, D. and Parker, M. (1998) *The New Higher Education: Issues and Directions for the Post-Dearing University*, Staffordshire University Press.

John, G. (2006) *Taking a Stand*, Manchester: Gus John Partnerships Ltd.

Kelly, T. (3rd ed 1992) *A History of Adult Education in Great Britain*, Liverpool University Press.

Kennedy, H. (1997) *Learning Works: widening participation in further education*, Coventry: Further Education Funding Council (FEFC).

Kirkwood, G. (1978) 'Adult education and the concept of community', *Adult Education 51* 145-151.

Lovett, T. (1975) *Adult Education, Community Development and the Working Class*, UK: Ward Lock Education.

Lynch, K. (2022) *Care and Capitalism: Why Affective Equality Matters for Social Justice,* Cambridge: Polity Press.

McCraig, C. (2016) 'The retreat from widening participation? The National Scholarship Programme and new Access Agreements in English higher education', *Studies in Higher Education* 41(2) 215-230.

Mandler, P. (2020) *The Crisis of Meritocracy: Britain's Transition to Mass Education Since the Second World War*, Oxford: Oxford University Press.

Marriott, S. (1984) *Extramural Empires: Service and Self-Interest in English University Adult Education 1873-1983*, University of Nottingham.

Martin, I. (1996) 'Community Education: The Dialectics of Development', ch 6 in Fieldhouse, R. and Associates (1996) *A History of Modern British Adult Education*, Leicester: NIACE.

Midwinter, E. (1975) *Education and the Community,* UK: George Allen and Unwin.

Nyland, J. and Davies, D. (2022) *Curriculum Challenges for Universities: Agenda for Change,* Singapore: Springer.

Oppenheim, C. (ed) (1998) *An Inclusive Society: strategies for tackling poverty,* London: Institute for Public Policy Research.

Pratt, J. (1997) *The Polytechnic Experiment 1965-1992,* UK: Buckingham.

Raffe, D. (ed) (1998) *Education and the Youth Labour Market*, Lewes: Falmer Press.

Ranson, S., Rikowski, G. and Strain, M. (2000) 'Lifelong Learning for a Learning Democracy' for Chapman, J. and Aspin, D. (eds) (2000) *International Handbook on Lifelong Learning,* Dordrecht: Kluwer.

Robertson, D. (1994) *Choosing to Change: Extending Access, Choice and Mobility in Higher Education,* UK: HEQC.

Robertson, D. (1995) 'The Reform of Higher Education for Social Equity, Individual Choice and Mobility', ch 3 in Coffield, F. (ed) (1995) *Higher Education in a Learning Society,* University of Durham on behalf of DfEE, ESRC and HEFCE.

Savage, M. et al (2015) *Social Class in the 21st Century*, UK: Penguin/Random House.

Scott, P. (1997) 'The Crisis of Knowledge and the Massification of Higher Education', ch 2 in Ronald Barnett and Anne Griffin (eds) (1997) *The End of Knowledge in Higher Education*, Institute of Education, University of London series, London: Cassell.

Simon, B. (ed) (1990) *The Search for Enlightenment: The Working Class and Adult Education in the Twentieth Century,* Leicester: NIACE.

Skrbis, Z. and Woodward, I. (2013) *Cosmopolitanism: Uses of the idea*, London: Sage Publications.

Sutton Trust (2004) *The Missing 3,000: State school students under-represented at leading universities,* London: Sutton Trust.

TASO (2022)-Transforming Access and Student Outcomes in Higher Education- UK: https://taso.org.uk

Tomlinson, S. (2019) *Education and Race: From Empire to Brexit,* University of Bristol: Policy Press.

Toynbee, P. and Walker, D. (2020) *The Lost Decade: 2010-2020, and What Lies Ahead for Britain,* London: Guardian Faber Publishing.

University World News (2013) UK higher education since Robbins- A timeline, 01 November 2013; see also House of Commons Library (2012) Education: historical statistics, Standard Note: SN/SG/4252; and HE providers- in 2019/20 http://www.hesa.ac.uk/support/providers.

Vogel, J. (2017) *The Ascendancy of Finance*, Cambridge: Polity Press.

Waller, R. et al (2015) 'Neo-liberalism and the shifting discourse of 'educational fairness'', *International Journal of Lifelong Education*, 34(6) 619-622.

Wilkinson, R. and Pickett, K. (2010) *The Spirit Level: Why Equality is Better for Everyone*, London: Penguin Books.

Williams, J. (2013) *Consuming Higher Education: Why Learning Cannot be Bought*, London: Bloomsbury. For earlier accounts of the need for a 'critical thinking university', see also Duke, C. (1992*) The Learning University - Towards a New Paradigm*, Buckingham: Open University Press and Watson, D. and Taylor, R. (1998) *Lifelong Learning and the University*, UK: Falmer Press.

Wilson, P. (2010*) Big Idea, Small Steps: The Making of Credit-Based Qualifications,* Leicester: NIACE.

# Chapter 4

# Meritocracy, the 'Free Market' and the Race to the Bottom in Education

From the perspective of the current era with its expectations of ecological catastrophe, its international conflicts, its brutal environmental wars and its growing authoritarianism, we might look kindly on the time of relative social stability and increasingly high living standards which emerged with the growth of mass participation in education towards the end of the 20th century. At least in the western capitalist nations which subscribed to social democratic norms this appeared to be the case. There was no apparent alternative to globalised capitalism and neoliberalism appeared to be triumphant in that no realistic alternative could be imagined by most people. One commentator remarked that it was easier for some people to imagine the end of the world than to imagine the end of capitalism (Fisher 2009).

However, beneath this surface appearance of a golden age of globalisation and economic growth with its fetishisation of the market and subjection of citizens as consumers of the goods within that market, was a reality of social control and manipulation. This was where meritocracy found its new voice and meaning. If it was mass education that could embody the aspirations of the many, it was also to sponsor the selection of elites. The selection of elites using education and schooling was nothing new in British culture but the more democratic times demanded a different approach. Education would need to justify the social inequalities that came with formal access to equal opportunities. The possibilities of large scale reform receded in the face of the successful marketing of meritocracy which asserted that talent and ability could be recognised in British life and that this would drive people to succeed, as if the only thing stopping them was their own inhibitions.

Meritocracy became one of society's most powerful myths and many people wish to live in a world that appears to be fair and where rewards go to those who deserve them through talent and hard work. Unfortunately this ideal did not and does not correspond to the reality in which we continue to live and struggle to improve. The socially stratified, unequal and divided country that is modern Britain already had a stratified education system which has been adapted over time to the modern era of mass participation. As a result Britain remains a country beset and ruled by elites in which the education system directs those born to privilege and wealth into the highest status jobs and positions of power. This unequal system is not neutral in its impact on those who do not succeed. The effects of privileging some children hold back those born to parents who have not benefitted from such opportunities. A recent editorial observed… 'Just 7 % of children attend private schools. Yet privately educated young people make up almost one in three undergraduates at the country's most selective universities. In the jobs market, the figures are even worse: seven out of ten members of the judiciary were privately educated as were six out of 10 civil service permanent secretaries, more than half of diplomats and more than four in 10 senior media editors. This is not a product simply of their raw ability, but also of the vast resources that go into their education, the social connections and favours it opens up and the other forms of cultural capital it endows… Private schools create social harms. In acting as a conveyor belt to the most sought-after jobs they shut out other, more able, young people who lack those advantages. They cream young people from disproportionately affluent backgrounds out of the state system, which has a negative impact on attainment for everyone else.' (Observer 2022).

As we proceed into the third decade of the 21st century the system has other in-built inequalities. Selective state-funded grammar schools are disproportionately dominated by the children of the more wealthy parents whose parents often pay for additional private tuition to support them through the selection examination (the 11 plus). Where there is selection for secondary school, children from poorer backgrounds do worse on average. In addition there is significant selection for comprehensive schools by postcode. The best performing comprehensive schools are least likely to accept children from disadvantaged backgrounds. The attainment gap between the affluent and the disadvantaged appears to be growing as poverty spreads and … 'there is no evidence that the government's academy reforms have done anything to improve standards across the board' (Observer ibid).

The university system, as we have seen, is stratified and hierarchized to a ridiculous degree. Many, many universities claim to be 'world class' but this cannot be the case in general without devaluing the notion an elite institution itself.

The university a person attends is now a proxy for her/his employment potential. The educational stratification is in reality a social stratification for life. The pupils from the poorest backgrounds, receiving the pupil premium, make up just 2 % of admissions to the most selective universities, in spite of the fact they are 13 % of all young people. This is now the context in which we must try to understand the meanings of mass higher education and the growth and persistence of Access as a narrative which is vital to today's education system and its need to open up opportunities regardless of class or family origin.

## From diversity to hierarchy

This book has suggested that Access was both a type of 'provision'- a set of courses and learning opportunities- *and* a countervailing movement to the established educational system which had failed large numbers of the mainly working class people of the country. A people who by the 1970s were increasingly characterised as 'diverse' and multicultural. It was widely felt that it was the education system that had failed to give them opportunities to progress in education and to achieve what society told them was possible- that if they had the talent and worked hard they could succeed and enjoy the benefits of Britain's prosperity. Access offered an alternative route to the so-called ladder of opportunity since many people could simply not get their feet on the rungs of the ladder itself. Nevertheless, at the same time the institutions and people offering the new route were within that same education system, albeit in many cases at the margins or in the lower status institutions and positions. This was the paradox of Access; it was a demand and demonstration of the need for challenge and change whilst simultaneously it accepted this distinctive type of learning for what it was- an immensely worthy but unequal part of the hierarchy of knowledge and institutions within the British educational system.

This system itself, however, was driven and justified by an ideology of meritocracy which asserted that an individual's position in society should depend on his or her personal qualities of ambition, talent and effort. Unearned privilege should have no part in such a meritocracy. Access to education through the ladder of opportunity was in theory rooted in a basic idea of equality- that only talent and ability should count in the competition for places and opportunity. Furthermore, it was supposed that the free market could best be the organising framework within which meritocracy could flourish. The realities of the British education system and the wider society were quite other than this. A highly divisive social and class structure was characteristic of Britain right up to the third decade of the 20th century (Savage 2015; Dorling 2018). Nevertheless, the notion of a meritocratic society had great traction and was a key element in the development of mass higher education in Britain.

Access in its original form raised questions about how education and learning outside and at the margins of the mainstream could advance social mobility, opportunity and equality for the previously excluded. This chapter explores some of the conundrums of meritocracy which make it relevant to today's system of higher education and to the future shape of learning.

Meritocracy was once the cry of the dispossessed. Only let us compete on the basis of our naturally or God-given talents and abilities and we can remove the evils and barriers of inherited privilege and distinction based on birth or inheritance. Once we are allowed to compete fairly then merit not birth will determine outcomes so that power, wealth and authority can be justly distributed. The same thinking informed feminists who argued that girls and boys should learn the same things so that women could free themselves from the constraints imposed by the patriarchy. In the working class it was the meritocratic principle that drove people to prove they were as able as their social superiors. Working class intellectuals, many self-taught, emerged in the 19th century and the early 20th century to show that it was immoral to deny opportunity to the lower classes (Wooldridge 2021: 14-15).

At its most simple, merit and meritocracy mean that those with talent and ability should get to succeed. Unfortunately the corollary of this is that those with less talent get to fail. Those that fail to rise are left at the bottom of the social hierarchy and what is worse, they are seen to be there because that is where they belong; they deserve their fate due to their lack of aptitude or talent or intelligence or whatever measure is used to decide on the selection and fate of elites. In the first two decades of the 21st century, however, a whole set of social and economic developments occurred which undermined the idea that western economic systems and societies had a system of meritocracy which rewarded the deserving. In the last two decades of the 20th century this became clear as a series of social developments showed how globalisation and technical change had killed off many manual jobs, destroyed wholesale domestic industries and thrust the planet into a crisis of climate and ecological instability which threatened everyone's future. The rise of a technocratic elite and new forms of digitised capitalism seemed to ensure the capacity of existing elites to pass on their advantages and wealth to their children rather than to ensure competitive fairness and access to the elite positions in economy and society. Meritocracy ensured the continuation of elites and privilege, though its rhetoric always told a different story. At its best meritocracy became a disguise for a sophisticated form of class privilege; at its worst it helped enforce class privilege and social division where universal rights and justice had been promised. It is salutary to realise that in 2018 Oxford and Cambridge recruited fewer students from some 3,000 state schools than they did from just 8 elite schools (Sutton Trust 2018). What could justify such glaring inequality?

Success in a meritocratic system does not come easily. Huge amounts of money and effort are spent on children by parents eager to ensure their offspring get into the right schools, the right elite universities and onto the right career paths. Meritocratic selection is never left to itself. It has to be organised and often it is 'colonised' on behalf of those with existing resources. There is not very much room at the top and occupying it takes struggle and effort both to get and stay there. It goes almost without saying that competition to enter the elite schools and universities is fierce, though for the wealthy and well-placed, money and connections smooth the well-trodden pathway to inherited and paid-for privilege.

## Merit is everywhere but the rewards are not: equal opportunities to become unequal

The fact is there are many different types of meritocracy. It can claim a presence in political life where suspicion of democratic and collective involvement means that representative democracy is absent. It is compatible with the election or nomination of elites so that democratic pressures are less likely to be used directly to influence government. We can identify technocratic, business and academic meritocracies where certain qualities are used to select for merit and others are excluded. In producing business or academic meritocratic elites there may be little need to recognise the positive value of 'character' or that of virtue. Success is deemed to be more important than the value of a person's work or contribution to the greater good, things which are difficult to value in monetary terms. Underpinning the growth of modernity there are widely held beliefs and assumptions that a progressive society allows a meritocracy to exist and thrive. Societies based on hereditary principles or selection based on personal preference and selection by favouritism are widely held to be incompatible with the requirements of a modern, industrialised and sophisticated economy and society.

The problem with meritocracy is that it requires *selection* and this can and does lead to the entrenchment of elites, not least where elites with money and access to power can see that such purchasing power can buy access to the supposedly meritocratic elites- mainly in the present generation through education.

This encounters criticism from the left on the grounds that such elite formation in a vast variety of forms, not just in school selection, is unfair and denies the need for social justice and a level playing field. Marginalised groups are thus able to point to the way in which elite institutions simply fail to live up to meritocratic principles (Wooldridge ibid: 17).

As levels of social mobility in recent decades have declined in many western societies educational meritocracy can be seen to have transmorphed into its opposite. 'Educational institutions, including the most self-consciously progressive universities, are vectors of race-based inequality.' (Wooldridge ibid: 6). Instead of promoting social mobility and opportunity amongst the excluded and marginalised in society, significant parts of the elite system have promoted elite-continuity and social closure rather than an opening of class, gender, race, and ethnicity borders. The moneyed elite, including significant elements of ethnic and racial groups, have worked to provide a form of caste closure which sponsors certain groups but excludes others. Meritocracy does not produce social justice either. As Selena Todd suggests in a ground-breaking study of social mobility in the UK, despite a majority of every generation since the end of the 19th century moving up or down the ladder of mobility...'over the past 140 years, birth and wealth have exercised a far greater influence on a person's social position than talent, effort or ambition' (Todd 2021: 1).

John Rawls, the influential Harvard philosopher, argued that even a system of fair equality of opportunity could not produce an adequate system of distributive justice (Rawls 1971). High intelligence could not be used to justify differences in social or economic outcomes since differences in talent are morally arbitrary and not a reward for merit. Talent distribution was as arbitrary as social class – both of which were essentially inherited. Rawls' solutions to the inevitable inequalities of natural and social endowments was 'compensatory'. The winners had to share their benefits through progressive taxation if there was to be justice. Neither did hard work entitle an individual to higher rewards since this capacity was, like intelligence, inherited and therefore arbitrary and unjustifiably unequal. The emphasis here could be said to be on limiting inequalities rather than on opening up opportunities (Wooldridge ibid: 292). Rawls called this the 'difference principle' in which natural talents are viewed as a common asset and therefore should be enjoyed by those fortunate enough to be endowed only in so far as those who were not so blessed are also rewarded. In other words, the social rewards of talent and effort should be fairly shared, collectively and communally. No such situation actually exists in reality at a societal level, which forces our attention onto the question of the equality dilemma in which it is argued there will always be significant inequalities between people in terms of wealth, status and power. There will always be winners and losers, people who succeed and people who do badly in the competitive struggle for advantage in this view, which is widely held in liberal and conservative circles.

Rawls' solution to this dilemma was the promotion of equality of opportunity, through what he called the principle of 'fair equal opportunity' in which those with similar skills and abilities should have similar life chances (Rawls ibid: 72-73). This was to be achieved within the efficiencies of the so-called free-market economy which itself contained systems of institutionalised inequality. For Rawls the system could be managed so that the 'difference principle' permitted social and economic inequalities only where they work to the advantage of the most disadvantaged. This gave the right to compete within a system of institutionalised inequality but not the right to choose amongst alternatives of equal value. The problem here is that formal equal opportunities between competing groups or individuals do not deliver what Lynch called a 'real prospect of achieving something valuable relative to others' (Lynch 2022: 108).

In Lynch's view a concern with prioritising notions of 'freedom' over equality mean that…'even the most left-leaning liberal equal opportunities policies cannot deliver social justice in any substantive form in an economically and politically unequal society, as those groups that are privileged will use their own institutionalised power and influence to defend their own interests… The inherent classed logic of social hierarchy under capitalism does not permit the election of the few to become the pattern for the many. The very constitution of a hierarchical society precludes the development of a meritocracy as privileged groups use their excess income, wealth, power and other forms of social and cultural capital to undermine meritocratic practices' (Lynch ibid:108). When we consider the cumulative and overlapping social, economic, political and affective dimensions of inequalities, as Lynch does in her ground-breaking work, we are forced to engage with the intersectionality of inequalities and with the question of what kind of meritocracy has become accepted in modern times where there is pervasive and extensive inequality?

## Business capitalism as a leading ideology of meritocracy

There was once in the minds of many a belief that the post-war period was one of meritocratic revolution. In America, perhaps most spectacularly, the research scholar became the meritocrat- in- chief who might be thought of as not just understanding the world but changing it for the common good (Wooldridge ibid: 250). Across the Atlantic universities became 'engaged' in the wider social agendas of the day including professional and business life. Business schools became the hand-maidens of corporate industry and developed business models using 'knowhow' and management financial expertise to drive profitability and shareholder value. The new meritocrats did not inherit their wealth; they generated it through their knowledge of business practice and the application of expertise and trained intelligence. Schools became routes for mobility, universities became research-based training schools and businesses became obsessed with selecting the 'brightest and the best' who had the brainpower to drive towards greater profitability for corporate America. Intellect and mind and intelligence were co-opted through education to produce a version of meritocracy which offered access to opportunities, but would lead to highly unequal outcomes.

In the era of neoliberalism of the 1980s and 1990s, which itself sponsored the emergence of the technocratic revolution of the digital age, the globalising business ethic became a persuasive and dominant ideology in which individuals looked to themselves, their families and their elite membership of social and educational groups to safeguard their interests and identities. The state and big government were anathema; only the privatised market had the power and capacity to solve problems according to this creed. Neoliberalism became a dominant discourse in public life and policy, and was particularly noteworthy in America and Britain. The connections this 'philosophy' had to ultra-conservative political movements was clear (Brown 2019) and it marked a reaction against a rising tide of demands for social equality, and in America for desegregated public higher education (Chun and Feagin 2022). The neoliberal view advocated so-called free markets but in reality they extended the power of large commercial corporations over government and public life. Social welfare expansions, taxes on businesses and the regulation of corporate activities for the public good or protection were viewed as government interference in private profit making. Formally, governments at this time pressed for 'austerity' and the reduction of government expenditure as well as the privatisation of public assets including education. The realities of government interventions were paradoxically very different and in this period state expenditure and debt grew exponentially in Britain, in America and elsewhere. It seems clear that this aggressive version of neoliberalism had destructive effects on both American and British economies and the lives of their citizens (Chun and Feagin ibid: 64; Toynbee and Walker 2020).

## Moral managerialism

In a society supposedly driven by the fundamental belief that individuals count more than collectivities, it is something of a paradox to encounter the collective activities of capitalist firms and corporations as being virtuous. Some of them claim to be solving some of the world's biggest and most problematical issues including climate change, poverty, racial inequality and of course economic development (Dunn 2021: 26). Many of them insist that their firms exist for a higher purpose than simply making a profit. This is not just a 21st century event; by the mid- 20th century the idea of corporate responsibility was widespread as companies realised their corporate balance sheets could be enhanced by treating their employees better and understanding how they felt. Workers of all kinds could be seen to share popular values such as patriotism and be seen to contribute to a growing and progressive affluence. A growing class of professional managers spread these ideas and by 2008 more than 100,000 MBA graduates were being employed each year across the globe.

In the same period we can also observe the breaking up of traditional social and economic ties and communities and perhaps their moral force being weakened as individualism and consumerism displaced older and more collective ways of life. In the 1960s half of British voters knew who they would vote for in a general election but by 2018 only 9 per cent of the electorate identified strongly with a particular party (Dunn ibid: 28). It was not that politics was no longer relevant but people had shifted their attention to issues and causes that they valued. The collectivist pull of class and party appeared to have been broken. The capitulation of former Labour Party 'Red Wall' seats in the English Midlands and North to Boris Johnson's Conservatives in the election of 2019 was seen as evidence of this. Issues- based politics were unable to deal with the complex and multi-level social and political crises of the era, which were many-sided and long standing. Nevertheless, populist slogans had a resonance for political parties (take back control!) and in business the rapidly growing digital sector in Silicon Valley, which was outgrowing and out-muscling the old giants of the corporate sector, was itself claiming the high moral ground with its claims to be doing no evil and to be changing the world for the better.

How does this allow us to better understand the meritocracy issue? The modern digital IT companies, clustered often in America, see major world social and economic problems as issues to be solved and understood by the genius of a few gifted individuals who happen of course to work for their companies. Climate change, ecological degradation, racial inequality, the future of research into medicine and artificial intelligence can all be 'solved' by the application of technologies and digital communications which they own and control. This is part of the new meritocracy where the billionaire owners of the companies are presented as saviours of humankind. The reality is that the businesses that underpin these ludicrous claims are not about science and knowledge; they are about highly qualified and skilled professionals selling targeted advertising, web-hosting and communication as entertainment. They have persuaded the world that unlimited consumerism, pervasive mass surveillance and the monetisation of what was once private space are progressive and desirable innovations (Crawford 2015; Zuboff 2019). They are in the business of profit not of changing the world.

## The case against meritocracy

Meritocracy undoubtedly helped shape the world of modernity but from the 1930s onwards, according to Wooldridge, a movement took place against its core propositions. It was difficult to measure 'merit', the key element of meritocracy and certainly almost impossible to identify a coherent and consistent set of principles for merit which could be applied to wide and differing areas of social, economic and political life. In addition there were alternative values which stressed community, or collective life or even equality and fairness which were inimical to the apparently inevitable twinning of meritocracy and elitism. Wooldridge states…'The revolt against meritocracy had a profound influence on social policy across the rich world: the British abolished grammar schools and introduced mixed-ability teaching; the Americans introduced affirmative action and waged war on elite secondary schools; several continental countries went further still and introduced open admissions to universities.' (Wooldridge ibid: 279).What might conceivably be called progressive public policy including the abolition of selective grammar schools or the use of positive/affirmative action to encourage more equal opportunities, is viewed by Wooldridge as a rejection of the benefits of meritocracy. He argues that the opponents of meritocracy may in fact come from the 'left' with their view of the need for more equality of outcomes, or from the 'right' where vested interests conspire to privilege their own families by purchasing access to the elites of a society and culture.

The impact of the Second World War in Britain and the post-war 'settlement' of the welfare state including the 1944 Education Act which had extended access to grammar schools based supposedly on 'merit' and selection by an open examination for 11 year olds, helped create a more open and socially democratic Britain. Compared with the pre-war era working class children had greater opportunities to attend selective grammar schools but only if they passed the selective entry examination – the 11 plus. The vast majority did not pass and attended secondary modern schools which were clearly a second best option with very limited access to the ladder of opportunity. By the mid-1960s it had become clear that the unprecedented expansion of the education system, whilst allowing the increased numbers of working class children to forge ahead and acquire qualifications and even enter university, the *relative* life chances and prospects of working class children had not improved. Middle class pupils retained their historical and inherited advantages over working class pupils in taking up grammar school places. Schooling reforms in the state system had not abolished social difference but rather seemed to underpin and validate the social distinctions which resulted from social and economic inequality. The middle class culture and ethos continued to dominate the grammar schools and the working classes were allocated in the main to secondary schools which were not just second class but rather viewed as third class options. At the pinnacle of this hierarchy private elite schools continued to educate the children, mostly boys, of the upper classes and provide a well-trodden route to the two elite universities of England and then onwards to the professions and eminence in politics and public life associated with historic wealth and privilege in Britain.

This reality should not of course be understood as a criticism of the students and teachers who attended and taught in these secondary modern schools. Each secondary modern school in the era was different from every other school and there were legions of students who went on to make successes of their careers and lives. This was a tribute to the resilience and fortitude that schools instilled in their pupils, notwithstanding the difficulties they faced. Each school was located in a geographical area with a distinctive local social, cultural and political character and a degree of local, democratic accountability and control was possible. National funding was channelled through elected local authorities and some autonomy was permitted. Each school was of course a social system on its own, with its internal structures, complex social relationships and culture (Hargreaves 1967). The truth remains, however, that grammar schools were much better funded than secondary moderns and that aspirations and expectations for the less academic children were low and so were achievements in the struggle for better jobs and lives. The ladder of opportunity rarely reached up to the commanding heights for those who had failed the 11 plus examination and were relegated to secondary modern schools. The grammar schools themselves were often less than beacons of success and a majority of their pupils left at the earliest opportunity and did not go on to take A levels and enter universities. They also had an internal culture which, according to the classic study of a grammar school, differentiated between different types of pupils and sponsored the mobility of some students whilst restricting that of others (Lacey 1970).

The meritocratic idea though shot through with inconsistency and ambivalence, was however a key aspect of progressive education which set out to right historic social injustices. The meritocratic 'ideology' accepted that individuals differed in their innate abilities and the role of the wider society or the state in particular was to discover ability and allow it to flourish through educational opportunities. This position argued for a humane and efficient form of meritocracy. There was widespread belief in the idea itself which was understood as being good and progressive, not just amongst academics and educators. Jean Floud (1961: 93) summed up an apparent consensus amongst social scientists... 'Some pupils will always do better than others, but it is desirable that the order of inequality should be, as it were, a natural one unmarred by fictitious and irrelevant social differences'.

The attack on meritocracy itself came from Michael Young whose work was often paradoxically thought to be a celebration of it (Young 1958). The key issue raised in the book is the notion that the meritocratic idea is in fact the opposite of the egalitarian idea of equality. Meritocracy supports competition and inequality and in so doing smuggles in equality of opportunity in the place of actual equality of outcomes. The argument runs that if meritocratic competition is allowed to flourish then economic efficiency will hold sway and social compassion will be held in check. The social and psychological conditions which ensure people protect their own kind will, under meritocracy, ensure prevailing unfairness and eventual rule by 'meritocratic elites'. Meritocracy offers upward social mobility for the few at the expense of the majority who are kept in subordinate positions. Worse perhaps was the fact that the winners were persuaded that their own talent was responsible for their successes, whilst the losers had nobody to blame but themselves for their failures.

The critique of meritocracy centred on the questions of what were the relevant social and cultural differences which helped explain inequalities if natural endowments and talents, including the propensity or desire to work hard, themselves were to be set aside as reasons or legitimations for unequal social and economic outcomes. For Pierre Bourdieu (1990), an influential theorist of culture, educational differences were due to the way in which 'cultural capital' was produced and circulated. It was cultural capital which allowed the privileged to control access to the professions and prestigious positions in social life and then to reinforce this by persuading the poor that they actually only deserved to be at the bottom of the social pyramid. There had in addition always been a conservative critique of meritocracy where idealised versions of the past were sought where 'communities' contained only people who knew their place and were bound to each other by unbreakable reciprocal and mutual obligations. This was essentially a religious version of society whose fundamental order and highly unequal structure was ordained by a superior entity such as God! The communitarian ideal of a society was, however, also shared by critics of modernity and its specifically capitalistic forms. This version wanted a vision of a future society which rested on oppressed groups and classes freeing themselves from the inherited inequalities which bedevilled their lives and communities. The loss of community became a key theme in social studies and educational discourse (Bauman 2001).

## No room at the top for group rights, gender and identity politics

The critique of meritocracy based on ideas and beliefs about the need for greater social justice found its expression in a growing concern for group rights. These were the social groups that seemed immune to individual upward social mobility and whose position vis-à-vis other more advantaged social groups did not change. Race, ethnic belonging, faith commitments and sexual orientation were at the root of such identities and were the basis and source of much political and social unrest. The scepticism about meritocracy which emerged in the 1970s was underpinned in the real world by the persistent realities of race and gender inequalities and the consequentially perceived lack of social justice around them. Increasingly, the wrongs suffered historically by black and ethnic peoples and by women were collectively felt yet were intensely and personally experienced and articulated (Hirsch 2018; Rankine 2020). The solutions to racism and sexism increasingly were called on to be collectively driven, since this was how they were articulated as conscious experience. They were sites of injustice (Lynch 2022) as group identity became a crucial key to understanding social development. Radical approaches to the long term effects of slavery and patriarchy argued that these wrongs had been imposed collectively on people because of their 'race' or their sex or sexual orientation (Olusoga 2016; Bhopal 2018; Thornton 2013; Lynch 2022 ibid). In such cases there could be no solutions based on individualistic ideologies embodied in meritocracy. Solutions had therefore to be collectively inspired and collectively determined (Wooldridge ibid: 298).

The power and influence of the notion of meritocracy- its power as an ideology in fact- is shown in the manner in which 'academic' women were treated in the post-second world war period in Britain. Social mobility became a key focus in this period and the role of the social scientist itself became critical to establishing social mobility as a focus for research and a political goal. Upwardly mobile men had established roles for themselves and education itself was a cockpit of contested ideas around mobility and social transformations that were thought necessary. In the universities themselves, however, all was not well. Whilst the New Left were debating how a modern and humane socialism might offer a viable alternative to capitalism *and* communism (which had been discredited by Stalinism), women were being systematically marginalised and excluded from viable careers not just everywhere in the wider society but in the very university departments which researched inequality and social mobility. The post-war breakthrough generation of social researchers was primarily male and their study focus was exclusively on men's or boys' attainment at school. Girls' and women's experience was rarely examined and the exclusive focus was on social class, even where evidence showed that mothers were hugely influential on children's educational performance (Jackson and Marsden 1962).

The upwardly mobile social researchers and writers of the 1950s and 1960s were rarely women and with rare exceptions such as Jean Floud (1956) and the work of Jackson and Marsden (ibid) differences between the sexes were rarely explored. The roles and contributions of women to social mobility were constantly under-estimated as was the assistance and often unpaid labour that mothers and wives gave to upwardly mobile men. Selina Todd lays bare the fact that women academics were edged out and that … 'They went only 'reluctantly', taking with them the principle that trained welfare workers' expertise should inform social policy just as much as concern over social class.…The focus on male experiences of mobility marginalised those women who did manage to get a foothold in universities.' (Todd 2021: 153). Of course 'academic women' were not the most exploited and oppressed category of female worker in the UK in the post-war period- not by a long way. But they were clearly oppressed and held back in their professional advancement and were part of the exploited female labour force and no less worthy of note than the others in that category.

The impact of meritocracy as an ideology, as a way of thinking and believing that certain ideas are true and essentially right, came to dominate male thinking. It shaped sensibilities and legitimated the assertion that male expertise was more valuable than that of middle-class educated women and was far above that of working-class women who had been denied any chance of getting on the ladder of mobility. 'They (men) stressed the importance of establishing a meritocracy, and of measuring its success by gauging how far men like themselves could succeed. By the 1960s they had succeeded in persuading senior politicians that male upward social mobility was the best means to measure Britain's social and economic progress. The great inequality that neither the welfare state nor economic growth resolved- women's limited political power and economic opportunities- was ignored' (Todd ibid: 155).

## Individual and group identity

What was better understood was the idea that meritocracy was really about selection and selective education rooted in individualistic ideologies that separated out elites from the rest of society. The elites tended to come from the existing elites who had found ways of preserving their positions and wealth and indeed their cultural capital from one generation to the next. Equality of opportunity was being viewed within the critical or radical perspective as being in opposition to equality of outcomes, since the former allowed the emergence of managerial elites who governed and ruled on behalf of and in place of people who might have been selected from the broader masses but who in fact were recruited primarily from existing elites. The so-called meritocratic elites were rewarded with the glittering prizes in life- better jobs, more money, improved lifestyles, higher social status and greater access to power and resources. There was little or no equality of outcomes for the masses and in fact in the 21$^{st}$ century there may have been an increase in inequality on a global scale as well as within single states (Dorling 2018; Toynbee and Walker 2020; Picketty 2020: 534-536). The masses themselves were of course always something other than just an undifferentiated mass. The masses existed as social groups with specific identities constructed around many different cultural and material factors such as class, gender, race, ethnicity, religion, geography, occupation, work, community, sport and myriad interests and identities, some of which inevitably overlapped and intersected. The rhetoric of meritocracy was often about the recognition of individual qualities and talent but the reality was always about the social groups into which individuals were socialised and whose characteristics they shared. It was the structure of society and the way groups related to each other and to the institutional make-up of communities and society in general that determined the unjust social outcomes. It is difficult to have meritocracy, where people think they have achieved or acquired what they deserve through their own merits and talents, and at the same time raise the outcomes and achievements of whole classes and groups, many of whom may not possess outstanding talents. For meritocracy to be inclusive and dynamic there are major contradictions to be overcome.

The practical means of securing elite status across the generations involved education. For the UK elite circles, academic, selective schools continued to provide routes to selective elite universities for the children of the ruling elites and groups. These groups were of course distinguished by the fact that they were in possession of wealth, capital and social and cultural power. They were in a position to buy access to private schools, to the most successful state schools, and to universities which in turn could confer privileged access to jobs, many of the professions and entry to political power and influence. The abolition of grammar schools nearly everywhere by the 1980s had abolished one set of elite schools which had provided a route to success and opportunity for the middle classes and to a lesser extent the working class. The even more elite and privileged private schools, which served the much richer families under the misnamed 'public schools', were not abolished. They were not even mildly reformed with their 'charitable' status left intact so they could avoid paying tax on the profits they made. They were in fact encouraged to cater for the approximately 7 per cent of the pupil population whose parents used these schools to buy-in to elite positions and wealth in British society (Cohen 2009; Green and Kynaston 2019). How was it possible that age-old institutions such as public schools and social class groupings that had exercised power and accumulated wealth over generations could continue to exercise control in modern meritocratic Britain?

## The new meritocracy

The 1980s and 1990s saw a significant change in the way capitalist economies worked. The pro-market ideologies of the Thatcherite years came home to roost. The information technology and digital industries took off world-wide and the networked society and knowledge economy boomed. The promises and limitations of the social-democratic societies that arose after World War Two became apparent as neoliberalism and the ideologies of free market capitalism took hold in many advanced economies. At the end of the twentieth and beginning of the 21-first centuries the rise of hypercapitalist societies seemed assured (Picketty ibid: 415; Fisher 2009). As the new 21st century dawned a new 'occupational elite' came into being to service this rapidly expanding sector and a large number of high-IQ (intelligence quotient) jobs, most involving computing skills, were created in both the public and private sectors. This was a global phenomenon but could be best observed in the financial centres of global capitalism such as London and New York. Universities expanded to meet the new requirements of the market for academic talent. Money was the touchstone of the new elite's success and the measure of all things of value.

The new elites bought into the old elite schooling systems as a way of acquiring privileges for their children whilst the capacity of the newer comprehensive schools in the UK to deliver upward mobility was brought into question by conservatives who clung to selective education for schools and universities as an established and proven means of access to opportunity. The comprehensive schools when they were established across the UK by the 1970s, did provide opportunities for the very bright and talented at least, whilst the wealthy could always buy privileged access where native intelligence failed to secure places at the most desirable schools and universities. The marriage of money and elitism may have continued to produce more inequality so that, for example, in the UK in the early 21st century about half the places at Oxbridge went to pupils educated at private schools- some 7 per cent of the total school population. Social mobility may have gone into reverse whilst operating under the false colours of 'meritocracy' and equal opportunities for all who can afford it! Those who possess significant wealth, the plutocrats, are now allied to those who realise they must succeed in the meritocratic struggle to get the best education at the best and most prestigious institutions. The elite universities and business schools where aspiring meritocrats augment their qualifications for leadership are also a location where naturally the offspring of the wealthy encounter each other and create the social milieu and contacts which it can be said are needed for successful business enterprise. It may be that some eventually marry and reproduce since elite universities and business schools where the children of the wealthy meet each other are a key location for creating cultural and social capital.

The significance of private elite schooling for the 'new meritocracy' can be simply seen by the fact that four private schools and one state sixth-form college (Hills Road, Cambridge) send more pupils to Oxford and Cambridge than do 2,000 other secondary schools (Wooldridge ibid: 309). The dominance in many spheres of British public life of privately educated people is now legion (Green and Kynaston 2019; Verkaik 2019). The ideology of meritocracy is now central to their existence and this has major consequences for the whole society. The marriage of merit and money distorts all attempts at 'levelling up' the unjustified and damaging social inequalities that beset our society.

## The free market model of education

In theory the market model of university funding and support, and more general education provision, which the Conservative governments pursued between 2010 and 2020, were to create a diverse and competitive arena for institutions. Individuals would be able to choose freely which institutions they attended. Competitive prices would ensure an equitable distribution of places and opportunities for all those qualified to attend. Universities were given the right to set their own fee levels and attract students on the basis of their quality and sense of value for money and services to students. All had to function according to market incentives (Ball 2015). However, as anyone with first-hand knowledge of education might have told them and even with the smallest modicum of sociological knowledge that is not quite how it works. Within a very short period of time an informal but unacknowledged cartel agreement had emerged which effectively set the student fees for all universities at the highest level possible (£9,000 plus, per year on average) with individual institutions discounting certain courses and offering financial incentives to certain kinds of students. Universities do not just exist in a market for student choice. They live and die, as it were, in a reputational struggle for predominance where various indexes of performance are manipulated to best effect. The net result are various league tables which are taken by the general public as indicators of value and performance. Schools, parents, careers advisors, employers and the general public accept these contrived judgements as to what is best without fully knowing or perhaps also without caring about the real factors which lie behind the league table numbers, which by quantifying objective judgements of value, actually serve to legitimise already existing and inevitable inequalities between institutions. In the league tables the approximately 160 universities and more than 400 providers of higher education in the UK do not, obviously, start on a level playing field either in terms of their financial viability or their reputational status.

The significance of this lies in the comparators that are used to calculate and assess the value of education– which at the end of the day amounts to students, courses, learning experienced and degrees awarded. If these are subsumed under a single model of financial efficiency where the bench marks are universities with large-scale recruitment and marginal efficiencies with cost savings at scale, then many HE providers could never have hoped to compete. When they were established they were never intended to compete in this way. The existence of mission diversity was intended to be an authentic alternative to the historic and inequitable selectivity of the older universities. Mass higher education had a different mission and was part of what was supposed to be the authentic diversity of British higher education.

If the market model of university education failed in almost every aspect (it did not drive down costs for students; it did not increase opportunity), it did facilitate the expansion of student numbers and the growth of education as an industry. However, the market in learning was not primarily responsible for this - rather, the disappearance of a viable labour market for 16 to 18 year olds in this period was the primary cause alongside the world-wide growth of mass higher education. A school leaving age of 18 was introduced in 2013 and leavers had few places to go to secure a future. All of this was consequent on the continuing collapse of traditional industries and their training and apprenticeship schemes which had been the bedrock of many working communities and the heart of the skilled working class in Britain. For many young people it was now university or nothing. At the same time as increased cohorts of young people were entering universities, adult students were disappearing from the universities and adult education colleges and centres. The funding models available to universities privileged full-time school leavers and later masters' degree students over and above those of part-time adult returners who were now subject proportionately to the same fees regimes as full-time students. Very many adult learners could not of course afford to take out loans to fund higher level learning, even if their home circumstances and family lives allowed them the time and energy. The net result of this was to shift the age profile of universities downwards to young people and the neglect and disappearance of much adult and community education including university extra-mural departments which had for generations tried to bring higher learning and opportunities to communities and individuals (Marriott 1984).

The fact was that as participation in higher education rose, the British people were living a paradox. As university student numbers rose to meet the target set by the Blair Government of 50 per cent participation in higher learning, those who would not go to university were bound in the main for a low wage, low skill economy where the prospects for lifetime, well-paid and secure work were rapidly diminishing. Meanwhile the prospects of graduate *under-employment* were rising as graduate jobs with secure lifetime employment prospects were themselves becoming ever more scarce. A first degree was no longer a guarantee of a secure job and many new graduates found themselves in what were previously non-graduate jobs in the clerical and service industries, many of which involved short-term and part-time contracts and flexible hours. For many jobs the premium qualification became a second or masters degree and a required period of unpaid 'internship' work- an impossible demand on those without existing finance and wealth, often provided by affluent families to their graduate children.

If universities in general were subject to financial constraints it was also the case that considerable freedom was granted institutions to make their own way in the neoliberal market place for education. For those who developed Access and widening participation, learning was not a unit of financial resource. Neither was it a commodity to be bought and sold as a marketable product; it was not 'provision' to be disposed of just as it was not available off the shelf as a consumer item or positional good. For the supporters of Access, learning in the newly expanded system was about engagement and renewal. It was about critical thinking applied to the issues and challenges of their students as they struggled to overcome barriers to learning and opportunity. The setting up of Access provision was a redeeming of pledges made to local communities - that they should also inherit what learning opportunities can yield: a better social product and a better chance at life for the people who were living in the here and now and future opportunities for their children.

## Is the free market model now broken?

The universities in the UK expanded and developed in a period when a consumer-based ideology which stressed the benefits of so-called free markets and individual choice, was in the ascendancy. Tuition fees were increasing and the importance of revenue streams meant all universities were becoming big businesses. The economic power of education meant that universities were a key contributor to the prosperity and futures of their host cities and towns. This was the context in which students began to be treated like consumers who were buying a product for sale by the university. Education could be viewed and marketed as a commodity. This had been happening during the previous two decades but accelerated after the coalition government's reforms after 2010 which began to ramp up student fees from £3,000 a year to £9,000 and beyond. Access and its related foundation courses did not generate such high fee rates and in any case were mainly located in further education colleges and funded from a different funding agency from that of the universities. Universities competed to attract the highest number of students and the income that came with them as well as maximising revenue from other sources such as student residences. The Access agenda was increasingly marginal to the financial constraints and choices faced by universities. The government let it be known that universities could become bankrupt as well as having the capacity to acquire other institutions through amalgamations. This had always gone on in some ways in the past, but never before as part of the principle of a marketised education system. This was an actual example of what John Gray (2021) called ... 'the centrist ideology in which the principle function of government is to re-engineer society as an adjunct of the global market... (which) has become the orthodoxy of a vanished age'. The global free market was compatible with the ideology of meritocracy which asserted the fact that self-made men, it was almost always men, deserved to be in the leading positions of economy and society. If they did not merit it, how else had they arrived at their elevated status?

The new system attached funding to student numbers and from 2015 limits on recruitment were removed with the exception of some specialist subjects such as medicine which required much more additional resources. The more students recruited the more income for the university was generated. David Willets the Conservative minister for universities boasted that ... 'more students in England now get their first choice, and I'm proud of it' (Observer 2021: 8-11). Universities had of course to compete as never before and some private colleges came into existence to take advantage of public money available for courses, many of which had low value and poor quality. All the universities competed and advertised their courses to try to convince school leavers that their shiny new campuses and facilities were the best. Foreign students were particularly valuable since they paid even higher fees. There was a boom in student housing which became another income stream for universities. Universities borrowed money to finance their operations and the sector's debt trebled in a decade to £12 billion (Observer 2021 ibid).

One result of this was the development of what is known as market conforming behaviour. For universities this meant raising revenue streams, maintaining credit ratings and committing to a continuous flow of students who bring in fees. Maximising student intakes is a key to this process and its counterpoint is raising league table ratings. At the same time there is an imperative to lower costs which impacts on staffing expenditure and contracts which in turn has the effect of destabilising academic life. All academic life came to be measured and monitored in these managerialist terms. Risk taking and creativity was suppressed in such circumstances. Cost cutting measures and retrenchment may present the easiest immediate solution where market conformity holds sway.

The metrics do not of course capture the full reality of what was going on. Larger and richer institutions, for example, are able to game the system. There is only a very imperfect market in higher education anyway as cultural and historical factors shape who goes where regardless of the ability to pay fees. At the end of the day university leaders choose where to put resources and where the focus of development and effort shall be. The rules of this game favour conformity and conservativism and corporate uniformity. These rules clearly did not favour Access and widening participation as uniformity and standardisation of higher education in the new universities proceeded up to the year 2020. The truth is though that Access provision was never meant to be a standardised version of a university. It was meant to challenge that uniformity of expectations where all the players resemble each other. It was meant to equip us with a better prospect to truly reflect the diversity of our communities.

# The ascendancy of finance in the continuous emergency

Education cannot exist in a vacuum and was part of an extended crisis of economic life in Britain, most vividly seen in the dramas of the financial markets of 2008-09. The international banks and financial institutions were threatened with collapse and bankruptcy on a world scale. Joseph Vogl (2017) has called this the 'politics of emergency' in which government and the role of the state come together with the 'markets' to reinforce their favoured policies. The crises serve to legitimate what can be claimed as exceptions and exigencies. The crisis of funding for education is an on-going reality; it is never solved but merely postponed until a later date. The withdrawal by the British Government of block and grant funding for universities via a funding council in favour of an artificially and far from perfect market via student fees, loans and credit, opened the way for a continuing crisis of funding. There is always a shortage of income for universities and thus an actual or potential crisis to be addressed or averted by those who have the power within an institution. Those who have authority in a university are those who have control of the political economy of the institution. Financial matters become paramount to the well-being of the institution and it is finance which determines what shall be regarded as the weak points in the system (Davies and Davies 2021: ch 8).

Financial measures to solve the problem which are in denial of the true causes of the crisis may well make matters worse if they damage the essential infrastructure and purposes of the university. Challenges of curriculum renewal and problems of student recruitment are the stuff of university management, yet when these are presented as financial and budgetary deficits and crises, cutting and closing and reorganising provision and people may be presented as the only and inevitable solution. Those who define the problem and frame the issues and present the arguments get to propose the solutions. Once made these decisions seem unavoidable and correct. Over time they become part of the accepted wisdom of a management group; sanctified by group pressure and management conformism. The logic of financial exigencies enables institutional senior management to make policy which sacrifices the well-being and interests of one part to the higher good and common interest. What are rescue measures for a crisis of its own making (failing to renew and invest) must be geared to the strongest, not towards the weakest. This is the logic of the ascendancy of finance and the monetisation of learning.

# Neoliberal meritocracy

The neoliberal free market model of capitalism may have been a marriage of merit and money but it was more than that. Meritocracy served over decades as a potent and persuasive justification of the injustices of capitalist societies and was an intrinsic part of neoliberal thinking. Yet in the public mind meritocracy became associated with the idea that the most gifted and deserving were somehow naturally those who had succeeded. The existence of their success demonstrated the rightness and justification of it! Wealth and privilege are therefore self-justifying. The individuals and social elites who benefitted deserved their positions, wealth and power. If they owned it they must have shown the skills and talent to deserve it. Such thinking also penetrated thinking about the growth of the knowledge economy and as a justification for selling off and privatising parts of the welfare state (Littler 2018: 45). In the 1980s neoliberal meritocracy found its fullest expression in the policies of the Thatcher government which vigorously asserted the idea that anyone could make it and that freedom was to be found through the acquisition of consumer goods, home ownership and the privatisation of public utilities and the social housing stock. Later New labour governments pushed through the privatisation of public services handing power to private business interests and letting them profit from, for example, education and prisons.

Meritocracy as an 'ideology' extended the idea of competitive individualism into everyday life, supported by public mass media and entertainment businesses and business entrepreneurialism. There was a withdrawal from the values of the welfare state and erosion of the sovereignty of the national state in favour of the rapidly globalising world economy. The issues of downward social mobility and the social value of lower paid jobs became ever more invisible yet ever more disavowed by powerful ruling elites.

Meritocracy under neoliberalism had many different guises: it asserted that it was your own fault if you failed to achieve your dreams and aspirations since those with merit deserved to succeed. Inequality could not be seriously denied but the solutions were in the extension of capitalist, market principles and solutions. The net effect of this was, throughout this period, to increase inequality and social division. Meritocracy was a powerful idea because it appeared to react against inherited privilege and to assert the possibility of individual effort in overcoming barriers to opportunity and success. At the same time meritocracy was used to market and sell the idea of equality whilst extending the power of those with wealth and privilege. It confused the idea of democracy with the power of choice in the market where all things are for sale (Brown 2019). Yet the reality is that not everything can be bought and sold. Some parts of our collective and social life cannot and should not be monetised and working and living together rather than competing alone is the only viable and worthwhile future.

The deepening inequality of income and wealth which have characterised British society since the financial crash and crisis of 2008-09 (Dorling 2018 ibid; Toynbee and Walker ibid) has been magnified by the meritocratic pride and self-justification shown by the winners of the globalisation race. The growth of neoliberal belief systems and the acceptance of the free market state have undermined belief and trust in modern welfare states in many places across the globe. Local communities have been fragmented and destroyed as economic investment and employment have moved to more profitable places, resulting in the undermining of social and communal solidarity (Bauman ibid). In his book The Tyranny of Merit (2021) the philosopher Michael Sandel argues that the people who reach the top of the social and economic hierarchies tend to believe that their success is of their own doing; that they therefore deserve the full benefits and rewards that the market bestows on them. Likewise those who fail in the system are deemed to have failed due to their own inadequacies. Sandel's argument is that prevailing liberal conceptions of personal and social freedom tend to assume that ultimately we are all self-made and self-sufficient, whereas the reality is that we live social and communal lives in which we are dependent upon one-another. Markets alone cannot ensure we have a proper social fabric and effective social justice (Sandel 2012; Lynch 2022).

## The meritocratic monarch as king of UKania

That success in a meritocratic system has to be earned, organised, managed and worked for has been noted, even when elites are able to self-justify and legitimate their privileges by massaging and manipulating the public media in their own favour and interests. For a society such as the United Kingdom which maintains an hereditary monarchy with real political and symbolic power exercised and legitimated through a parliament, this represents an ideological challenge of some size and scope. How can a meritocracy exist at all when the apex of the social, political and status hierarchies is occupied by someone who is there by the accident of birth? No-matter how much credence is given to the value of continuity, stability and mystical identity of the queen or king, there is no such thing as a meritocratic monarch in today's modern society. The Enlightenment and subsequent revolutions and constitutional reforms put democratic constraints on European royals and banished the corrupt aristocracies from democratic government. At least that in theory is the story democratic nations have told themselves.

Yet in many parts of Britain and in particular in England, there is a widespread and collective delusion that somehow the monarchy and specifically the late queen was somehow a 'blessing' which had been bestowed on the people- perhaps by god so that the monarch was, even in this modern and agnostic age somehow 'divine' or at least somehow divinely inspired as the embodiment of the nation and its identity. Her majesty, it was widely touted by a fawning and infantilised press and media, had somehow earned the trust and love of her people (who were her *subjects* – not *citizens* of an independent and democratic nation) by having shown no political opinions or attitudes to the great social issues of the day and era over a very long lifetime during which her immense wealth had been preserved and her family's privileges maintained. A delusion has been created and systematically broadcast that the monarchy is somehow magically and meritocratically achieved and is a deserved existence. By 2022 Queen Elizabeth II had reigned for 70 years and would be succeeded, as expressed by commentator Nick Cohen (2022), by a man who had announced his willingness to break the connections which controlled the head of state.

The hereditary power in a monarchy inevitably 'throws up a duffer' (Cohen ibid) and Charles III as succeeding monarch does not accept that his authority has nothing to do with his ability and is simply an accident of birth. There is an incipient assumption that this accident of birth and heredity is ordained by some higher power. And yet whereas people may have believed they were blessed to have a queen, many of them wished to have a queen without the rest of the royal family. When we examine the circumstances of the queen's accession to the monarchy and head of state even the most pro-monarchist members of the public could have hardly believed that god had deigned to appoint this particular woman to the job since she was only there because parliament had deposed her uncle, the nazi supporter Edward VIII. The house of Windsor- Battenberg survived but war, revolution and egalitarianism had destroyed the Habsburgs and the Romanovs and many another European monarchy. The queen stayed out of politics and was modest in her demeanour and attitudes. Nobody outside her personal circles knew her politics or personal beliefs, or even if she had any serious convictions beyond her obvious obsessions with dogs and horses. She was a blank sheet on to which anybody might project their own version of what she really was. The in-coming king Charles, according to Nick Cohen, had no such sense of caution, but only a sense of entitlement when the future monarch wrote in 2003 … 'What is wrong with everyone nowadays? Why do they all seem to think they are qualified to do things far beyond their technical capabilities? People seem to think they can all be pop stars, high court judges, brilliant TV personalities or infinitely more competent heads of state without ever putting in the necessary work or having natural ability. This is the result of social utopianism which believes humanity can be genetically and socially engineered to contradict the lessons of history.' (Cohen ibid). There is no awareness here of the genetic fluke which benefitted a less than modest pretender and later inheritor to the throne. In his mind his long apprenticeship to his mother equipped him as a self-made monarch who succeeded to the crown and all its trappings, wealth and power on merit rather than by sheer luck and accident.

In reality and historically, argues Krishnan Kumar (2022), …'it was the strength of the rule of primogeniture in the European empires which allowed them to escape the ferocious succession struggles that plagued so many of the non-European empires- Ottoman, Mughal, Chinese- where brothers, cousins, uncles and nephews fought for the throne. On the other hand, as the Habsburg and to some extent the Romanov families well illustrate, primogeniture could mean succession by the weak and feeble-minded rather than by those who had proved themselves in battle or superior court politics (often fought out by ambitious mothers of the harem)'.

The story of the meritocratic monarchy in the UK is of a presumptuous heir to the throne who believed, like Boris Johnson the ex-British prime minister in his breaking of the Covid 19 Rules and in his misleading statements to Parliament, that the rules did not apply to him. The king, according to Cohen expects to lead as monarch not just to follow protocols which mean rubber stamping decisions made elsewhere by others (Jobson 2018). The conventions which kept his mother in check may not serve to constrain him which is especially concerning as Britain moves into a constitutionally unstable future with a border in the Irish Sea and a separatist government in Scotland. The new monarch Charles has shown his fondness for dictatorial monarchies in the Middle East who have no time for the democratic niceties of European democracies.

The case of monarchy somehow claiming meritocratic value for itself highlights the absurdity of inherited elitism where accidents of birth give rise to immense privilege and social inequality. Absurd they may be, but they are sign-posts of the much more extensive and pervasive ideologies of meritocracy which serve to obscure and to legitimate inherited and culturally transferred social and intellectual capital as well as 'real' capital wealth and assets which are passed on down through the generations to secure the private access and ownership of what is after all society's wealth and the property of us all. As Polly Toynbee (2023) remarked the world may laugh at our monarchistic absurdity but we must take it seriously… 'Monarchy is a cast of mind that blocks reform, an unholy religion made of these remarkably unremarkable people. Despite the best education for generations, their most useful genetic function is to demonstrate that talent and intelligence is randomly assigned. Monarchy breeds in Britain a feudalism of the imagination that gives a stamp of approval to inheritance and to the inequality, risen rampantly in recent decades, that is, at the root of our social and political malaise.'

## Lessons learned

This chapter is part of a narrative about Access as an educational movement which came about at a point in British history when change was desired by many but was frequently denied. Access came at a democratising moment in education when people were demanding more learning opportunities. It was also a time when fundamental social change was underway in the economy and culture. The social imperative was for mass further and higher education as economy and society adjusted to global change; the personal imperative was of a desire for a more fulfilled life and future for self and family. Much of the Access agenda was ultimately concerned with work and employment for its students and therefore with social mobility and moving up the ladder of opportunity which was thought to exist.

The fastest growing occupations between the 1990s and the 2010s were managerial, professional and technical jobs (Todd ibid: 321). However, these jobs though 'professional' and 'managerial', actually lacked the income and security previously associated with senior posts. There was job title inflation with little lifetime career path development available. Meanwhile heavy industry declined and skilled manual workers also experienced job insecurity. People entering the labour market in this era believed that only by being upwardly mobile could they succeed in life and politicians encouraged this. Older strategies for improving life were diminishing such as trade union power and collective bargaining, whilst social mobility through meritocratic effort was supported for the talented few. Individual drive and ambition was said to be the real solution to the need to equalise opportunities (Milburn 2009). Social mobility was the central social policy objective for governments of all stripes in this period (Mandler 2020), yet upward mobility was not achieved for those at the bottom of the social and economic hierarchies. The fact is the most desirable and best rewarded jobs and careers remained in the hands of the wealthy elites and ordinary people in trouble were told to save themselves by individually climbing the social mobility ladder. Secure manual and clerical jobs continued to be harder to find. In 2006 Alan Johnson the Labour minister for education stated that the Labour Government would no longer fund further education courses which had... 'little value to the economy...so more plumbing (and) less pilates and flower-arranging' (Todd ibid: 323). Unfortunately this decision alongside the introduction of market-led conditions and valorisation of vocational education helped ensure the closure of many of the adult education courses of the pre-Access kind which had brought women back into education in the 1970s. The introduction of university tuition fees by Labour also hit mature students hard and working class students were disincentivised. Mature student numbers and part-time enrolments fell as we have seen in earlier chapters of this book, and arguably study opportunities were diminished for those who most needed them. These were consequences of polices and programmes which were hardly commensurate with the rallying cry of New Labour-Education, Education, Education.

Social class continued to matter even when working class students did manage to enter elite universities. Such students, said to be among the 'brightest and the best', were significantly less likely to enter the professions or management than graduates whose parents were themselves professionals. The striving for upward mobility offered no challenge to the embedded inequalities of class, race and gender.

In general successive governments in this period encouraged free-market and neoliberal policies that benefitted the rich and which effectively closed off routes to ambitious young people from the lower social and income groups. Without family wealth and support young graduates could not afford to be geographically mobile as they could not afford to own a home of their own, especially not in London and the South East where paradoxically most of the graduate jobs were located. By 2017, 37 per cent of graduates were employed in non-graduate jobs, mostly in clerical and service- sector posts (Todd ibid: 328). Many people who came from London could only afford to live there if they shared the family home and London became the most socially polarised city in Britain...'wealthy inhabitants lived in expensive neighbourhoods and had very different kinds of jobs to most local people. And they did not choose to let their wealth trickle down the ladder. Instead they worked hard to secure their own and their children's prospects by investing in their homes, education- these cities housed elite private schools as well as universities- and their own savings. This was a perfectly understandable strategy in such an uncertain, unequal world. But it did not produce any engines of social mobility.' (Todd ibid: 329).

The political spirit of the age seemed to be that talent would best be helped by competition rather than social welfare. The acquisition of wealth was the key signal for ambition and effort and the favoured route towards it and the justification of it was supposed to be upward social mobility. One result was an increase in poverty and an associated increase in the wealth and earnings of the wealthiest 10 per cent of the population who by 2015 owned 45 per cent of the nation's household wealth. In the housing market by 2017 councils owned just 7 per cent of housing while 63 per cent was owner occupied and an increasing proportion – 30 per cent by 2017-was privately rented (Todd ibid: 335). Home ownership for the precarious and young workforce became a distant dream as house prices rocketed upwards. Whilst this damaging and depressing scenario was evolving governments were inventing and being assisted by what Selina Todd (ibid: 338) calls the 'social mobility and diversity industry'. After 2000 there was a growing number of charities, lobby groups and private businesses which focussed on and worked for social mobility through education and employment. The central tenet of this work was the idea that disadvantage can be overcome by personal aspiration and ambition allied to hard work by the individual. The fact that poverty, deprivation, discrimination, marginalisation and exclusion may have social and economic causes which can never simply be countered by personal motivations and aspirations to succeed was generally ignored. Little criticism was offered by the social mobility industry of the preservation of their wealth by the nation's richest people or of the ways in which the private schools and elite universities hoarded their resources. Similarly the large commercial banks and financial institutions which had been rescued by government intervention following the great banking crisis of 2008/09 were allowed to continue their businesses without control in favour of the majority. Even though the themes of meritocracy and diversity were touted and extolled by governments and agencies, the majority of businesses and the professions were left unreformed. A minority of talented black and minority ethnic people were recruited into the higher echelons of the businesses and institutions but the masses of the ordinary people were left unaffected... 'The social mobility and diversity industry had failed to challenge the working patterns and hierarchies that ensured most people ended up at the bottom of the ladder. While ethnic and social difference could be celebrated as evidence of 'diversity', the emphasis was always on raising people's aspirations, resolutely ignoring the limited room at the top.' (Todd ibid: 344-5).

After two turbulent decades the 21st century revealed a Britain which was divided between a small wealthy elite who were becoming richer and the broad masses, many of whom were becoming poorer. The elite did not create a meritocracy with greater opportunity for everyone. Far from it, Britain was perhaps a more unequal society than we had seen for at least a century. Neither did this culture produce happiness and contentment since research showed that the more equal societies enjoyed greater happiness, better health and higher levels of educational attainment (Wilkinson and Pickett 2010; Dorling 2017). By 2020 it was clear that getting to the top was more difficult than it ever had been and that poverty and deprivation were on the increase; whole new concepts such as 'food poverty' and 'energy poverty' were conjured into existence to describe the dire straites so many people were in. Life for the middle classes was also getting harder as job security and opportunity diminished, especially for young people. House prices continued to rise making the future less and less certain for those without access to family wealth. Those who contemplated climbing the slippery ladder of opportunity were probably outnumbered by those who lived in fear of sliding down that same ladder.

# A future postponed

There is an argument that globalisation and the marketisation of so much of our social life has somehow run its course. The Covid-19 pandemic which broke out in 2019 has often been cited as signalling the end of an era and the need for a 'new normal' (Nyland and Davies 2022). This came at the end of a period in which austerity was the major public policy driving down expenditure and investment in public services of all kinds including net per capita expenditure on education and health, allied to an explosion of market-driven and debt-based consumption. The net effect was to create new forms of poverty and deprivation so that differences in life chances between the rich and poor are virtually as great as they were one hundred years ago. In Europe Britain appears to be uniquely tolerant of inequality. No other large European country according to Dorling (2017) taxes the rich so little and lets them take so much wealth and income at the expense of the poor. Britain spends less on health than other comparable countries and is alone in seeing the life expectancy of some of the poorest people begin to fall. No appeals to meritocracy have been able to rectify these levels of inequality. Neither did meritocracy come to the aid of the sick and dying during the Covid crisis when only a universal public service could be effective and protect all the people of the nation. The persistent inequalities we endure disfigure British society and make unfairness an abiding and familiar feature of our lives (Toynbee and Walker ibid). What is to come next, it is said, must be better and fairer than what went before. Equality of opportunity must be more than an aspiration and become a reality and result in equality of outcomes. A new sense of common purpose can perhaps be generated which can re-instate a more socially just society in which poverty, deprivation and social exclusion can be challenged and overcome. The inequalities we have listed earlier as being part of the 'wicked issues' are unsustainable for the future. A sense of something needing to be done to atone for the failures of the last decade is palpable in the wider society as the 21$^{st}$ century enters its third decade.

The origins of the problems of meritocracy and equality of opportunity, however, go back much further within the collective experience, psychologies and ideologies of the British people and on some of the most critical issues the people have yet to speak. That these issues will involve education is hardly in doubt and the lessons of Access may yet speak to the promise of a better future and transcend the ideologies of a meritocracy and the free market in opportunities. They can be said to be ideologies because they are not realities, yet they are still powerful beliefs and practices which shape behaviour and thinking and have been widely celebrated over a long period. Our understanding of education in modern life requires us to grasp the historical development of ideas and ideologies as they impact on our lives and futures as material forces. It can be reasonably argued that the 1960s were the high point of liberal, democratic humanism with respect to education but were followed by a reaction as capitalist interests invested in and supported Thatcherism and Reaganism. Their neoliberalist economic strategies helped transform the remnants of the social democratic welfare state settlement into a more rapacious and global force (Brown 2019). This was part of the spread of economics into all walks of life associated with globalisation. Neoliberal economics had at its heart an assumption of the economic and moral rightness of individualism. It was a moral issue because it was said to be innate to human nature and life. Only free markets and states that allowed property, wealth and capital the freedom to prosper could guarantee a free society. There is a sub-text also here – that the right of the state to act on behalf of us all is in question if it contradicts the rights claimed by individuals. The collective and communal interests of a society can be undermined in this way by powerful economic and social interests (Zuboff 2019). Education itself cannot be immune from the debate as we have seen. A neoliberal form of meritocracy has become the basic commonsense of British society which justifies hierarchies and vast inequalities and this has become embedded in our social spaces, our culture and in our educational institutions (Ball 2015). It is surely the task of critical thinkers and educators to challenge this and rejuvenate the Access agenda.

The original Access movement raised questions about knowledge and learning in the context of social mobility and equal opportunity which remain with us some forty years later. We continue to live, however, with these two 'ideological' myths - that of equality of opportunity and that of meritocratic selection- which have had a pervasive and sometimes pernicious effect on our social and intellectual life. Both have been used as ideological masks (Lynch ibid: 151) to conceal their own false promises and perpetuate a deception. The reality is that few people can achieve their full potential where social inequality and injustice are pervasive and unchallenged and it is surely the task of educationalists to bring this challenge into the central focus of our learning and teaching.

# References

Ball, S.J. (2015) 'Living the Neo-liberal University', *European Journal of Education,* Vol 50, No 3, 2015.

Bauman, Z. (2001) *Community: Seeking Safety in an Insecure Wor*ld, Cambridge: Polity Press.

Bhopal, K. (2018) *The Experiences of Black and Minority Ethnic Academics: A Comparative Study of the Unequal Academy*, London: Routledge.

Bourdieu, P. and Passeron, J-C. (1990) *Reproduction in Education, Society and Culture,* London: Sage Publications.

Brown, W. (2019) *In the Ruins of Neoliberalism: The Rise of Antidemocratic Politics in the West,* New York/Chichester, West Sussex: Columbia University Press.

Chun, E. B. and Feagin, J. R. (2022) *Who Killed Higher Education? Maintaining White Dominance in a Desegregating Era,* New York and London: Routledge.

Cohen, N. (2009) *Waiting for the Etonians: Reports from the Sickbed of Liberal England,* London: Fourth Estate.

Cohen, N. (2022) Unlike the Queen, Prince Charles will have no sense of caution, only of entitlement, *The Observer*, London Sunday 5 June, 2022.

Crawford, M. (2015) *The World Beyond Your Head: How to Flourish in an Age of Distraction,* UK: Viking/Penguin.

Davies, D. and Davies, E. (2021) *A Fair Go: Learning in Critical Times and Places,* UK: Amazon.

Dorling, D. (2017) *The Equality Effect: Improving Life for Everyone,* UK: New Internationalist Co-operative.

Dorling, D. (2018) *Peak Inequality: Britain's Ticking Time Bomb*, University of Bristol: Policy Press.

Dunn, W. (2021) 'Woke Capitalism! How the managerial class created the dangerous myth of the virtuous company', *New Statesman* Vol 150, no 5642, 22-28 October 2021.

Fisher, M. (2009) *Capitalist Realism: Is There No Alternative,* Winchester UK/Washington USA: Zero Books.

Floud, J.E. (1956) *Social Class and Educational Opportunity*, UK: Heinemann.

Floud, J.E. (1961) 'Social Class Factors in Educational Achievement' in Halsey, A.H. (ed) (1961) *Ability and Educational Opportunity*, Paris: OECD.

Gray, J. (2021) 'The great sell-out' London: *New Statesman* 16-22 April, 2021.

Green, F. and Kynaston, D. (2019) *Engines of Privilege: Britain's Private School Problem,* London: Bloomsbury Publishing.

Hargreaves, D.H. (1967) *Social Relations in a Secondary School*, Oxon: Routledge.

Hirsch, A. (2018) *Brit(ish): on race, identity and belonging,* London: Jonathan Cape.

Jackson, B. and Marsden, D. (1962) *Education and the Working Class*, UK: Penguin.

Jobson, R. (2018) *Charles at 70: Thoughts, Hopes and Dreams*, UK: John Blake Pub. Ltd.

Kumar, K. (2022) 'King of Kings: A collective biography of emperors in world history', The Times Literary Supplement, no. 6219 June 10 2022, a review of *In the Shadow of the Gods: The emperor in world history* by Lieven, D. (2022), UK: Allen Lane.

Lacey, C. (1970) *Hightown Grammar: the school as a social system*, Manchester University Press.

Littler, J. (2018) 'Narratives and Values: Young and old meritocracy - from radical critique to neoliberal tool' *Renewal* 26, 2018.

Lynch, K. (2022) *Care and Capitalism: Why Affective Equality Matters for Social Justice,* Cambridge: Polity Press.

Mandler, P. (2020) *The Crisis of Meritocracy: Britain's Transition to Mass Education Since the Second World War*, Oxford: Oxford University Press.

Marriott, S. (1984) *Extramural Empires: Service & Self-Interest in English University Adult Education 1873-1983,* University of Nottingham.

Milburn, A. (2009) Panel on Fair Access to the Professions, *Unleashing Aspiration: The Final Report of the Panel on Fair Access to the Professions*, London: HMG 2009.

Nyland, J. and Davies, D. (eds) (2022) *Curriculum Challenges for Universities: Agenda for Change,* Singapore: Springer Press.

Observer 17.01.2021, London. Observer 04.12.2022, London

Olusoga, D. (2016) *Black and British: A Forgotten History*, London: Macmillan.

Picketty, T. (2020) *Capital and Ideology*, Cambridge, Mass. /London, England: The Belknap Press of Harvard University Press.

Rankine, C. (2020) *Just Us: An American Conversation*, UK: Penguin/Random House.

Rawls, J. (1971) *A Theory of Justice*, Cambridge, Mass: Harvard University Press.

Sandel, M. J. (2012) *What Money Can't Buy: The Moral Limits of Markets*, Great Britain: Allen Lane.

Sandel. M. J. (2021) *The Tyranny of Merit: What's Become of the Common Good?* UK: Penguin.

Savage, M. et al (2015) *Social Class in the 21 Century*, UK: Penguin/Random House.

Sutton Trust *'Access to Advantage'* 7 December 2018, UK.

Thornton, M. (2013) The mirage of merit, *Australian Feminist Studies,* 28 (76): 127-143.

Todd, S. (2021) *Snakes and Ladders: The Great British Social Mobility Myth*, London: Chatto & Windus.

Toynbee, P. (2023) *The Guardian, Journal- opinion*, London, 10.01.2023.

Toynbee, P. and Walker, D. (2020) *The Lost decade 2010-2020 and What Lies Ahead for Britain,* London: Guardian Books.

Verkaik, R. (2019*) Posh Boys: How English Public Schools Ruin Britain*, UK: Oneworld Publications.

Vogl, J. (2017) *The Ascendancy of Finance*, Cambridge: Polity Press.

Wilkinson, R. and Pickett, K. (2010) *The Spirit Level: Why Equality is Better for Everyone*, London: Penguin Books.

Wooldridge, A. (2021) *The Aristocracy of Talent: How Meritocracy Made the Modern World,* UK: Allen Lane/Penguin.

Young, M. (1958) *The Rise of the Meritocracy: An Essay on Education and Equality,* London: Thames and Hudson.

Zuboff, S. (2019) *The age of surveillance capitalism: The fight for the future at the new frontier of power*, UK: Profile Books.

# 'ACCESS' FOR INNER-CITY STUDENTS

*The Vice-Chancellor (far right) with students on the 'Access' course and Linda Loy (second from left), one of the organisers, and the Chair of the course, David Davies (back row, right).*

On Friday 9 May, the Vice-Chancellor visited the 'Access' course at the Octagon Building in Grove Street and met teaching staff and students.

The 'Access' course is a new route into higher education for adults from the inner city, and it grew out of the belief that for many people, particularly black people, the education system has failed them. The aim of the course is to provide a positive educational opportunity for adults within the inner city who have little or no formal qualification, and it is designed for mature students over 21, particularly members of the black community, who wish to return to study to prepare for entry to a higher education course.

Access is a partnership between Old Swan Technical College and Mabel Fletcher Technical College. This University is also interested and involved in the project, and Professor Noel Boaden and other staff of the Department of Continuing Education have participated in the course. Other establishments participating include Liverpool Polytechnic, Liverpool Institute of Higher Education, the Charles Wootton Centre and Elimu Wa Nane, an educational institute run by the Methodist Centre.

The elements of the Access course include study skills, English, mathematics, social studies, black studies and computer studies. An emphasis is placed on individual counselling and support throughout the course, and students will also be given the opportunity to gain practical experience in a chosen area of professional work.

The Access Course teachers with the Vice Chancellor of Liverpool University 1983

# Chapter 5

# Race, Racism and Access

The official origins of Access in Britain are in the government letter of 1978 which encouraged the setting up of 'special Access courses' and in effect invited local authorities and by extension their educational institutions to extend opportunities and access to higher education and the professions to black and other ethnic groupings and communities (John 1993: 10). Was the recognition of black and ethnic groups' needs for 'special Access courses' a recognition of the position and experience of these communities in British life and society? The answer must be ...only to a limited degree since the whole question of institutionalised racism and the embedded and long-term cultural and social exclusion and marginalisation of black and ethnic groups from 'mainstream' life could not be addressed by a small number of worthy courses staffed by relatively junior teachers and volunteers. Nevertheless, it signalled a change.

Access as a *movement* arose in a milieu in the 1970s and 1980s, at the point when working people were seeking a better life and a more secure future; a point at which the reforms in schooling and higher education which the post-war settlement had delivered were being experienced by many people as failure. Comprehensive schooling and the expansion of universities had stalled by the 1980s and social inequality was on the rise. At the same time black and other ethnic groupings were increasingly marginalised in the inner urban areas of United Kingdom cities. Black youth were alienated in particular as cultural integration was seen to fail and as racial discrimination was perceived as somehow embedded in British society. Black students often came from the battle-grounds of the inner cities. This had a profound impact on what was acceptable as educational knowledge to black people themselves. The emergence of Access courses served to assert the presence of black people in further and higher education and signalled the need for changed priorities and to the need for a commitment to alternative means of entry to further and higher education.

From the start there were those who insisted that we need to locate Access in the wider debate about who has access to power, to resources and to the professions via the education system (Tomlinson 2019: ch1 and 2). If Access in general was about contesting some of the wider and historical inequalities of British society (as proposed earlier in this book) then, as Gus John suggested...

'We need to talk not about black Access Courses, but about a black access movement that takes on the educational rights of all people, whatever their background...Although Access Courses may address the issues of black people, and to a lesser extent women seeking to enter HE, they don't address the issues of what happens to these people, what these institutions are about, and what their responsibilities are as institutions of higher learning in meeting these students' needs...Governments and the universities themselves are very reluctant to raise questions about the so-called mainstream...They are reluctant to discuss who should validate knowledge and who decided that we should screen certain things out and study other things. Why should there be such a major divergence between the pedagogy and curriculum of Access Courses and those of the HE institutions to which these students progress?' (John ibid: 10-11). That there was discrimination against black and some ethnic groupings in the wider society and in employment was clear; the evidence within education broadly was less clear but there was a widely perceived sense of alienation by black people and participation was lower than their white and Asian counterparts (Taylor 1993).

The historical aspects of race and racism were often hidden from view (Hiro 1973; Fryer 1985; Walvin 1973; Olusoga 2016; Scanlan 2020), however, the contemporary ones have seldom been far from the headlines. A deep seated and complex racial problem exists in the United Kingdom which has often over the decades exploded into public consciousness (Foot 1969; Rex 1973; Moore 1975; John 2006; Tomlinson 2019). More than four decades ago Stuart Hall (1978) argued that race, racism and its disavowel- its lack of recognition amongst the dominant classes and in their discourse- was a key theme and signifier for a society that was careering into a series of crises that was accompanying the decline of British economic and social life. Unemployment, violent crime, urban decay, the breakdown of public order, street violence and demonstrations were all laid at the door of ethnic and racial minorities. Black youth in particular were perceived to be a threat to the tolerance, order and stability of British society (Dhondy 1974,1979; Davies 1981; Hebdige 1981; John 1981, 2006) The language and perceptions used to describe, for example, black youth in 2011 in London boroughs and other cities (Tomlinson 2019:183) was remarkably similar to that used 40 years previously.

The troubling and sensitive issues of race relations were never absent from struggles and disputation around education. The material basis for these concerns lay in the inner urban working-class districts which bore and continue to bear the brunt of Britain's material poverty, destitution and social disadvantage. This is the underpinning of the institutionalised racism and discrimination in employment, housing and education that racial minorities and many black people experienced.

The evolution of race relations in Britain and the ways in which the racialisation of British society were perceived by black people and ethnic groups impacted on the meaning and outcomes of Access education. By the 1980s the attempts at integration and assimilation of black and other ethnic groups was seen as seriously deficient (Rex and Tomlinson 1979; Ben Tovim et al 1981a, 1981 b; Lawrence 1981) and came to be replaced in much public discourse by the idea of multiculturalism which emphasised the existence and validity of cultural diversity. The major emphasis here was on the multiplicity of cultures and ethnically diverse populations with which education had to cope and acknowledge as being equally valid. Multiculturalism endured much criticism including the belief that institutional racism involving access to power, resources, employment, housing and relations with the educational system is not a question of ethnic or cultural qualities, but rather is about the structural aspects of social life rooted in the organisation and cultures of British institutions and life (Allen 1971 and 1982; Tomlinson 2019).

The growth of Access to HE took place in the context of rising unemployment, especially for young black people where it was estimated to be three times higher than for white school leavers (Cross 1978). A racial division of labour and a black underclass existed as a structural feature of the general division of labour in Britain (Hall et al 1978). None of this of course is to deny the importance of social class, gender, age and skill in shaping labour market opportunities but black workers were disadvantaged within a series of cross-cutting hierarchical divisions of the labour market. Black and ethnic minority populations suffered the multiple problems of disadvantage and deprivation experienced by residents of the inner cities. They experienced the effects of massive, persistent direct and indirect discrimination in many aspects of social and public life (Smith 1977; Allen 1982). All of this was 'intersected' in the historical and contemporary manifestations of racism, much of which was disavowed and unacknowledged in British society and culture (Hall 2017: 23 and 73).

# From invisibility to social justice

Racism is often disavowed and invisible to white people precisely because it is routine and unconscious. That Britain could be a racist society was not thought possible by many white people, especially when acts of Parliament had ruled racial discrimination in employment, in housing and education illegal. However, the non-legality of racism did not prevent its occurrence. Education had a role both at school and in adult, further and higher education to assert the principles of social equality and social justice which hidden and institutionalised racism denied. Access courses from their very inception insisted that it was necessary to challenge and remove racism in education itself. Practices and procedures within education in general which discriminate against black people and their traditions, language and cultures were to be combatted and replaced. The black experience was not to be ignored or made invisible by educational providers and cooperative work between educators and black and ethnic communities was designed to recognise and then resist and remove racism from British social life and culture. All of this was to be reflected in the Access curriculum which was to articulate humanitarian concerns with social justice. In the process of developing courses and curricula to reflect and give expression to black people's experience and aspirations the Access movement came into being. This process was eclectic, locally focussed and even parochially driven (Ben Tovim 1981a; Clay 2020), however, it was to have national significance as the demand for educational opportunities spread and as black and ethnic groupings organised themselves to improve their educational prospects (John 2006).

# Race and education

'There are no guarantees against the growth of a popular racism, but there is always, in the factual everyday struggles of those who resist racism, the possibility of anti-racist politics and pedagogy' (Hall 1980: 69).

Educators committed to Access were faced with the realities of racism and of how race actually worked in British society. Race and the issues associated with it were the flash points for historical and continuing crises and conflicts in the last decades of the 20th century and educators could not ignore these. The lived realities which confronted the black population- their 'lived experience' of racism and their resistance to being treated as subordinate and inferior - were of the utmost importance to educators regardless of their own ethnic or racial identity.

Cultures of resistance took many different forms; some were forced to the margins such as Rastafarianism which challenged the role of the state and its institutions and culture. In some cases opposition was expressed through 'style' where dress codes and music sought to disrupt the dominant and commercially viable (profitable) cultures (Campbell 1980; Hebdige 1981).

Race and racism was a daunting challenge to education beyond school where attitudes in the wider society were shaped by the inadequacies of previous schooling and the damaging continuities of empire and British attitudes to foreign nations and peoples (McIlroy 1981; Tomlinson 2019). Access courses involving black people and ethnic minorities were part of a broad set of contemporary and controversial issues of the most potentially explosive kind.

## Contexts and origins of Access courses

It was possible in the late 1970s to discuss the idea of *Higher Education for All* (Roderick and Stephens 1979) and *Higher Education for Everyone* (Edwards 1984) and omit separate consideration of the concept of Access. Neither did race nor the likelihood of institutionalised racism feature in the dominant discourse. The government's Department of Education and Science had, however, in August 1978 invited seven local education authorities to establish pilot courses for entry into higher education and by the mid-1980s it would have been inconceivable to discuss the issue of increasing opportunities to enter higher education without tackling the significance of Access (CNAA 1984; Evans 1984; ILEA 1984). Clearly the wider context was one of expansion of the generic system of higher education and there was 'social demand for education from below' (Harrop 1984: 200). This was commensurate with what Richard Johnson (1988) described as a demand for 'really useful knowledge' which working people had wanted historically as a means of improving their prospects and though he was writing about the 18th and 19th centuries he drew relevant comparisons for us today in the 21st century.

By the 1980s wholesale economic and social change was underway as new economic conditions emerged to shatter the older industrial and commercial communities. Britain's adoption of neoliberal, marketised economics, led by the Thatcherite politicians in the Conservative Party was only one instance of a world-wide trend which re-shaped much of the global economy and disrupted both local and global life nearly everywhere. Technology and the shifting logics of capitalism were forcing a new phase of development on a world-wide basis.

The value of all things was increasingly to be found in the market-place and higher education itself was increasingly seen as part of the 'knowledge economy, subject to the laws and disciplines of the market just like any other commodity. The vocabulary of educational change and opportunity was nevertheless often positive and found a resonance amongst many of those who had been failed by the old system. This was the meaning of the opening-up and expansion of university education in the UK in the 1970s and 1980s and which had been signalled by the Robbins Report of 1963.

Visionaries at the time could see the world-wide expansion of 'lifelong learning' (Faure 1972; Freire 1972) which questioned many of the old distinctions between academic and vocational learning and skills and sought the abolition of old distinctions between elites who had access to learning and the masses who had been alienated from educational knowledge. Education and the possibilities of learning outside the conventional systems seemed to offer at the very least an encounter with the social order and its educational institutions. This was the real meaning of Access which attempted to re-draw the educational map on a very limited scale admittedly and to pose new questions for new audiences and learners. If we can accept that new forms of education can tell us a great deal about wider social developments, then Access opened up questions about what counts as knowledge and how it is articulated and experienced by people whose existence and culture were often seen as challenges to existing education. These challenges were of course rooted in the lived experience of discrimination and racism in employment, housing and education itself by members of the ethnic minority and black communities. Such experiences generated the will to resist and to find knowledge and learning that would equip a successful struggle for improved outcomes.

Access courses emerged at the end of the 1970s in response to the needs of minority ethnic and black communities which were not being met by the existing educational systems. A rather fragile and tentative alliance was established involving national and local government, higher and further education and Access courses themselves and their black communities. Although the first London course was established in 1975 (ILEA 1984: 6) it was not until 1978 that Access courses more generally received government approval and even then they were to receive no national funding and were to be dependent upon the political and financial support of local government.

# The need for Access

Access courses began in a period of disillusionment and conflict about education, especially in relation to black students and pupils. The reforms and innovations in education in the 1960s and 1970s had proved inadequate in meeting the needs and aspirations of the black populations of Britain. Serious levels of under-achievement were apparent in the schools and black pupils were making their way into the further education sector not as a second chance but rather as a first and only chance to acquire learning (Eggleston 1986).

The understanding and explanation of the reasons for the failure of the education service to deliver success for black people varied greatly depending on the stance of those making the judgement. Educational debate in the 1970s at national level frequently contained criticism of 'progressive' approaches to learning and teaching (Black Papers 1971; Flude and Parrott 1979) and multiculturalism in schools and the wider culture was widely disparaged by conservative opinion (Jeffcoate 1979). There was open polarisation of views on the education of minorities in a system that had been designed for white children (Tomlinson ibid: 108). Educational nationalism persisted with the myth that black and other minorities in Britain possessed full opportunities to assimilate and integrate into the British way of life and culture. If there were barriers, they had been created by the minorities themselves. The national government tended to view failure by black students in both schools and colleges as a function of people's cultural deficits especially in respect of language deficiencies (Edwards 1979; ILEA 1984: 17-18).The black communities on the other hand considered institutional racism to be the major problem to be tackled (Smith 1977; Runnymede Trust 1980; Sivanandan 1982).

# The invisible problem of the disadvantaged

Higher education institutions at this time did not feel compelled to re-assess the failures of previous reforms and innovations. The universities, polytechnics and colleges of higher education, with few exceptions, felt that their provision gave expression to the liberal progressive ethos in education and this was combined with a belief that their paramount duty was to preserve the high standards of quality associated with the British first degree. It is interesting to note that in 1984 the National Advisory Body (NAB) (for public sector higher education) issued a report of its Continuing Education Group with over forty detailed recommendations for broadening access for mature students, none of which mentioned the needs of minority ethnic groups and black communities. Only a handful of years earlier two influential publications on higher education *for all and everyone* failed entirely to mention race, ethnicity and racism as aspects of our society which impacted on education in any way at all (Roderick and Stephens 1979; Edwards 1984). At the time their very invisibility and assumed integration and assimilation was seen as an indicator of progressivism and liberalism by teachers and leaders in higher education. This was hardly surprising since the educational needs of a multi-racial society in schooling had been widely associated with a general category of 'disadvantaged'. All minority children, children of immigrants and those from racial minorities had been lumped together as part of the disadvantaged population. This was a euphemism for 'poor' argues Tomlinson (2019 ibid: 105) that endured for years. The government Department for Education at the time asserted that minority children shared with the indigenous children in urban areas 'the educational disadvantages associated with an impoverished environment' (DES 1974: 2). Members of black and minority communities were being exhorted to accept their poor housing and neglected urban environment and the failure of their children in schools because they shared these conditions with poor whites. The language of disadvantage and deprivation was used to disavow and deny the racial and ethnic issues which were there for all to see, if they had eyes to do so. For black people and many members of ethnic communities it was confirmation that both overt and covert forces were at work to exclude them from participation in education and the rewards available for those who could succeed.

The first Access courses emerged in the decade from 1975 to 1985 but the origins and causes of Access lie in the period of the post-war boom of the late 1950s and early 1960s. All the major political parties of the time were agreed that technological progress could be used to sustain affluence and deliver rising living standards. A widely if not universally shared consensus was reached on the desirability of a conflict-free mixed social market economy which could deliver full employment and a greater measure of shared national wealth. Education, it was thought, could simultaneously liberate individuals into an increasingly classless and affluent society and train the skilled workforce required for the generation of future national wealth. Expansion of the economy and the labour force, partly through immigration from the so-called new-Commonwealth countries including the Caribbean states, was the order of the day. Education policy focussed on expanding the quantity of education available whilst questions of content and of pedagogy (learning and teaching) and what was to count as valid knowledge remained exclusively the concerns of the teacher professional

(CCCS 1981: 163-164; Johnson 1981: 43). Barriers to access to educational opportunity became anathema to all shades of political and educational opinion and comprehensivisation of state schooling progressed. The Robbins Report of 1963 had pointed the way to the expansion of universities and there was a broad consensus that it was necessary to widen the basis of educational access. Just how far this expansion reached eventually and just how much the key issues of Access to HE had impacted on conventional universities some 50 years later is moot. In the case of the London School of Economics, which hosted a commemorative event and book on the Robbins Report (Barr 2014) and had employed not only Robbins himself but other LSE academics who worked on the Report, LSE was a university which had social justice in its DNA. Its academic engagement with progressive social policy, critique and debate was not in question. However, in common with the original Robbins Report the anniversary event managed to evade the key dimensions of inequality and injustice that revolved around race, ethnicity and identity, although David Watson in his contribution was aware of the specific issues concerning women and higher education (Watson 2014).

There was, however, no automatic connection between the expansion of HE provision and the reforms of state schooling and the dire need for social justice and equity for the disadvantaged ethnic groups and black communities. They were in policy terms still 'invisible' in this great shift of emphasis on the need for equality of opportunity. They themselves still had to speak fully for their interests but would do so with increasing authority and sometimes anger (John 2006 ibid). The principles of national policy were increasingly to view black people as bearers of educationally disadvantageous behaviour and as the inheritors of a deficient culture. There was no automatic connection linking expansion to equality and ethnic minorities benefitted less than their white counterparts from the growth in provision. Compensatory intervention programmes failed likewise to break the cycles of advantage and disadvantage conferred by the proxies for class and race such as 'father's occupation'. As early as 1964 J.W.B. Douglas had concluded that far from breaking the hold parental position had on school success, the selection and streaming functions of schooling actually reinforced the school's role in maintaining class inequalities rooted in the cumulative under-privileging of children in working class homes. Meritocratic ideology, however, was gaining ground and emerged triumphant at the expense of equality of educational opportunity. By the 1970s it was plain that the problems of education and equality needed to be posed in new terms (Halsey 1972: 7) It was also clear that by the 1970s race and ethnicity were intersecting with social class to make the connections between educational reform and social and community experience that much more problematical.

It is hardly surprising then that the demands for Access came from outside the conventional educational institutions and called for a radical approach to learning which could embrace community experience and learning which in turn needed to express the black and minority ethnic experience itself.

## Reshaping the curriculum from above or through resistance?

The reality of formal government policy and much of the educational establishment focussed on the so-called 'Great Debate' about the need to compel the teaching profession to address the vocational needs of industry and to curb the commitments to progressive ideologies, styles and fashions which were blamed for the alleged decline in standards in schools and elsewhere (Donald 1981; Green 1983). By the mid-1980s the national government had intervened massively to re-shape the curriculum in schools and colleges of further education. The emphasis was on job-preparedness and technical and vocational skills acquisition for young people whose employment prospects had in many places simply collapsed as British industry and productive capacity imploded under the Thatcherite neo-liberal economic programme. It was not the government's job, it was stated, to rescue unprofitable industries and concerns. The market had to be left to its own devices. Vast swathes of factories closed in this period and youth unemployment rose spectacularly- whilst among some inner-city black youth populations ethnic disadvantage reached majority proportions (Allen 1971).

The issues faced by indigenous black communities were compounded by the continuing force for social division and conflict engendered by immigration to Britain. The assumptions of acculturation and the supposed benign effects of the melting pot metaphor, which it was hoped by some would overcome the temporary disjuncture produced by the requirement for foreign labour, for example, were not borne out in reality. Immigration in the 1950s and 1960s did not lead to successful multicultural integration and a harmonious social settlement. The fact that cities such as Liverpool had experienced black settlement for generations with no significant eradication of racial prejudice or diminution of institutional racism was largely ignored (Henfry and Law 1981; Ben Tovim et al 1981a; MAPG 1986; Clay 2020). There was in effect little comprehension of the experience of post-war immigrant generations who were forced into low pay employment, sub-standard housing, insecure conditions of life and marginalisation in respect of cultural and social as well as economic life in this period. Once the relative permanence of their stay in Britain was confirmed by the apparent lack of alternatives and lack of job opportunities in their countries of origin, many black immigrants projected their hopes and aspirations on to their children. The children born to black immigrants in the 1950s and 1960s were the first generation of British-born black people to be present both in terms of substantial numbers and widespread geographical location. This fact should not lead us to underestimate the historical significance of the black presence in British history and society (Fryer 1985; Olusoga 2016). Neither should we overlook the fact that many immigrants with professional and academic qualifications were excluded from 'professional' jobs when their qualifications and experience were deemed to be less than equivalent to the British standard. Unemployment and under-employment had even in the good times been far worse for black people than for comparable white groups (Allen 1971 ibid; MAPG 1986).

The need for Access courses was not recognised in the 1950s and 1960s and it would take another two generations for the absences from British public life of black people and ethnic minority members to be recognised and addressed. Even in the third decade of the 21st century there are major areas of our social and economic life where the black British presence is missing. Migration did not cease to be highly contentious in the new century and questions of white and black identities along with the ideologies of populism and nationalism challenged democracy and democratic engagement with the globalising world (Eatwell and Goodwin 2018; Garton Ash 2018).

Although the education system tended to ignore the needs and potential of many of its black students in the 1960s, there was innovation and critique throughout the period (Allen 1971; Rex 1973; Dhondy 1974; Moore 1975). Black parents began to be organised so as to voice the needs of their own children which were not being met by schools (Coard 1971; Humphrey and John 1971). Criticism of education policy began to strike resounding notes throughout the 1970s. In the wider society, relations between the police and black people and ethnic groups were disintegrating; there were disturbances in Southall in 1979, where 342 people were arrested after a whole day of fierce fighting with police (Kettle and Hodges 1982: 20-21). Social conflict around race issues became more marked and race riots took place in Brixton, Liverpool and other cities in 1981 and in Toxteth and Handsworth in 1985. Oliver Letwin a minister in Margaret Thatcher's government advised her that race riots were caused by individual bad character and attitudes. The reality was of course entirely different.

When the first significant government support for Access arrived in 1978 it was arguably as a palliative and form of crisis management rather than a result of rational policy development within a coherent analysis and plan of action.

Significantly the first proposals were in relation to the need for ethnic group members to be involved in initial teacher training. By the mid-1970s the revolt of black youngsters in state schools was becoming alarming…'Genuine cultural integration… foundered against the fact of massive under-achievement of black children in British schools' (Raynor and Harris 1977: 187). Increasingly in the 1970s black pupils resisted and rejected white schools. Many black students became 'unschoolable' making the institutions themselves, and the teaching strategies and styles that even the reformists had introduced, redundant and ineffective (Dhondy 1974, 1979; Little 1978).This experience was to have a significant impact on what was to be considered the appropriate pedagogies and content of the Access courses that subsequently emerged. Conventional cultural practices and forms of knowledge which had served to discredit black people's experience in the past and had, in their view, legitimated their failure were not likely to generate support from black communities wanting Access courses.

Although teacher training was the initial focus of government interest in Access in 1978, it was soon apparent that Access was required for black students to higher education more generally. Access to social work, nursing and youth and community work were specifically mentioned at this time by the Department of Education and Science (DES) showing their concern with vocational and community-based training rather than with raising the standards of deprived or marginalised groups or addressing social injustice in general. Millins (1984), an early supporter of Access, noted that the level of DES support at that time did not include an offer of help to the seven Local Education Authorities involved in Access development. (Avon, Birmingham, Bradford, Haringey, Inner London, Leicestershire and Manchester). Student grants were to be discretionary and LEAs were exhorted to give priority to such awards but no actual funds were forthcoming (Tsow 1983: 4).

The lack of public finance for Access contrasted with the contemporary expansion of government backed schemes in further and vocational education and training. The government of the time was hugely invested in education and training but arguably on the basis of compensatory interventions to mitigate the effects of historically high youth unemployment. It was widely thought at the time, though without direct evidence to support it, that much of the country's North Sea oil tax revenues went into efforts to keep masses of unemployed and disaffected young people off the streets. In the further education colleges and in community-based organisations, YTS- youth training schemes- soaked up the excess youth labour market. However, these schemes did not provide 'real' jobs and proper apprenticeships over a long term period for the unemployed young people. They did keep them off the streets and allowed the unemployment statistics to be manipulated so as to appear less of a problem than it really was. It was notable that unemployment among black youth in the inner cities was often spectacularly high and these mainly vocational initiatives failed to grapple with the issue of race and racism in employment and across the wider British culture and society (Brown 1984; Gleeson 1985; Dale 1985). Most Access courses at this time were focussed on mature people rather than on the younger adolescent cohorts, many of whom were leaving school to face a future without prospects for well- paid work or training for a career.

The funding that was made available for Access was earmarked for monitoring and evaluation rather than for establishing and maintaining provision. Local Education Authorities did, however, continue to support and establish Access. ILEA and Manchester, for example, established full-time grant-aided courses. By 1983 some 1,800 students were involved on Access courses in sixteen LEAs and involving some fifty institutions. Women outnumbered men by three to one with approximately 60 per cent of students coming from ethnic minorities, the great majority being of Caribbean origin (Millins 1984). Access as an alternative form of learning for mature students had found a significant resonance across a range of institutions of further and higher education. It was a period in which non-traditional students of all kinds were apparently highly valued (NAB 1984; JMB 1986) in higher education, but for ethnic minorities and black communities in particular Access signalled the possibility of an improved social result which could give recognition to their learning needs within their own cultural and community settings (Millins ibid; FEU 1986).The main emphasis was on community-based and relevant provision negotiated with local HE institutions. The 'commanding heights' of the elite universities were not involved in a systematic way in these Access developments and the ultra-selective and often arcane and secretive selection methods used by elite universities would remain unchallenged by the established education authorities for some considerable time. Meanwhile the growth of mass attendance in higher education proceeded along with new forms of hierarchy and differentiation. The status distinctions of higher education continued to act as the most difficult barrier to cross for non-traditional students and especially for those on the Access route.

## Race and education 1997 - 2022: a divided society

The election of the New Labour government in 1997 should have marked a decisive point of upswing for egalitarian policies benefitting the deprived and disadvantaged, and for addressing the historic inequalities experienced by black and minority ethnic communities in Britain. Despite the new government's commitment to a socially and racially just society, the realities of the 1980s and 1990s turned out somewhat differently. Anti-immigrant sentiment grew in Britain in this period and wars in Afghanistan and Iraq heralded a perceived and increased threat from some young and alienated, radicalised Muslims who were susceptible to ultra-conservative and fundamentalist views on Islamic culture and the supposed islamophobia of some western societies. The neoliberal economic policies of New Labour contributed perhaps paradoxically to growing inequality and poverty, in spite of the brave attempts to redistribute rising tax receipts from the burgeoning financial sectors of the economy to the poorer people and the introduction of Sure Start children's centres across the nation. In these years the rich got richer and the poor got poorer (Dorling 2017).

From the early 2000s there was an historically unprecedented flow of immigrants into Britain and claims were made that the immigrants were taking jobs away from British workers because they were willing to work for lower pay (Murray 2017: 38). Many people believed that immigration had been bad for the economy and had undermined British culture as well as viewing it as a burden on welfare (Eatwell and Goodwin 2018: 34). It was suggested by some right-wing political interests that low paid workers felt threatened by economic migrants and refugees from Europe and this added to the tensions and hostility towards former colonial British citizens who had migrated to Britain. Mass migration from within the borders of the European Union and from former colonies were different phenomena but collectively resulted in strong concerns being expressed as to how immigration was changing the nation. Britain was becoming ever more diverse but in some respects ever more disunited as many people were concerned about perceived threats to their identity and social group. Education could not absent itself from the potent cocktail of race, ethnicity and immigration and the ethnic transformation of the West. Radical lifestyle changes in 'modernity' were underway in developed and developing economies and societies and education once again was an existential issue which cut through (intersected) and across the lines of class, race , ethnicity and faith and whose outcomes were uncertain.

Schooling became the focus of contradictory policies. Comprehensivisation was the formal policy adopted by New Labour but individual competitiveness was encouraged by pupil testing and targeting. The neoliberal viewpoint on the inevitability of globalisation and market competitiveness in which Britain seemed destined to be a player confirmed the direction of travel for education. Competition would ensure that standards were maintained and the outcomes could be claimed as right and proper since meritocratic principles had been applied. None of this shifted the dial on the under-achievements of some black and ethnic group pupils and the questions of what is actually taught in schools and universities (the curriculum) could be ignored in so far as they might contribute to our understanding of how race and the racialisation of our culture and society had actually occurred and still impacted on our lives (Hall 2017; Elias 2020).

By the early 2000s poverty and inequality had reached levels not known since the 1930s. British society was plagued by division and dissent, including the decision to go to war in Iraq and the ever present issues of mass migration, including that from the enlarged European Union. Education was fragmented and the market competition between schools and the support from government for 'diversity' of schools, including support for 'faith schools', increased the segregation of the school population. By 2005 the Labour Government was promising a commitment to a place in school, college or training for every 16-19 year old and in 2008 all young people up to the age of 18 had to remain in education or training. The youth labour market had effectively been abolished and 'nationalized' (Dale 1985 ibid).

Community cohesion was supposed to be possible within an ethnically diverse British society but the realities were far from the ideal. Trevor Phillips, chair of the Commission for Racial Equality, claimed in 2005 that multiculturalism suggested separateness and that the country was sleepwalking into segregation (Tomlinson 2019: 164). The year 2005 also saw two major terrorist bombings in London by young Muslim men educated in English schools. What it meant to be British was increasingly questioned by minorities and by many in the traditional majority white populations who had not come to terms with the changed demographics of a multi-racial and multi-ethnic society that was modern Britain. The politics of immigration and Islam were often poisonous and frequently associated with racism in the minds and experiences of some of the black and minority ethnic communities.

The second decade of the century saw concurrently the outworkings of the international finance/banking crisis which in the UK consolidated the power of finance capital and the onset of a decade of austerity. This impacted most severely on the poor and led to the reduction of budgets for public education. After being rescued by the central national banks including the Bank of England, the financial markets went on to demonstrate their 'meritocratic' rights to award themselves huge bonuses and payments. The Labour Party went ahead with its 'academy' programme which was a means of creating 'independent state schools' free from local authority and democratic control. The divesting of ownership and control of schools from the elected local councils- an effective privatisation at one level to 'trusts' and organisations of many different types-meant the breaking up of labourist power and influence in many towns, cities and local communities and was a deeply political act. The Conservatives were to complete this project in the second decade of the century. The funding for most of the schools and colleges remained in the hands of the central government who also retained considerable power to shape curriculum content.

The period from 2010 to 2020 was one in which free markets and shrinking state institutions increased the gap between rich and poor. Education and the racial divisions were key features of this divided nation where many members of the governing elites had been educated at private schools and gone on to Oxford and Cambridge. Privatisation continued in both school and university sectors and university fees rose to unprecedented levels. A rhetoric was used to suggest that 'excellence' for all children was available and that this was a form of social mobility accessible for all, but the realities were quite different. The entire board of the Social Mobility Commission set up in 2011, resigned in 2017 because the nation had become more divided by income, geography and generation (Tomlinson ibid:176). The language of 'diversity' used by politicians masked the realities of an unequal and divided multi-ethnic and multicultural society. Moreover it was a society which had not come to terms with its imperialist past and was intensely divided over its place in modern Europe. No formal and significant reckoning was made with the structures of white supremacy, the history of colonial violence and the diasporas and migrations that have shaped modern Britain (Elias 2020). The traditional subject-centred curriculum remained entrenched in schools and universities with minimal progress towards a universal literacy which might have enabled learners to better understand the role of the British Empire and what replaced it including the true significance of the European Union.

The formal approach to the kind of society Britain was in the first two decades of the 21st century, and emphasised in the guidance given to schools, focussed on the values of democracy, the rule of law, individual liberty and mutual tolerance and respect for different faiths and beliefs systems. Few right thinking people would disagree with this list, but on the other hand these values are not limited to any single nation or country. Neither did their existence in British society ensure that education would be the fulcrum through which such values were experienced. To the contrary, schools in England were in the frontline of religious and political/ideological dispute and division in this period. Democratic beliefs in racial justice were often called into question (Hirsch 2018; Tomlinson 2018). The privileging of the offspring of the wealthy continued and the elite universities consistently recruited fewer black and minority students than could be justified on the grounds of equity and fairness. Division and inequality on the bases of race and class and area of domicile continued to characterise both the wider society and the educational institutions within it. Selective education and social mobility for a few working class and black/ethnic minority students continued to be the basis for official policy and educational institutions came into line with this.

The first two decades of the 21$^{st}$ century produced much heated debate if not light on the themes of assimilation, integration and living in a multicultural society (John 2006; Murray ibid: ch 6). The language and rhetoric of integration was used to berate those who were seen as refusing to integrate into a supposedly homogenous majority British society and culture. It was never of course homogenous and it was never truly socially integrated. At times race and immigration became toxic within the social and political discourses of British life. The history of Britain is about the many different social groups and their co-existence over many generations; it is about how the diversity of history sometimes achieved social consensus and how the apparent homogeneity of British culture in fact masked the differences (Malik 2023). Education might have been the means by which a genuinely pluralistic and multiracial and multicultural society was made and it is hard to speculate how this might be done *without* education. Nevertheless, a tolerant democracy which recognises diversity and ensures a fair degree of access to life's chances and opportunities for all is a key value for educators. It infused the work of the early Access movement and gave a voice to racial and ethnic minorities who were seeking better educational lives and outcomes.

Access emerged at a time when public authorities could begin to see the advantage of incorporating articulate and often angry community leaders into the system. The riots of the early 1980s and Access courses emerged practically in tandem when the hopes and aspirations for equal opportunities for *all* had seemingly been jettisoned by both political and educational leaders. Self-improvement and economic advancement was on offer for some of the articulate members of oppressed groups and a proportion of black and ethnic groups could be sponsored into a more middle class environment whose function was to ameliorate racial tensions and conflicts. The rewards for participation would be personal success and some upward social and economic mobility for members of a meritocratic and industrious elite. The tension between the benefits on offer for individuals who could get ahead and the need for the transformation of a whole social and ethnic group were clearly evident to communities themselves at the time (Hall 1983; MAPG 1986). It was not a tension that could be resolved by the Access movement alone which bought in to the meritocratic ideal by sponsoring individual achievements whilst simultaneously acknowledging collective and community aspirations. There remains also the question of what it was that black Access students were getting access to? The wider society with its cultural discriminations, its sense of embedded racism in parts of its institutional life, in employment, in policing, in aspects of sporting life and still in wide swathes of education had not removed the stains of supremacist associations. The educational rights of all people were still to be fairly and equitably shared but Access had opened up possibilities and points of departure for black and minority groups in British society which could not be denied.

# References

Allen, S. (1971) *New Minorities, Old Conflicts: Asian and West Indian Migrants in Britain*, New York: Random House.

Allen, S. (1982) *Ethnic Disadvantage in Britain,* Unit 4 of Open University course E354, *Ethnic Minorities and Community Relations*, Milton-Keynes: the Open University Press.

Barr, N. (ed) (2014) *Shaping higher education: 50 years after Robbins*, London: LSE- London School of Economics and Political Science.

Ben Tovim, G. et al (1981a) 'The Equal Opportunity Campaign in Liverpool' ch 6.4 in Cheetham, J. et al ( 1981) *Social and Community Work in a Multi-racial Society,* London: Harper and Row and the Open University.

Ben Tovim, G. (1981b) 'A political analysis of race in the 1980s' in Husband, C. (ed) (1981) *Race in Britain*, London: Hutchinson.

*Black Papers on Education* (1971) – Cox, C. and Dyson, A.E. (eds) London: Davis Paynter Ltd.

Brown, C. (1984) *Black and White Britain*, PSI. (see Gleeson 1985:70).

Campbell, H. (1980) 'Rastafari: Culture of Resistance', *Race & Class* Vol XXII No 1 Summer 1980.

CCCS- Centre for Contemporary Cultural Studies-(1981) *Unpopular Education: Schooling and Social Democracy in England since 1944*, University of Birmingham and London: Hutchinson.

Clay, D. (2020) *1919-2019 A Liverpool Black History 100 Years: A Liverpool Black Perspective,* Liverpool: Beatentrackpublishing ISBN: 978 1 78645 469 0.

CNAA- Council for National Academic Awards-(1984- August) *Access to Higher Education: non-standard entry to CNAA first degree and Dip HE courses,* London: CNAA Development Services 6.

Coard, B. (1971) *How the West Indian Child is Made Educationally Sub-normal,* UK: New Beacon Books.

Cross, C. (1978) *Ethnic Minorities in the Inner City,* London: Commission for Racial Equality.

Dale, R. (ed) (1985) *Education, Training & Employment: Towards a New Vocationalism?* Open University/Oxford: Pergamon Press.

Davies, D. (1981) *Popular Culture, Class and Schooling,* Unit 9 Open University Course E353 *Society, Education and the State,* Milton-Keynes: Open University Press.

DES (1974) government Department of Education, *Educational disadvantage and the needs of immigrants,* London: HMSO.

Dhondy, F. (1974) 'The Black Explosion in Schools', *Race Today*, February 1974.

Dhondy, F. (1979) 'Pupil Power', *Teacher's Action*, 13 November 1979, London: Teachers Action Collective.

Donald, J. (1981) 'Green paper: noise of crisis' in Dale, R. et al (eds) (1981) *Schooling and the National Interest*, Milton Keynes: Open University Press and the Falmer Press.

Dorling, D. (2017) *The equality effect: Improving life for everyone,* Oxford: New International Publications.

Douglas, J.W.B. (1964) *The Home and the School: A Study of Ability and Attainment in the Primary School*, London: McGibbon & Kee.

Eatwell, R. and Goodwin, M. (2018*) National Populism: The Revolt Against Liberal Democracy,* UK: Pelican Books.

Edwards, E.G. (1984) *Higher Education for Everyone,* Nottingham: Spokesman.

Edwards, V.K. (1979) *The West Indian Language Issue in British Schools: Challenges and Responses,* London: Routledge and Keegan Paul.

Eggleston, J. (1986) Education for Some: The Educational and Vocational Experiences of 15-18 Year Old Members of Minority Ethnic Groups- A Report, UK: DES.

Elias, H. (2020) 'Time and race in history education', *Renewal: a journal for social democracy,* 28.4 UK: Renewal/Lawrence & Wishart.

Evans, N. (1984) *Access to Higher Education: non-standard entry to CNAA first degree and Dip HE courses,* London: CNAA Development Services publication 6.

Faure, E. (1972) *Learning to Be,* London: UNESCO/Harrap.

FEU (1986) Access to Further and Higher Education, draft paper to the Board of Management 9 October 1986.

Flude, R. and Parrott, A. (1979) *Education and the Challenge of Change: a recurrent education strategy for Britain,* Milton-Keynes, England: Open University Press.

Foot, P. (1969) *Immigration and race in British politics*, Harmondsworth: Penguin.

Freire, P. (1972) *Pedagogy of the Oppressed*, London: Sheed and Ward Ltd.

Fryer, P. (1985) (2nd impression) *Staying Power: The history of Black people in Britain*, London: Pluto Press.

Garton Ash, T. (2018) 'A humiliating deal risks descent into Weimar Britain', *The Guardian (Journal)* 27 July 2018.

Gleeson, D. (1985) Privatization of Industry and the Nationalization of Youth, ch 4 in Dale, R. (ed) (1985) *Education, Training & Employment,* Open University/ Oxford: Pergamon Press.

Green, A. (1983) 'Education and training: under new masters' in Wolpe, AM. and Donald, J. (eds) (1983) *Is there anyone here from education?,* London: Pluto Press.

Hall, S. (1978) 'Racism and Reaction' see John, G. (2006), 'Antiracist Education: A movement for change in education and schooling, Manchester 1985', ch 1.7 in *Taking a Stand: Gus John Speaks on education, race, social action & civil unrest 1980-2005* (p.100), Manchester: Gus John Partnership.

Hall, S. et al (1978) *Policing the Crisis; Mugging, the state and law and order,* London: Macmillan.

Hall, S. (1980) 'Teaching Race' in James, A. and Jeffcoate, R. (eds) (1981) *The School in the Multicultural Society,* London: Harper and Row/the Open University Press.

Hall, S. (1983) 'Education in Crisis', ch 1 in Wolpe, AM. and Donald, J.(eds) (1983) *Is there anyone here from education?* London: Pluto Press.

Hall, S. (2017) *The Fateful Triangle: Race, Ethnicity, Nation,* Cambridge, Mass/ London, England: Harvard University Press.

Halsey, A.H. (1972) *Educational priority,* London: HMSO.

Harrop, S. (1984) 'Adult Education and Literacy: The importance of post-school education for literacy levels in the eighteenth and nineteenth centuries', *History of Education* 1984 Vol 13 No 3: 191-205.

Hebdige, D. (1981) *Subculture as Style*, London: Methuen.

Henfry, J. and Law, I. (1981) *A History of Race and Racism in Liverpool; 1660-1950,* Merseyside Community Relations Council.

Hiro, D. (1973) *Black British, White British*, New York/London: Monthly Review Press.

Hirsch, A. (2018) *Brit(ish): On race, identity and belonging*, London: Jonathan Cape.

Humphrey, D. and John, G. (1971) *Because They're Black*, London: Penguin.

ILEA- Inner London Education Authority- (1984- September) *Access to Higher Education: Report of a Review of Access Courses at the Authority's Maintained Colleges of Further and Higher Education,* London: County Hall.

Jeffcoate, R. (1979) *Positive Image: Towards a multicultural curriculum*, London: Harper & Row.

John, G. (1981) 'Black Youth as an Ideology' ch 4.7 in Cheetham, J. et al (eds) (1981) *Social and Community Work in a Multi-Racial Society*, London: Harper and Row/ the Open University Press.

John, G. (1993) Say NO to "Ethnic Minority", *Access News* No 16, June 1993, ACES, University of North London.

John, G. (2006) *Taking a Stand: Gus John Speaks on education, race, social action and civil unrest 1980-2005*, Manchester: Gus John Partnership.

Johnson, R. (1981) *Education and Popular Politics*, Unit 1 Open University Course E353 *Society, Education and the State*, Milton Keynes: Open University Press.

Johnson, R. (1988) 'Really useful knowledge 1790-1850: memories for education in the 1980s' in Lovett, T. (ed) (1988) *Radical Approaches to Adult Education,* UK: Routledge.

JMB- Joint Matriculation Board-(1986) *The Progress of Mature Students*, report, Manchester: JMB.

Kettle, M. and Hodges, L. (1982) U*prising: The police, the people and the riots in Britain's cities,* London: Pan Books.

Lawrence, E. (1981) 'White Sociology Black Struggle', *Multi-Racial Education* Vol 9 No 3.

Little, A. (1978) Educational policies for multi-racial areas, inaugural lecture, Goldsmiths College, London University.

McIlroy, J. (1981) 'Race Relations and the Traditions of Adult Education', *Studies in Adult Education* Vol 13 No 2 October 1981 pp. 87-97.

Malik, K. (2023) *Not So Black and White: A History of Race from White Supremacy to Identity Politics*, UK: Hursta & Co Pub Ltd.

MAPG- Merseyside Area profile Group- (1986) *Racial Discrimination and Disadvantage in Employment in Liverpool,* February1986.

Millins, P.K.C. (1984) *Access Studies to Higher Education, September 1979-December 1983: A Report*, London: Roehampton Institute, Centre for Access Studies to Higher Education.

Moore, R. (1975) *Racism and Black Resistance in Britain*, London: Pluto Press.

Murray, D. (2017) *The Strange Death of Europe: Immigration, Identity, Islam,* London: Bloomsbbury.

NAB- National Advisory Body (1984) Report of the Continuing Education Group.

Olusoga, D. (2016) *Black and British: A Forgotten History*, London: Macmillan.

Raynor, J. and Harris, E. (eds) (1977) *Schooling in the City*, Milton-Keynes: Ward Lock Educational/The Open University Press.

Rex, J. (1973) *Race, colonialism and the city*, London: Routledge & Keegan Paul.

Rex, J. and Tomlinson, S. (1979) *Colonial Immigrants in a British City: A Class Analysis,* UK: Routledge and Keegan Paul.

Robbins Report (1963) *Report of the Committee on Higher Education*, Cmnd 2154, London: HMSO.

Roderick and Stephens (1979) *Higher Education for All*, Sussex: Falmer Press.

Runnymede Trust (1980) *Britain's Black Population,* London: Heinemann Educational Books.

Scanlan, P.X. (2020) *Slave Empire: How Slavery Built Modern Britain*, London: Robinson.

Sivanandan, A. (1982) 'From Resistance to Rebellion: Asian and Afro-Caribbean Struggles in Britain' in Sivanandan, A. (1982) *A Different Hunger: Writings on Black Resistance,* London: Pluto Press.

Smith, D.J. (1977) *Racial Disadvantage in Britain*, Harmondsworth: Penguin.

Taylor, P. (1993) Ethnic Group Data for University Entry: findings of a Report for the CVCP, *Access News* No 16, 1993, University of North London.

Tomlinson, S. (2018) 'Enoch Powell, empires, immigrants and education', *Race Ethnicity and Education*, 21 1: 1-14.

Tomlinson, S. (2019) *Education and Race: From Empire to Brexit*, Bristol: Policy Press.

Tsow, Ming. (1983) *Access to Higher education: Forum*, London: Millins/ Roehampton Institute of Higher Education.

Walvin, J. (1973) *Black and White: The Negro and English Society 1555-1945*, London: Allen Lane the Penguin Press.

Watson, D. (2014) 'What happened later? The British road to mass higher education,' ch 3 in Barr, N. (ed) (2014) *Shaping higher education: 50 years after Robbins,* London: LSE.

Wolpe, AnnMarie. and Donald, J. (eds) (1983) *Is there anyone here from education?*, London: Pluto Press.

# SCHOOLKIDS FACE JOBS DISASTER

## Jobs gloom 'is recipe for race alienation'

NEARLY 200,000 schoolchildren will step straight from the classroom into a crisis this summer.

They are the ones who won't get a job, the Manpower Services Commission said yesterday.

The Government com-

BY ROGER TODD, Home

## Better on the dole than back in the classroom

## Ministers back £168M plan to beat youth unemployment

# School leavers send jobless figures soaring

Birmingham Post Business Editor

Jobless school leavers have sent West Midland unemployment figures rocketing to record heights this month. And there are fears that the position will be even worse in August.

### New jobs hope for school leavers

About 170 youngsters in the Midlands have been found temporary jobs through the Government's Work Experience Programme, which was launched last month.

## Dangerous rise in coloured jobless

# Jobless total hits 1,613,956: union leaders protest

## £1½m scheme to help young jobl

# Young jobless hit by dole

# Challenge over delays jobless by TUC

## Work experience makes sense

# Left defeated

## 1977 – 'the worst year of all'

### DEMAND FOR COMPLETE CHANGE

The crisis of social and economic life impacted unequally and unjustly on young people.

# Chapter 6

# Open Colleges for an Open Society

The growth of the Access movement took place co-incidentally with the emergence of what were known as 'Open Colleges'. These colleges were in fact collaborations between education providers who were interested in discovering and using new forms of open learning so that more people could be brought into mainly adult learning. New organisations were needed that could operate outside the conventions of formal state schooling and the divisions between vocational training and academic scholarship which bedevilled British society and hindered equal opportunities through learning. The open college idea also found a ready response among providers of basic skills education who were in the business of addressing the large numbers of illiterate and innumerate people in the United Kingdom and who had been failed by their school experience. Many Access courses would not have been organisationally possible without the parallel development of open colleges.

Demand for continuing education was growing throughout the 1970s and 1980s as mature adults looked for opportunities to retrain or to enter academic and professional life. Public sector higher education had in particular identified adult non-traditional students as a worthy enterprise (NAB 1984), yet the new growth point was different. Its objective was that of designing courses specifically for adults who had little experience of study and who lacked confidence but who had hopes of succeeding in new ways. Ethnic and black communities, women in particular whose employment prospects had been limited by social expectations and patriarchal attitudes, those who had been made redundant by the closure of old industries and technological change and millions of people whose literacy and numeracy skills were under-developed, all constituted the new learners. Open colleges were for all those schemes which provided an alternative form of preparation for future learning (Lucas and Ward 1985) and they ranged from courses which were subject- specific and taught in only one college to the multi-institutional arrangements such as the Open Colleges of Manchester and Merseyside, and the Open Colleges of the North- West and South London which each recruited at least 2,000 students annually in the early 1980s. A Manpower Services Commission (MSC) report (1985) noted that nearly 50 per cent of Access schemes had been initiated between 1982 and 1985 and that the success of Access was not in doubt. These initiatives which were to be so significant in opening up study and work opportunities for access students were intrinsic to the open college movement. They gave expression to the important principle that an inclusive system should be capable of recognising all learner achievement.

What was remarkable, however, was not the emergence of another non-standard type of entry to higher education, equivalent to A Levels- important though this was. More important was the recognition that Access could not, nor should not, be limited to one level of provision but ought to encompass the whole range of adult educational provision- from basic education up to university entrance. Credits awarded at the different levels could be accumulated to ensure progression for an individual right through to university entrance. It was envisaged that a complete range of courses at all levels could be incorporated in Access education, if they were part of an open college. Credits for learning achievements in an open college could be accumulated and awarded without reference to a particular target or qualification, giving the learner in theory a huge amount of flexibility over what was learned and when. So it was that credits became part of the educational landscape in the UK and drew on the experience of the American credit-based degree system which involved universities and community colleges and on that of the Open University (OU). The credibility of the credits relied on the support of the HE institutions supporting the open college(s) and threw great weight for Access courses in particular on the quality of the courses rather than focussing on the assessment of learner's achievement. The relationship between the specific Access course and the receiving HE institutions became paramount for this level of provision with the higher education partners in the driving seat in defining and 'validating' the standards and quality of the courses.

The argument for such new open college institutions, networks and federations was as follows: traditional forms of schooling, further education and higher education were continuing to fail the majority of the population who were excluded from the benefits of further learning and the opportunities in life and work which resulted from education. A new system, capable of recognising and validating different forms of experience and of meeting new and emerging learning needs was required. A far wider definition of learning was needed which could reach out to the broad masses who continued to be excluded from opportunities and life chances through education. A massively more flexible and adaptable system was required to help transform the learning prospects of the dispossessed and socially excluded. People at all stages and ages in their lives would have to be able to accumulate credits, not just for courses taken at different times and in different places and in different subjects, but also for life and work experience of a wide variety of types for which paper qualifications did not yet exist. It was widely conceded amongst Access teachers that these issues could only be tackled through open education which would redefine the notion of widening participation as an option for the majority. 'Open College' would potentially do for the sub-degree student- the ordinary person in the street and in the community and in the workplace- what the Open University had tried to do for undergraduate education – make available and possible for ALL to achieve a better life through education.

## The learning society and the need for change

There was evidence in the mid-1970s that mature students were attracted by schemes of independent studies (Percy and Ramsden 1980) and that they appeared more likely to have clear ideas about issues and themes around which their studies could be organised. As adults they wanted to study freely and draw on other disciplines which were not available in conventional study. The work of Alan Tough (1979) in America had established that 'learning projects' were common amongst the ordinary adult population and that people were learning all the time- they just did it in ways not recognised by professional educators. In addition to formal education providers a vast range of unofficial educational opportunities were being created by voluntary organisations, private and commercial organisations, community support and development organisations, adult education centres, trades unions, local and regional authorities and employers' organisations providing training as well as providers of systematic adult learning. One research study calculated that over 20 per cent of the adult population of the North-West of England in 1979-1980 was participating in post-school education. It concluded that '… we are, in fact, a learning society… learning adults are the norm, although they may not know, or wish to acknowledge, that they are involved in education' (Percy 1988: 111).

The first such open college, that of the Open College federation of the North West, based on Lancaster University and Nelson and Colne College, was a scheme for the development of courses which could serve as alternative qualifications to A Levels, success at which would make possible entry to institutions of higher education. It began in 1975 on the initiative of the Nelson and Colne Principal David Moore and Charles Carter, Vice Chancellor of Lancaster University. At a later stage other LEA colleges throughout Lancashire and the Lancashire Polytechnic became actively involved. There were open colleges and open college networks (OCNs) and federations set up in Manchester, in South Yorkshire and in London and eventually across the whole country including Wales, Scotland and Northern Ireland. The various schemes quickly outgrew the earlier idea for a replacement of the A level entry for university matriculation, though this was always a key objective for the Access courses themselves. There was simultaneously a community of interests which wanted to develop learning opportunities and recognition which a credit framework could help satisfy. There was also a wider set of interests which favoured the development of a broader and critical curriculum- what Stuart Hall (1983) called a 'universal literacy'. This involved the idea of an open curriculum which in the minds of its supporters could help bring about change and awareness and a new kind of learning and education. When they looked around at the issues confronting the changing world this transformational learning was direly needed.

## Open College as an encounter with the educational order

Open colleges came about as part of a movement in the 1980s which wanted to address the changing educational needs of a society undergoing a fundamental transformation. Traditional industries and their communities and associated labour markets and employment opportunities were disappearing. Once prosperous industrial towns and many coastal communities were becoming 'hollowed out' as economic investment dried up and young people began to look elsewhere for a viable future in a post-industrial world. Educationalists developed a wide range of imaginative responses and continuing education for all was seen by many as part of the solution. Economic and social change was influenced by the application of new technologies, the changing age structure of the population, the erosion of the traditional manufacturing base and the stabilisation of the then current high levels of unemployment and its attendant social evils. Uncertainty and precarity became endemic especially for poorer and vulnerable people. Education was viewed as a potential solution and means for bringing about social and cultural change. For those who had for whatever reason been excluded from learning opportunities in the past, continuing education through a more open system offered some hope for a better future (ACACE 1982a: 7-8; Percy 1983).

The world of full employment and adequately funded leisure time, if it had ever existed as a basis for participation in post-school learning, was no longer capable of meeting the needs of a society faced with mass youth unemployment, sustained adult unemployment and the collapse of traditional industrial employment and skills amongst a large proportion of the working class. How could education help solve such issues when half the population of Great Britain had had no post-school education at all and only 20 per cent of the population had participated in spite of the lip service paid to its value? (ACACE 1982b: 107). The fact was successive British governments had only ever given adult and continuing education a low priority (Russell 1983, para.80). And yet the 1980s were not the 1930s or even the 1950s. Social attitudes and perceptions had decisively shifted and aspirations were in play that would not accept a bleak and hopeless future for the broad masses! If education were to be part of the solution it had to be of high quality, it had to be more comprehensive and inclusive than in the past and it had to be accessible and relevant to the lives of learners. Only then could it engage successfully with the evolving self-perceptions and attitudes of learners and only then could it address the problems of social order and fragmenting communities. As the barriers to education became better known, the need to remove them became more imperative. The practices and procedures of the universities and higher education institutions themselves became the object of scrutiny and it was becoming clear that they were in the business of sorting out applicants and were not simply 'gate keeping' but 'gate closing' institutions (McPherson 1972; Davies and Davies 2021: 8).

Open colleges emerged at a time of significant social change and disruption, including within and across the educational landscape. They were locally based and organically linked to their hinterlands. They were voluntary and autonomous and democratically accountable to their local owners who were mostly accountable themselves to elected local authorities. Because of this an organic process of development could develop between the stakeholders in which differences of opinion could be resolved. There was no imposed or centralised single perspective on how a curriculum should develop or on the correct method of validating a course of study. A relative equality of participation by partners was the order of the day. These things emerged in dialogue and discourse and within a shared vision of what an open college might achieve (Black 1982; Wilson 2010: 21). Across the country the new needs of the labour market were responding to the changing patterns of industrial investment and the historic centres of manufacturing in the heartlands of the Midlands, Lancashire, Yorkshire and the North East were in transition to a bleaker immediate future for the unskilled and semi-skilled workers and their families. Education itself was under considerable pressure to adapt with further education no longer able to rely on a steady stream of craft and engineering apprentices as it had in the boom years of the 1950s and 1960s. At the same time Access courses were being established throughout England and the other home nations, although in an uncoordinated way, and adult education initiatives for second chance education and community development threw up creative attempts to bring learning to bear on social issues and challenges (Lovett 1975 and Lovett et al 1983).

## Open colleges as an alternative

In the 1970s and early 1980s Access courses played an integral part in the development of alternatives to traditional routes into universities and into adult education in general. It was not just that groups and communities that had been marginalised such as the black and other ethnic groupings and communities that were involved in the encounter with the social order. Wide sections of the working class were alert in the 1980s to the need for change and social conflict was a dominant social and political reality in this period (Hall ibid). The middle classes, as we have noted, were increasingly taking up the opportunities offered by continuing education and massive structural alterations in domestic, occupational, financial and lifestyle circumstances across all social groups were occurring. Nevertheless the issues of race and minority ethnicity groups were still paramount for some sections of the population. In 1986 the Commission for Racial Equality reported that there was a continuing failure to remove institutional racism and indirect discrimination practices from the education system (CRE 1986: iii).This was one example of many in which institutional conservatism restricted access and participation across a wide section of the population. The higher education institutions in particular were bounded by their articles of government, by their funding arrangements, by their staffing and management structures and by their organisational ethos and ideological orientation so that they could not respond to the emerging needs and demands. Courses in HE had mostly to be award bearing and be 'poolable' for purposes of governmental funding. A host of institutional prescriptions effectively prohibited these institutions from developing a comprehensive learning offer to the upcoming and previously excluded students. The point, however, was that the new needs of adult learners whether younger or older, was precisely that they were both *continuing* and *comprehensive.* That is to say, the new learning offer needed to bring together many of the post-school learning opportunities including re-training and skill updating for working people and the learning needs of the whole community going way beyond existing award bearing courses. This was why the open college schemes referred to their claim to both provide access to provision which was *continuing and comprehensive* and to develop it where it was needed (Black 1982; Wilson 2010).

Priorities for this agenda were identified in a report by the Advisory Council on Adult and Continuing Education (ACACE 1982a: 190) and included:

- development of more part-time provision
- expansion of short full-time course provision
- help with practical difficulties facing adult students, particularly those wanting part-time study
- positive support for educational release from work, particularly for those working unconventional hours
- development of modular courses
- the provision of a national information service on credit transfer and development of operational arrangements for transferability of credit.

Most of these priorities had been identified almost a decade before the ACACE report (Houghton and Richardson 1974) and by the 1980s it was open colleges which were making the claim for the distinctive educational experiences and interests of both working class people in particular and on behalf of the economically deprived and socially excluded. The open colleges were in later years to spread, covering most areas throughout the country. A national open college network (NOCN) was later founded with the aim of co-ordinating and linking the many OCNs that had sprung into existence in the founding period of the 1980s and early 1990s.

## The origin and development of open higher education

The term open college evokes immediately consideration of the Open University which demonstrated its presence through a variety of communication and pedagogic methods including television, radio, video, correspondence tuition, computer-aided learning and face-to-face situations (Perry 1976; Rogers and Groombridge 1976; Venables 1976). The OU provided open access and routes to formal higher education qualifications and learning to those who had been denied them for whatever reason. The need, the motivation and the ability to learn were the entrance qualifications for OU study. For those without any formal qualifications this route was not at all easy but with persistence and the right motivation and support, it was possible to succeed. The ability to learn and the basic talent for academic success was demonstrably present in the lives, the capacities and experience of ordinary people who had previously never considered themselves capable of advanced study.

Open college extended the possibilities of open learning first explored at higher education levels by the Open University. The social, economic and geographical circumstances which had been barriers to university entry had to be countered by 'openness', flexibility and an insistence that the student become a critical agent in identifying his/her own learning needs and the strategies necessary to meet those needs. This approach raised the question of what can be defined as open learning? Educators identified more than one style or form of open learning available in the United Kingdom, mainly through conventional providers (FEU 1985). There were also flexible and innovative learning schemes and systems in particular local institutions such as schools, FE colleges, adult centres and in voluntary adult and community centres throughout the land. Students attended such centres which offered face-to-face courses and classes. There were locally based flexi-study systems where institutional providers gave basic guidance and learner support together with library and tutorial facilities with students working mainly at home (FEU 1984; Lewis 1984). For students living at some distance from centres there were correspondence courses and packages of learning materials which could be bought or rented by students, and there were occasional residential sessions available. The OU and the government's Open Tech scheme were examples of this approach using distance learning techniques.

It was likely that an open college system would begin primarily with a commitment to a locally based or college based course or programme and would develop over time the flexible and outreach systems designed to support non-traditional learners on a journey into higher education. All the open colleges shared a certain basic rationale for their development and committed to acknowledging a range of unmet learning needs within their spheres of influence and localities. All of them were committed to the principle that a system was needed that recognised *all* learner achievement. The main means of doing this was to be via credit-based courses and the recognition of different kinds and levels of learning, but the exact nature of 'credit' and the thorny questions of the value and standards of credit and indeed just exactly what did one mean by an 'educational credit', took the best part of a generation to become clear (Wilson 2010).

Access courses had a close and umbilical relationship with open college networks across the nation, many of which became Authorised Validating Agencies (AVAs). Each AVA was a consortium of further education providers and polytechnics/universities and by the early 1990s there were about 30 such local consortia whose main task was to ensure the quality of Access to HE courses and to issue a license to operate to the providers. The quality of learning on an Access to HE course was the focus for AVAs rather than on the quality of assessment leading to an Access to HE Certificate (Wilson ibid: 70). The differences in the conception of what exactly credits were and of their comparative value would occupy the developers of credit-based systems for many years. There were differences between the culture of quality that informed the AVAs and that of the awarding bodies for vocational qualifications and this led to difficulties when the emergence of a national qualifications framework came on the agenda. Many AVAs transformed themselves into OCNs especially after the further education sector was 'privatised' and incorporated in 1992. Access to HE programmes became in the main credit-based provision through the OCNs but the OCNs did not offer qualifications themselves. A version of this credit system came eventually to underpin the national Qualifications and Credit Framework (QCF).

Though the credits awarded by the OCNs to learners were recorded in a credit record there was no concept of national credit accumulation within traditional OCN systems. The confusion of what was a credit and what was a qualification which was credit based, persisted well into the 21$^{st}$ century. Credit transfer between different university-level institutions never took flight in spite of attempts by some HE institutions and the Open University in particular to validate each others' credits.

## The needs met by open colleges

The primary need for open colleges was to combat educational disadvantage. By providing courses directly related to community needs and by widening curriculum aims, providers aimed to overcome discriminatory provision against adults and in particular against black people, ethnic minorities, the unemployed, women, the handicapped, those with learning difficulties, the isolated and working class people with no developed tradition of adult or further education. In the 1980s the numbers of adult returners into FE and HE remained low. Amongst the 16-19 age group participation nationally was low in both schools and colleges (Kedney 1985) and open colleges could offer a partial remedy here. In London and Manchester claims were made for the successes of open colleges in increasing the participation rates amongst black and ethnic communities, women and the working class (OCSL 1984; Millins 1984; MOCF 1985).

There was a need to provide greater flexibility and movement within the whole range of courses and learning on offer. Open colleges offered learning opportunities and progression from basic skills and literacy right up to entry to higher education so that an escalator was available which people could join or leave at any point of their own choosing. These were effectively alternative routes to progressive learning which were separate from the old ordinary and advanced (O and A level) GCE pathways followed by traditional provision and aimed at mainly young people. Entry to study within a whole range of academic and vocational subjects was guaranteed to *anyone* at an appropriate level at any time in their life. The only requirements for entry and progression were the capacity to demonstrate learning ability and that the learning outcomes of the course had been met. The motivation and capacity of the students to complete the course of study was never in doubt in the minds of Access tutors. These capacities were brought to bear by the students themselves, rather than being imposed by the institution. The Manchester Open College provided hundreds of courses at four different levels, whereas the Open College of the North West provided two levels of attainment, principally for accessing higher education degree courses. These were the early pathfinders in the creation of credit based learning and over time a variety of different credit based schemes emerged to meet what were thought to be local needs and circumstances. Qualifications were claimed and awarded when the commensurate number, level and combination of credits had been achieved by the learner. OCNs were not normally the awarding bodies for the qualifications; they awarded credits and aimed at providing huge flexibility and opportunity for creative and generative types of learning.

Open colleges subscribed to what was thought to be a democratic curriculum where the affiliated members decided on the courses to be offered and the modes of teaching and learning to be used. No external body or examination board determined the curriculum or its assessment procedures. Power within the federation of members was shared between teachers, students, communities and providers and it was claimed the curriculum content was client and learner-centred and student-negotiated. Any curriculum area could in principle be put forward for validation and approval in the Manchester version. The MOCF offered what it called an alternative ladder of learning. If people wanted an educational activity in the broadest meaning of the term, then it could offered and credit awarded. The governing body of an open college could in principle reflect democratic control over curriculum planning and over its pedagogical practices. One result of this was the release of enthusiasm and imaginative creativity in course design and planning in academic staff. These features served to distinguish open colleges from conventionally owned and managed institutions though the ultimate sources of funding and hence ultimate control lay with formal local and national government and its agencies.

At the time of their formation there is no doubt that open colleges thought of themselves as the harbingers of a genuinely comprehensive education system which could facilitate a break with some of the features of the then existing system which consigned so many people to failure at the age of 16 and offered few routes back into learning for later life. The narrow and elitist educational system was widely perceived as failing a large section of the population. By providing alternative educational routes to success and by recognising the dignity of each individual within it, open colleges were thought to be capable of overcoming some of the negative effects of educational segregation and of raising the overall educational standards of the majority. The question of how significant such aspirations were and how much of a serious threat they were to the nationally entrenched educational establishment has unfortunately been answered by subsequent history. No long term *fundamental and decisive* change in educational opportunity can be said to have occurred as a direct result of the Access movement or the open college movement. The structural and systemic educational culture remained in place with institutions adapting and modifying their curricula and admissions systems at the margins so as to accommodate some aspects of the demand for change and renewal. The growth of education as an 'industry' was underway and expansion appeared to offer more opportunities to more people than earlier. However, following the election of the Thatcher government in 1979 the trend was towards a marketised and ever-more commercialised version of educational development. Mass higher education was underway, certainly, but the learning society was to be driven by neo-liberal principles and a market economy rather than by the educational needs of working people or the principles of social justice and fairness.

The period of development for both Access and open colleges was marked by political assaults on and criticisms of educational progressivism (CCCS 1981; Hall 1983; Wolpe and Donald 1983; John 2006). Paradoxically, there was support within the educational profession for the advance of progressive ideas and schemes such as the recognition of life skills within the formal curriculum, and support for the validity of experiential and prior learning. The Further Education Unit- a part of the government's ministry of education- played a progressive and innovative developmental role in the acceptance of a wider curriculum for post-school learners (FEU 1983). Open colleges gave expression to new sets of questions and helped define new priorities for new types of learners. They were a generative source of innovation in new types and forms of learning. The beginnings of a new approach to what knowledge and learning might possibly be could be glimpsed in the missions and aspirational demands of Access and its associated movement for open college learning.

# A model for an open college?

There was no single model for the development of open colleges. Some operated as alternative accreditation networks with supposedly a democratic ethos in which all partners participated on an equal basis. There was no unified curriculum model for all open colleges, though Access to HE courses figured in all provision and were a defining feature. Some open colleges had 'top down' development models embedded within their procedures and organisational cultures; some espoused community-oriented provision which could reflect the need for social change at street and neighbourhood levels. Some versions stressed their links with black and ethnic minorities in local communities; some were closely linked with a single institution whilst others had connections with a range of HE and FE providers. The Open College of South London (OCSL) was substantially funded by ILEA, the powerful and influential local education authority for London, and had a well- resourced development team. Its range of Access courses covered almost every subject discipline including science, maths, food studies, computing, electronics, and engineering as well as various generic, humanities and social science options. OCSL was notably successful in recruiting students of African-Caribbean origins (Millins 1984; OCSL 1984) whereas Access courses in general were less successful in recruiting women and men of Asian origin. The original Access courses in both Manchester and Liverpool were developed with the educational needs and demands of black communities in mind and open college developments in both those cities were conscious of their specific educational needs (Davies 1987: 104; John 1993). The diversity and greater numbers of ethnic groups in London were a distinctive feature of OCSL developments and outside of the capital by the mid1980s there was nothing to compare with the number of courses nor the range available in the South London model. The Manchester Open College Federation was linked to a number of HE institutions including the Open University and provided courses at four levels from basic education to Access to HE in a variety of different subjects. It also had a funded development team employed by the Manchester local authority (Black 1982). Students received a study 'passport' which recorded their credit achievements. The first open college-The Open College of the North West- retained its academic support from Lancaster University and Lancashire Polytechnic but existed on marginal levels of funding (Percy 1988).

In the mid to late 1980s the open colleges in the UK appeared to be a significant potential force for educational and hence for social change. Access courses were a central feature of the movement and reflected the growth of mass access to higher education which itself gave expression to a growing sense that education was the key to opportunity and personal fulfilment in a world where older traditional forms of work and career were disappearing at an alarmingly fast rate. The universities were expanding rapidly and their higher status and greater resource base meant that they tended to dominate developments, yet each individual HE institution was separate with its own specific history and culture. Each university had a relative autonomy both academically and financially, with little reason or motivation to collaborate across formal boundaries. At the same time a competitive and marketised system of post-school education was being encouraged by government to maximise its resources through aggressive student recruitment of fee generating students. This was to prove damaging to the cause and ethos of open college with its roots and philosophy lying partly at least in the voluntaristic adult learning tradition. In addition the long term relationship of national to local government was diminishing the financial resources and capacity for making decisions available to local authorities. More and more power was accumulating to central government so that local governments were becoming 'agents' for national concerns and priorities. The progressive and potentially transformative capacity of open colleges with their local demands and focus were by no means the priority for a radicalising national government concerned to limit the powers and capacities of the local state whilst privatising wherever it could the provision of education at all levels. Quite the opposite in fact, especially since open colleges were a challenge to the dominant ideology of the ruling elites in Britain which supported selection and privilege for a minority in education.

The significance of the open colleges could be seen in the willingness of many of the newer universities to attract adult and mature students. Concessions were made to the removal of barriers by the higher education institutions and some recognition of the curriculum changes implied by the Access movement was given. Some argued at the time that what mattered more to the universities were the effects of the declining birth-rate of the decade and a half leading up to the 1990s (Percy 1988: 119). Students were needed to fill empty places and institutional survival was paramount. What mattered more generally for the individual, however, were the lessons of the open college learning experiment where the starting point was the experience of the learner. The outcome was not always a place in a university, though much university thinking about Access was founded on such an assumption. One lesson learned was that the curious and perhaps aspiring adult would turn to the universities when they made their offerings flexible and attractive enough to fit in with the learner's interests and goals. Goals and aspirations were naturally enough difficult to separate from the texture of ordinary life in the communities from which people came and to which most would return after their education was formally completed. Whether open access education and open colleges actually touched people's lives is more than a matter of conjecture. The claims made at the time and the evidence of progression into university life for working-class and disadvantaged people suggest it had significant impact (Millins 1984; MOCF 1985). Open colleges showed the world of universities that the life-worlds and interests of working class and ordinary people were really quite extra-ordinary and deserved their place in the systems and cultures of learning.

The open colleges made a significant contribution to the growth and consolidation of Access as a movement which supported multi-level access to learning and its accreditation. They allowed learners to progress from basic skills and literacy classes to university level study and qualifications whilst remaining in their home communities and institutions and within their cultural 'habitus' or everyday world. This was an important feature for many adult learners who still had many barriers to overcome if they wished to succeed in higher education. The open college federations sponsored collaboration across all 'binary divisions' and linked adult and further education with universities in new and innovative ways (Sanders and Whalley 2007; Wilson 2010). They did not transform the post-school educational landscape, though that was a prospectus some had thought was possible if Access could be part of the critical learning needed for community action (Lovett et al 1983). Open colleges as credit based awarding bodies were not immune from the forces and circumstances which incorporated much adult and continuing education into the vocational maw of government funded provision. That proved a false prospectus as argued in chapters 3 and 4 of this book. Its original supporters thought that OCNs were a movement; they were never simply conceived as awarding bodies for credit and/or qualifications. There was a community of interests (Wilson ibid: 19) for the development of an 'open' curriculum that would create new opportunities and new access routes for new and different learners. The open colleges were, in the beginning, always much more than credit systems with their complex and arcane sets of technical specifications. Each open college was locally based and completely autonomous though the Manchester model became very influential in the North and far beyond.

In the year 2000 there were 31 open college networks which worked in collaboration with the NOCN ( National Open College Network) that had been set up in 1991 (Opencoll 2020). In 2005 these were merged to form 11 larger OCNs (open college networks) and they continued to offer provision in various centres including schools, colleges, voluntary organisations, community centres, prisons, training providers and employers. The OCNs continued to offer Access course diplomas as Access Validating Agencies, recognised by the official Quality Assurance Agency for Higher Education. The credit based learning opportunities, based on OCN credits, continued to expand with government support. In 2010 it was claimed that OCNs had developed hundreds of thousands of learning and accredited units in every conceivable subject and vocational area (Wilson ibid). These included tens of thousands of Access to HE units. Some 6,000 or so organisations that used the units had been involved over the years in their development. There is a note of caution to this undoubtedly successful and expanding picture of educational development. The link between what was on offer within the Qualifications and Credit Framework (QCF) which eventually emerged in 2008 from these developments, and the original conception of a movement of critical learning, became ever more tenuous as the privatisation and commercialisation of publically funded education took it away from the founding vision and values of the 'open colleges' as a radical and transformative force in education. The QCF operated between 2008 and 2015 and was replaced by the NQF- national qualifications framework- which in turn was replaced by the Regulated Qualifications Framework (RFQ). Credit and qualifications frameworks had become a part of the conventional qualifications topography.

By the early 2020s the remaining open college networks that existed across the country continued to offer credit- based courses and work-based learning programmes and this was in fact commensurate with the governmental policy agenda developed over the previous three decades. The open colleges were not able to reform the traditional institutions of further and higher education. Indeed they did not set out to do so and they were umbilically attached to them. Neither could they offer an alternative system of learning opportunities since the intended outcomes for most students were conventional further and higher qualifications delivered in the main within conservative and publically funded institutions. In spite of the very real innovations and opportunities they had carved open for generations of adult students, the open colleges had no real independent existence apart from the 'mother' institutions which sponsored and helped fund them and were never likely to be able to resist pressures to conform to government funding and regulatory requirements. They had to adapt to the more powerful institutional and political trends to survive. Nevertheless, at that point in time there were some 40,000 Access course students nationally and it was clear that the alternative to the conventional school-based qualifications for entry to higher education had stood one test of time and that open colleges had made their own vital contribution to widening participation.

# References

ACACE – Advisory Council for Adult and Continuing Education- (1982a) *Continuing Education: From Policies to Practice,* Leicester: ACACE.

ACACE (1982b) *Adults: Their Educational Experience and Needs*, Leicester: ACACE.

Black, A. (1982) *The Development of the Manchester Open College Federation*, London: FEU.

CCCS (1981)-Centre for Contemporary Cultural Studies (at Birmingham University) *Unpopular Education: Schooling and social democracy in England since 1944*, CCCS: University of Birmingham and London: Hutchinson.

CRE- Commission for Racial Equality- (1986) (summer), *New Equals*, UK: ISBN 01040.

Davies, D.W. (1987) New Approaches to Access to Higher Education in England: Issues and Prospects, M.Ed. thesis, University of Liverpool, May 1987.

Davies, D. and Davies, E. (2021) *A Fair Go: Learning in Critical Times and Places*, UK: Amazon.

FEU (1983) – Further Education Unit of the Department of Education- *Curriculum Opportunity: A map of experiential learning in entry requirements to higher and further education award bearing course*s, London: FEU.

FEU (1984) *Flexible Learning in Action: three case studies of flexibility*, by Birch, D.W. and Latcham, J., London: FEU.

FEU (1985) The Experience of Open Learning: A Summary Document, London: FEU.

Hall, S. (1983) 'Education in Crisis, Part One: The politics of education', in Wolpe and Donald (eds) (1983) *Is there anyone here from education?* London: Pluto Press.

Houghton, V. and Richardson, K. (1974) *Recurrent Education: A Plea for Lifelong Learning*, London: Ward Lock Educational.

John, G. (1993) Say No to "Ethnic Minority", *Access News*, No 16 June 1993, London: ACES/University of North London.

John, G. (2006) *Taking a Stand: Gus John Speaks on education, race, social action & civil unrest 1980-2005,* Manchester: Gus John Partnership.

Kedney, R.J. (1985) *Further Education Management Audit Studies: 1984-85: Student Enrolments: Forecasting Trends*, Coombe Lodge: FESC. IBN 2037.

Lewis, R. (ed) (1984) *Open Learning in Action: case studies,* London: Council for Educational Technology (CET).

Lovett, T. (1975) *Adult Education, Community Development and the Working Class,* London: Ward Lock Educational.

Lovett, T., Clarke, C. and Kilmurray, A. (1983*) Adult Education and Community Action,* London: Croom Helm.

Lucas, S. and Ward, P. (1985) *A Survey of 'Access Courses' in England*, University of Lancaster.

McPherson, A. (1972) *Eighteen –plus: The Final Selection, Units 15-17 Educational Studies: A Second Level Course, School and Society.* Prepared by Andrew McPherson, Donald Swift and Basil Bernstein, Milton Keynes: The Open University Press.

Millins, P.K.C. (1984) *Access Studies to Higher Education, September 1979-December 1983: A Report*, London: Roehampton Institute, Centre for Access Studies to Higher Education.

MOCF (1985)-Manchester Open College Federation, *Update,* Spring 1985.

MSC- Manpower Services Commission (1985) Newscheck, November 1985.

NAB (1984) - National Advisory Body for Public Sector Higher Education, Report of the Continuing Education Group, London: NAB (August 1984).

NOCN (previously National Open College Network) see *opencollnet.org.uk*

OCSL (1984) - Open College of South London, Access Courses in the Open College of South London: Some Questions and Answers; see Davies (1987) pp. 102-105.

Opencoll (2020) see *opencollnet.org.uk*

Percy, K. et al (1983) *Post-Initial Education in the North-West of England: A Survey of Provision,* Leicester: ACACE.

Percy, K. (1988) Opening access to a modern university, ch 12 in Eggins, H. (ed) (1988) *Restructuring Higher Education*, Milton Keynes: SRHE/Open University Press.

Percy, K. A. and Ramsden, P. (1980) *Independent Study: Two Examples from English Higher Education,* London: SRHE.

Perry, W. (1976) *The Open University*, Milton Keynes: The Open University Press.

Rogers, J. and Groombridge, B. (1976) *Right to Learn: The Case for Adult Equality,* London: Arrow Books Ltd.

Russell Report (1983) *Adult Education: A Plan for Development*, London: DES/HMSO.

Sanders, J. and Whalley, P. (2007) *Celebrating Achievement-25 years of Open College Networks,* Leicester: NIACE/NOCN.

Tough, A. (1979) *The Adult's Learning Projects: A Fresh Approach to Theory and Practice in Adult Learning,* Toronto: Ontario Institute for Studies in Education.

Venables, P. (1976) *Report of the Committee on Continuing Education*, Milton Keynes: Open University Press.

Wilson, P. (2010) *Big Ideas, Small Steps,* Leicester: NIACE.

Wolpe, AM. and Donald, J. (eds) (1983) *Is there anyone here from education?,* London: Pluto Press.

# Chapter 7

# Access as Critical Thinking: Contested Knowledge

This book has argued that Access courses were not only a new method of facilitating entry to universities but were also at the same time a 'movement' involving significant parts of the post-school education scene right across the country. Access was not just significant because of the student numbers involved- these were always a small proportion of the totals, even as these numbers began to rise in the 1970s towards mass participation of each succeeding cohort of school leavers in the 1990s. Access implicitly questioned the traditional forms of teaching and learning and of how we think about academic and public knowledge. It was a competing claim for how knowledge is organised and transmitted and applied within and beyond our educational institutions. Put simply, Access was an alternative to the dominant paradigm in which formally organised knowledge and academic learning functioned to exclude most people from learning opportunities in higher education. Access was the means for some to move up the ladder of opportunity and become socially mobile whilst the education system in which it was embedded functioned to legitimate the economic and social inequalities of the wider society. Access challenged a system habituated to the filtering and screening out of those who would not be allowed to enter the academy and the professions. In its theory and actual practice it suggested a new paradigm might be possible.

The concept of 'paradigm' used here derives from the work of Thomas Kuhn (1970) and refers to the way we understand and apply knowledge to particular practical situations. Kuhn's main concern was with the analysis of types of scientific explanation which led him to explore the conceptual basis and organisation of science as ways of looking at the 'natural' world. He argued that a field of scientific enquiry rests on a set of assumptions and taken for granted axioms which set out the conceptual boundaries within which the enquiry takes place. These scientific parameters included the models of analysis in use, the problems for which solutions were necessary, the validating standards used to assess results and the normal modes of thinking applied to a particular scientific enterprise. All of these constitute a paradigm within which a scientist carries out 'normal' science. Kuhn suggests it is not normal practice for a scientist to examine the assumptions upon which her/his work rests. The significance of Kuhn's work for other fields of enquiry in the social sciences or education lies in its ability to help us explain our understanding of the ways in which knowledge is organised, transmitted and recognised.

Access courses questioned implicitly and explicitly some of the conventional axioms and assumptions of conventional educational practice. Access programmes were often overtly related to collective experience and forms of knowing which were rooted in the perceived needs and experience of disadvantaged groups and communities. It was not the numbers of Access students and courses that were most significant but rather the fact that this movement appeared as a practical realisation and expression of a possible alternative educational paradigm. The knowledge paradigm in which Access courses operated took as its central concern the idea that the mind and intellect is capable of infinite development. An individual has an unlimited capacity for educational development and as such has an entitlement to learning at each and every stage of a life. In the Access movement this perspective was passed on to students through a curriculum which stressed the need for useful knowledge which could be acquired by any person who was sufficiently motivated and dedicated to learning. The barriers were not insurmountable as the Open University had already demonstrated as thousands of students completed their degrees without having had entry qualifications. Access became part of self-understanding; it became knowledge which could be acted on; learning was externalised in students' social actions and practice (Freire 1972; Lovett 1983) and possibilities were opened that had once been closed.

## Access as critical thinking

Access courses showed a wide public that knowledge could potentially be emancipatory (Habermas 1972) and could lead to what Mezirow (1983) called 'perspective transformation' by which he meant a critical theory of adult learning that could transform our understanding of why we are the way we are and enable us therefore to be different. Knowledge was not just enshrined in existing syllabuses and institutions of higher education. Access was a movement of learners and teachers who looked for change in the way institutions managed and selected their students and the knowledge they were deemed to require to get ahead in further learning- and all that might follow from that. If perspectives were to be transformed as part of this then Access was also a process of *critical* learning. But what exactly was critical learning and could it lead to a paradigm shift in learning? These were the sorts of questions that were being asked by proponents of critical thinking and adult learning in the 1980s (Mezirow 1983; Griffin 1983; Gibson 1986) - the point at which the Access movement was asking questions about the dominant paradigm for entry to higher education.

There are many claimants as authentic antecedents of Access and the history of adult education in modern Britain includes the diverse and innovative contributions made by, for example, the Workers' Education Association, by community educators, by local authorities, by university extra-mural departments and by adult colleges (Fieldhouse 1996). We have already noted in chapter 2 above the immense role played by women in the history of adult learning and its contribution to social justice issues. A good deal of debate took place in the 1970s and 1980s on the best way forward to produce higher education for all. The social policy aspects of increasing provision and the economic implications of increasing state intervention in higher education were widely discussed (Roderick and Stephens 1979) and a change of emphasis in academic and public concern could be detected. A wave of interest occurred in what was called lifelong education and which later was transposed into the idea of lifelong learning. The famous Faure Report in 1972 stimulated policy developments in a number of countries in Europe, Australasia, Canada and Japan (Richmond 1974; Field 2004a, 2013; Elfert 2016). A key aspect of the new approach was that there should be a focus on the promotion of learning rather than on teaching and training. There was a second wave of interest in the notion of lifelong learning in the 1990s when globalisation and the pace of technological, economic and cultural change pushed competitive economies to greater rivalry in the fields of financial investment and economic growth (Field 2001). Education and hence lifelong learning became part of the burgeoning knowledge economy which focussed primarily on the individualistic benefits that could accrue from an instrumentalist approach to learning (Field 2004b). It has been suggested in this book that this trend is at odds with ideas of a broad learning 'Access' culture which favoured wider participation and social transformations through critical learning. As a trend it was to grow in influence as the century reached its end and the fruits of neoliberal policies began to shape learning and especially continuing education for economic purposes.

Knowledge and learning in Access, however, were problematised- that is to say, the processes of knowing, and hence learning itself were thought to be properly located at least in part in the student's experience and consciousness. Knowledge was not simply incorporated within objective syllabuses and curriculums, as in the traditional and conventional paradigm. Knowledge had to be interpreted and re-experienced in the mental structures of the mature student where the student had greater responsibility for her/his own learning. This 'phenomenological' approach put the student's subjectivity and understanding of self at a more central locus than the older, more 'objective' view of what knowledge actually was. Access courses had in general a commitment to process rather than to curriculum content. This was the basis for critical learning and social development and was rooted in collective, communal experience and social practice rather than individualistic concerns for self- advancement. At least this was in theory a rationale for the distinctiveness of Access courses which focussed on the teaching and learning methods appropriate to the (adult) learners who were the students. It involved what we can call a pedagogy of 'dialogue' and questioning in which learners were seen as creators of knowledge rather than as consumers of knowledge produced somewhere else by others who were considered to be experts. How the more subjective and 'phenomenological' approaches to learning experience could challenge the embedded, unequal and socially unjust material and cultural factors which constituted huge barriers to learning, however, was unclear. That the Access curriculum or approach to learning had significance for how knowledge, culture and power were conceptualised and distributed could not be denied. New forms of knowledge and experience were emerging which would eventually be admitted to a more problematical and contested curriculum (Seidman 1998).By the end of the last decade of the 20th century, higher education in the United Kingdom was said to be in crisis, though different voices identified different crises (Griffin 1997). Significantly, academics identified a crisis of knowledge with implications for the values of a liberal democratic society as mass higher education along with its Access variant took hold of the modern world of education (Scott 1997).

## New knowledge: contested knowledge

Access as defined in this book arose as part of the transition from an elite to a mass system of higher education in a period when the social and class structure of Britain was in flux and when the historic achievements of British society – its solidity, its pragmatism, its sheer massive traditional industrial might, the apparent immovability and persistence of its class structure– were being undermined and replaced by very different conceptions. By the 1980s *progress* was being identified with change and modernity and postmodern thinkers such as Lyotard (1984) thought it denoted a condition of perpetual motion in which new desires would come and go along with new technologies which would replace the old ones. The neoliberalism of the 1970s had produced a new capitalism which gave birth to a culture of the flexible and provisional. Little was fixed and everything was changeable and for the short term. Individuals were faced with endless consumption and new satisfactions, including the possibilities of shifting and multiple identities. Zygmunt Bauman (2000) called this 'liquid modernity' and suggested it was capable of dissolving traditional values and behaviours. By the middle of the second decade of the 21st century there was debate and concern that contemporary life, that is to say the advanced capitalist forces of production, were 'accelerating' and dissolving our social life beyond the limits of control (Noys 2014). The economic force driving the changes was neoliberal capitalism which was busy deconstructing the old economic order in favour of 'open markets', global free trade and unhindered global expansion of productive capacity in search of profit. Being postmodern by the end of the 20th century meant joining a global order which was inevitably far greater than the single nation state and which would inevitably dominate world development.

## The new modern and growth of techno-capitalism

The general mood of postmodernism was optimistic with a sense that old boundaries and constraints could be removed, new identities formed and old elites moved aside in favour of the new. The rise of new inequalities brought about by neoliberalism could be masked by the growth of credit-led consumerism and where necessary for the poor and dispossessed, the interventions of the welfare state. These changes indicated a shift in the way knowledge and learning was used in postmodern society. Driven by science and technology the logic of capitalism was merging knowledge and science into capitalism itself so the two were becoming indistinguishable. Science was no longer a scholarly endeavour and pursuit of knowledge for its own sake but was now itself a force of production and a part of the circulation of capital. This idea is in effect an anticipation of the notion of the 'knowledge economy' which was to be taken up in the 1980s by universities which were encouraged to exploit their knowledge resources and be more entrepreneurial. Capitalism itself was on the cusp of using the digital revolution to connect international business and trade with financial markets whose authority depended on owning the capacity to process vast amounts of digitised information and data. The dawn of Silicon Valley was about to occur where big finance and advanced technology could create 'platform capitalism' where the acquisition of data and information of consumer preferences could simply outperform traditional capitalism in favour of 'surveillance capitalism' (Zuboff 2019). Science and knowledge could be privatised and turned into assets in ways simply not conceived in earlier times.

## Redefining inequality through education

Modernity and postmodernity in this sense undermined traditional forms of community and solidarity which were no longer capable of protecting people whose economic security was linked with skilled and unskilled labour in traditional industries and communities which were being dissolved. Education was called upon to respond as a key means of responding to these pervasive changes and this involved the expansion of higher education of which Access was an intrinsic part. The growth of Access to higher education was part of the reconstruction of types of traditional adult education which had emerged from the long history of struggle for education and learning. Often such struggles were organised at a local level and had elements of democratic control built into their practices and procedures. Later developments in the 20th century favoured state-funded and state-controlled provision geared towards a vocational perspective and the needs of a 'knowledge economy' in which the UK might improve its performance and position. And yet Access provided unheard of opportunities for tens of thousands of people who had been denied access to higher education. What could be more progressive than that?

The transition to a mass higher education system brought with it massive investment and growth of institutionalised learning. The demise of the diverse voluntary and locally accountable and generally speaking 'adult' education tradition was accompanied by the explosion of university places and institutions, and by the consolidation of FE colleges into a central government controlled sector which was highly sensitive to market demands for vocational learning. The ideology behind this growth asserted students were the main beneficiaries of higher education and therefore they should pay for the investment in their own 'human capital'. This was the justification for the raising of university student fees and for the incorporation of much Access, pre-access and second-chance learning into the formal governmental funding system within the FE sector.

Educationalists and Access movement supporters faced a dilemma since they generally supported the expansion of higher education and their product, as it were, was in high demand from both intending students and the universities keen to grow their student numbers and enhance their funding. Furthermore it seemed abundantly clear that the more people were educated the better society would be and few denied that higher participation in higher education was one mark of a progressive and more liberated society. Economic growth and development was also seen to be correlated to the growth of learning opportunities. For families without access to wealth or conventional cultural resources and cultural capital, education for their children was not just the obvious way forward it was probably the only one. It was difficult for anyone to argue that increasing investment in education was not desirable.

The problem was and remains- the growth of education in this era and beyond also saw the continuation and even acceleration of inequality and social injustice (Dorling 2018). What remained below the horizon was the possibility that education itself was itself generating this inequality alongside the economic and social conditions driving modernity. If we choose to view educational activity through the lens of individual experience and development then we are likely to see positive outcomes. This was the case as argued earlier when highly talented individuals from BAME groups were recruited to Oxbridge in an attempt to signal progress towards a more fair and just society (James 2018). However, if we see education as contributing to social differentiation and to an ideology of meritocratic justification of privilege, then we are forced to engage more critically with the core values of a democratic society. This can mean asking how education lives up to its claims to open up opportunity and advancement on the basis of merit and worth for more than the very talented individuals within a given social group?

## Social inequality and class remain as the market develops

One of these key claims to democracy concerns the salience of social class. Despite the rising of inequality over the last two decades there has been a tendency in the wider society and culture to deny the significance of class. Assumptions have been made that class is now consigned to a more divisive past (James ibid; Savage 2015) and many people do indeed operate as if class bears no relevance to the practical and applied aspects of education. It seems as if it has been banned from the policy discourse around university entry and displaced by a more acceptable vocabulary of the 'disadvantaged'. This category can include the lower income or status groups, or under-represented groups of different types and often proxies are used such as postcodes, POLAR (participation of local areas) or free school meals data (Harrison 2018: 61). Definitions and the meanings of social class are notoriously difficult to assess and they change in significant ways over time (Savage 2015; Picketty 2020 ch 14), however, the relevance of class to understanding the unequal wealth and power relations of modern society continues to be demonstrated (Dorling ibid 2018: ch 2.4; Todd 2021). There is also misrecognition of the nature and extent of the social and educational 'advantage' and privilege. One of the most significant features of meritocracy is its capacity to legitimise and reward existing privilege under the guise of 'justified reward' to those who succeed in the competitive struggle for places in prestigious universities or have access to the best careers.

The significance of this for Access has been the marketisation of widening participation – a key theme in the original Access agenda. Since universities were able to define widening participation in different ways they were able to construct institutional agreements with partners and providers which reflected their own needs and privileged their own programmes. There was no national view or consensus on what the wider system objectives actually were. The net effect of this was to consolidate the distinctions between the high status and lower status universities after 1992. There was little commonality in the way elite universities sought to recruit a small group of high-ability, but socially disadvantaged members of ethnic groups and the mass recruitment amongst ethnic minority groups to the lower status 'convenience universities' in the urban centres. The relative superiority of elite universities, measured in terms of performance league tables which themselves reflect and consolidate a range of pre-existing distinctions including endowment wealth, has arguably been increased in recent decades, even though some elite institutions have increased their intakes of students from working class backgrounds. The access agreements that universities had to make with the government agency in England, OFFA ( Office for Fair Access) in order to charge higher fees had only weak sanctions for non- compliance, and furthermore ... 'Higher education providers with the most unequal student bodies are the least likely to hit access and progression targets' (Havergal 2016; and see OFFA 2016).

The access and widening participation efforts of recent decades undoubtedly expanded provision and opportunities for literally millions of students who historically would have been excluded from higher education. But there is a cycle and structure of advantage which continues to hold sway in British and especially in English life. It is spectacularly unequal and unfair, though it may be meritocratic in some limited senses it is a rigged and managed system. It is not an aberration or malfunction in an otherwise rational and fair system. The inequalities are predictable and intended to privilege those who benefit from them. The accidents of birth and social placement associated with owning wealth and accessing power and influence determine social and educational outcomes far more than talent and natural ability which are randomly distributed across the social landscape. A small number of private schools dealing with about 7 per cent of the school population take a very high proportion of undergraduate places at the most prestigious universities. The economic power of the parents of these children is able to be converted into educational and cultural capital and so advantage can be purchased and transmitted to each succeeding generation (Green and Kynaston 2019). The power of such factors is shown in the way in which these HE institutional hierarchies are deeply embedded in wider social and economic structures- such as that of the graduate labour market and the professions (Savage ibid). The way in which different institutions are valued in the wider society has significant implications for careers and opportunities for graduates. The degree classification an individual achieves and its location can be crucial for opening opportunities in the workplace. Oxbridge in particular is renowned, or perhaps better described as notorious, for the social and cultural capital it manages to transmit to its graduates and which fosters their careers long after they have left university life. In terms of their on-going social networks many never leave these communities of interest; why would they when they continue to confer benefits down through the generations.

The market of course implies 'choice' is available which in turn connotes for many a sense of freedom to select for oneself the education fit for one's children or oneself which may in turn allow a sense of control over what the uncertain future may hold. The problem is that market forces in education do not operate in a free market for everyone. The market is managed in favour of certain social and economic interests whose privileges ensure unequal and unjust outcomes for the less well- off and the working classes. The ideology of choice along with that of meritocracy, often glibly conflated with ideas of 'freedom' and respect for the rights of individuals, has held sway in wider political debate and find expression in educational policy developed and imposed by conservative elitist interests.

There is in addition the difficult problem of how and why people appear to willingly accept the domination of technology, media and communication systems which position them as consumers of a world made somewhere else and which generates vast profits from doing so whilst so many of the consumers are in fact poor and disadvantaged? It raises also the question of why people are willing to insert themselves into grids of surveillance and control and their willingness to pay for this as part of the market economy in which we exist?

# A critical curriculum and pedagogy

One of the striking features of Access education was that learners and teachers did not only have in mind access to a particular kind of institution or system but rather to a particular kind of knowledge itself. The theoretical potential of the idea of Access was, and is, in the area of the curriculum content of education. In fact Access was significant for a range of providers including those involving further and higher educational institutions and for government policy. But perhaps its most significant feature involved the knowledge content of higher learning and the learning and teaching methods best suited to critical thinking. However, it was clear from early on that achieving a greater degree of openness and rationalising access to classes and using distance learning methods could all be achieved without radically affecting the curriculum content of the traditional education system, including that of the universities. The Open University showed how previously excluded students could be recruited and engaged in successful degree level study, using radically different tuition methods without abandoning a very traditional knowledge structure of subjects and academic faculties. Access historically and traditionally, including that provided by the Open University, was in many if not most cases, conditioned and shaped by the curricular considerations of traditional and conservative institutions. The barriers maintained by these institutions which people faced when trying to gain entry to universities were not merely physical, technical and economic. There were also additional barriers… 'constituted by the "social construction of knowledge" …(and) cultural restrictions upon access to high-status knowledge' (Griffin 1983: 82-83). In other words, universal and democratic access to knowledge is restricted where knowledge itself is stratified. Access was allowed to challenge institutional resistance to the entry of, for example, working class students or members of ethnic and racial groups, but did not challenge the curriculum content and meaning of education and learning. This would have been a step too far for the guardians of traditional knowledge in the elite universities.

The Access movement came to fruition in a time of growth for mass higher education, but it was a mass system of education *without* a common culture of knowledge- what Stuart Hall referred to as a universal literacy (Hall 1983). Where the emphasis was on gaining entry to a socially conservative and culturally elitist system, the structures of knowledge were left unchallenged and unchanged. The realities of a mass education system, where knowledge and qualifications were highly unequal and stratified, could be by-passed and these realities exposed a major paradox for the Access movement. Access opportunities were developed under conditions of social conservatism where there was little or no re-construction of social knowledge. A mass system of education was encouraged in the absence of a common culture of knowledge and an absence of what a 'university education' might be if it focussed on what knowledge might best contribute to a fairer world (Ashwin 2020). The strategies associated with Access included removing financial barriers, making positive interventions and developing counselling and guidance services and the introduction of well-designed individual study and intensive group-work, along with the use of innovative technology exemplified by the Open University. All these improved educational methods were to the good and to the benefit of students and teachers. What they were not, however, was the kind of radical change that mass higher education might have implied- that is to say, a correspondingly radical change in how society is understood, how knowledge is defined and how it is translated into qualifications and opportunities which transform people's lives. In order to achieve this, a critical curriculum is required. The Access movement did not achieve this breakthrough in any conscious or coherent way; no single unifying narrative emerged to spell out the key principles for all who were part of the movement. But the movement was a beacon and guiding light for those who thought and worked towards such principles. We might term them for convenience 'points of departure' for the future of engaged and committed knowledge and for which Access, however incomplete, was an early and notable example.

## Points of departure for a critical curriculum

Access was about more than gaining places in educational provision, on courses and into previously elite-recruiting institutions. It was concerned with all of that of course, but it engaged with the problematic knowledge-content of learning (who learns what and for what purposes?). This was a deeply cultural issue and raised problems about identity, belonging, social justice and the sources of social division and solidarity which would continue to bedevil British society for generations to come. It also raised questions about the interplay of material and cultural factors which constitute the barriers to learning and alert us to the ways in which Access could be conceptualised in terms of knowledge, culture and power (Griffin ibid: 87).

Over and above the fact that Access was about gaining entry to provision, it was primarily important in engaging and challenging the *content* of that provision. It did not do this as a principled and coherent theoretical proposition but rather it achieved this by calling into question the previously unchallenged, unproblematic categories which defined educational achievement. It could not overthrow these categories (the disciplines are hard to dislodge) but it could bring to light, directly through personal and collective experience the fact that the content of education is socially defined, distributed and evaluated. The content of education had historically failed to deliver its promises to broad masses of people and yet Access, through its students, demanded an alternative. The students wanted learning which resonated with their lives and aspirations, including their identities. This potential alternative did not ignore such matters and focussed on the curriculum problems of the wicked issues of the moment, of poverty and injustice, of racial and ethnic experience, of women's issues and perspectives and on themes of inclusion and the need for social change and better outcomes.

It would be unjustifiable to claim that all Access provision fulfilled the claims made for it here! Clearly there was significantly diverse provision, and courses were spread across the United Kingdom and Northern Ireland amongst very diverse and different communities. There was historically no single point of condensation which could have captured the learning and work of many thousands of people in many different locations and who thought of themselves as delivering Access. There was no single 'conjuncture' and no unified or universal model for Access. There was, however, a sense of there being a movement for change and growth underway which could shift the dial on how learning and education might open up opportunities previously denied. Access was about the widening of purposes and the generation of knowledge for social progress. A number of key themes for an Access curriculum can be identified within this generic approach and for the type of pedagogy (learning and teaching) adopted by Access programmes. These themes were by no means imperatives but they served as guidance to practice.

## A summary of themes for a critical curriculum within Access:

- the character of communities, including their demographics and cultures should be expressed in the curriculum at every level so that lived experience and critical self-reflection becomes crucial to learning
- cultural diversity and tolerance should contribute to healthy social integration and social justice; this is an educational challenge to be met and overcome
- education should be a democratising process which can challenge damaging and persistent inequalities, including those of class, race and gender
- engagement with the new technologies and digital communications so that they contribute to socially progressive outcomes is needed

- that the self-elected group of mega businesses that exercise monopoly functions over our digital lives should be made to accountable to democratic procedures
- the mass-psychology of passivity and consumption of goods and services as the 'highest' form of value must be questioned by critical learning
- the social purposes of learning and knowledge need to be re-instated in public and communal life
- learning should be for democratic citizenship not just widening participation
- the existential challenges of climate change and ecological disaster facing the planet must be central to our learning.

## A brief summary of themes for a critical pedagogy

No single university academic discipline or subject can yield up a handy set of concepts to be applied to the issues of Access and diversity of learning outlined in this book. There is, however, reason to believe that the process of critical thinking and research and progressive learning might offer a way forward. Some of the steps in this process of reform involve reformulating the role of learning and teaching for critical social and political engagement and in the re-conceptualisation of public education in the lives of thinking citizens. Some of the steps in curriculum planning for engagement in this process can be identified as follows and may serve as guidance for practitioners:

- identifying real world problems which can be expected to be complex and involve contested knowledge
- establishing learning sets, groups and teams which can draw on the different 'discipline' approaches and knowledges and use knowledge for action and transformation
- starting inquiry using curiosity, problem solving, reflection and openness to critique as a basic and democratic form of learning and knowing
- an insistence that learning and action for change and transformation go hand-in-hand and should be geared towards the solution of problems
- generating and testing knowledge solutions with those whom it affects so that knowledge becomes really useful
- personal commitment to learning and critical reflection on the status of knowledge about what is to be studied

- a realisation that the monopolies held on knowledge creation and its distribution can no longer be maintained by conventional universities but must be re-thought in the new contexts
- the unlocking of human potential through critical thinking and learning, especially for those who have not had learning opportunities or cannot afford them
- a challenge to the conservative and traditional notions of the neutral and objective observer who is capable of exercising judgement from the 'outside'
- adopting a learning methodology which supports mutuality and reciprocity and encourages and facilitates participants' visions for the future and views learners as active agents for positive change
- acknowledging that the educational purpose of a higher education degree is to help students/learners develop a transformational relationship to knowledge. By doing so they can critically understand themselves and their environments and be better prepared for changing both themselves and the society in which they live.

All of these processes and activities involve what was once called pedagogy and represent part of the viable basis for critical thinking and learning which needs to underpin learning and teaching (Davies and Nyland 2022). Using some of these approaches, the Access movement showed us an example of how learning could be re-thought and re-conceptualised and can still serve as a model for the future.

## New knowledge is contested knowledge

Whatever the future holds, the present demands that we as educators look at our real experience in the real world and this can only be done by knowing others in some direct and meaningful way and by sharing the thoughts and insights we gain as a result. Is this not the great challenge of change to all of those involved in public education in this as in every generation? The Access movement provides us with a lived example of educational change whose historical meanings still resonate strongly.

To meet the challenge we need to acknowledge that social practice in modern life is modified in the light of new information and knowledge which comes from an increasingly diverse range of sources. These include the social spheres as well as the academic and employment fields. The old monopolies on access to knowledge and learning can no longer suffice. Family, community, education, government, internet, social media and 'infotainment' all help comprise the social and cultural processes which are institutionalised as part of social life and practice and therefore impact on education. They throw up both some of the great benefits of modernity but also the great threats it poses. This means learning must be shaped and organised for an improved and democratic social result if we are to engage and overcome the daunting challenges facing an increasingly precarious ecology and a fragile world. The continuous production and incorporation of new and contested knowledge through critical learning into institutional practice is the driving force of modernity (Giddens 1991). It is one of the essential social practices which sustain our lives and should serve the interests of the many and exist for the benefit of society.

# References

Ashwin, P. (2020) *Transforming University Education: A Manifesto*, London: Bloomsbury Academic.

Barnett, R. and Griffin, A. (eds) (1997) *The End of Knowledge in Higher Education*, London: Cassell.

Bauman, Z. (2000) *Liquid Modernity,* Cambridge: Polity Press.

Davies, D. and Nyland, J. (2022) 'A Crisis of Knowledge: Themes for an Engaged University Curriculum' ch 4 in Nyland, J. and Davies, D. (eds) (2022) *Curriculum Challenges for Universities: Agenda for Change*, Singapore: Springer Press.

Dorling, D. (2018) *Peak Inequality: Britain's Ticking Time Bomb*, University of Bristol: Policy Press.

Elfert, M. (2016) 'Revisiting the Faure Report (1972) and the Delors Report (1996): Why was UNESCO's Utopian Vision of Lifelong Learning an 'unfailure'?' ESREA Triennial Conference 2016, Maynooth, Ireland.

Faure, E. (1972) *Learning to be*, report, Paris: UNESCO; see also Elfert, M. (2015) *UNESCO, the Faure Report, the Delors Report and the Political Utopia of Lifelong Learning*, European Journal of Education, Research, Development and Policy, Vol 50 No 1 March 2015.

Field, J. (2001) 'Lifelong Education', *International Journal of Lifelong Education*, 20 (1-2), 3-15.

Field, J. (2004a) *Lifelong Learning and the New Educational Order*, Stoke-on- Trent: Trentham Books.

Field, J. (2004b) *Lifelong Learning and Cultural Change: A European Perspective,* conference on Lifelong Learning and New Learning Culture, National Chung-Cheng University, Taiwan, 1-2 October 2004.

Field, J. (2013) 'Adult education as a social movement: inspiring change or fading dream?', *Adults Learning*, Summer 2013.

Fieldhouse, R. and Associates (1996*) A History of Modern British Adult Education,* Leicester: NIACE.

Freire, P. (1972) *Pedagogy of the Oppressed*, Harmondsworth: Penguin.

Gibson, R. (1986) *Critical Theory and Education*, London: Hodder and Stoughton.

Giddens, A. (1991) *Modernity and Self-Identity: Self and Society in the Late Modern Age*, Cambridge: Polity Press.

Green, F. and Kynaston, D. (2019) *Engines of Privilege: Britain's Private School Problem*, London: Bloomsbury Publishing.

Griffin, A. (1997) 'Knowledge under Attack: Consumption, Diversity and the Need for Values' Introduction, in Barnett, R. and Griffin, A. (eds) (1997) *The End of Knowledge in Higher Education*, London: Cassell.

Griffin, C. (1983) *Curriculum Theory in Adult and Lifelong Education*, Beckenham, Kent: Croom Helm.

Habermas, J. (1972) *Knowledge and Human Interests*, London: Beacon Press.

Hall, S. (1983) 'Education in Crisis' Part one: The politics of education' in *Is there anyone here from education* (1983) edited by AnneMarie Wolpe and James Donald, London: Pluto Press.

Harrison, N. ( 2018) 'Patterns of participation in a period of change: social trends in English higher education from 2000 to 2016', ch 4 in Waller, R. et al (eds) (2018) *Higher Education and Social Inequalities: University Admissions, Experiences, and Outcomes*, London and New York: Routledge.

Havergal, C. (2016) Elite universities least likely to hit access goals, *The Times Higher.* (see James, D. (2018) p.242).

James, D. (2018) 'Social class, participation, and the marketised university', in Waller, R. et al (eds) (2018) *Higher Education and Social Inequalities: University Admissions, Experiences, and Outcomes*, UK: Routledge.

Kuhn, T. (1970) *The Structure of Scientific Revolutions*, University of Chicago Press.

Lovett, T. (1983) *Adult Education and Community Action*, London: Croom Helm.

Lyotard, J-F. (1984) *The Postmodern Condition: A Report on Knowledge*, Manchester University Press.

Mezirow, J. (1983) 'A Critical Theory of Adult Learning and Education' in Tight, M. (ed) *Adult Learning and Education*, London: Croom Helm/The Open University.

Noys, B. (2014) *Malign Velocities: Accelerationism and Capitalism*, Winchester UK: Zero Books.

OFFA- Office for Fair Access (2016) *Outcomes of Access Agreement Monitoring for 2014-15,* Bristol: Office for Fair Access.

Picketty, T. (2020) *Capital and Ideology,* Cambridge, Mass/London, England: the Belknap Press of Harvard University Press.

Richmond, W.K. (1974) Foreword- in Husen, T. (1974) *The Learning Society*, London: Methuen & Co.

Roderick, G. and Stephens, M. (eds) (1979) *Higher Education for All,* Lewis, Sussex: The Falmer Press.

Savage, M. et al (2015) *Social Class in the 21st Century,* UK: Pelican.

Scott, P. (1997) 'The Crisis of Knowledge and the Massification of Higher Education', ch 2 in Barnett, R. and Griffin, A. (eds) (1997) *The End of Knowledge in Higher Education*, London: Cassell.

Seidman, S. (1998) *Contested Knowledge: Social Theory in the Postmodern Era,* (2nd ed) Oxford: Blackwell.

Todd, S. (2021) *Snakes & Ladders: The Great British Social Mobility Myth*, London: Chatto & Windus.

Zuboff, S. (2019) *The Age of Surveillance Capitalism: The Fight for a Human Future at the New Frontier of Power,* London: Profile Books.

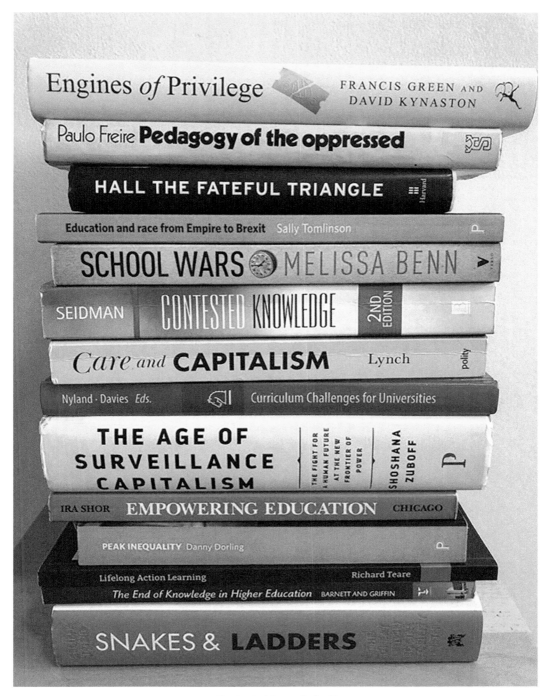

Contested knowledge?

# Chapter 8

# Access and University Engagement: Towards a New Framework

## Future prospects

The Access movement may have been part of a relatively brief period of growth and optimism in modern British education. This book has argued that its significance went beyond the relatively small numbers of adults involved in learning and teaching in the 1970s and 1980s as widening participation and mass higher education took off in Britain. It showed us an alternative way of developing education, firstly for those who had been excluded from higher learning and then more widely for those who struggled for an improved curriculum. Access put the social issues that matter right in the forefront of learning and in doing that raised a series of questions that continue to resonate into the third decade of the 21$^{st}$ century. Access was really an attempt to engage educational institutions and their stakeholders in a different type of learning. As a movement it had an impact right across the various levels and types of educational institutions in Britain and it fed into and contributed to the growth of mass higher education. Since Access for students was primarily concerned with accessing higher level study it had particular meaning for universities. Access raised for universities the possibilities of a different kind of engagement with students themselves, with communities and ultimately for the wider society. It raised the question of what university engagement itself is and might yet be.

There are few who would disagree with the assertion that we need to invest in the public realm and services in order to build a more resilient economy and society, and education must be right at the heart of this. Can the promises made in the past about the need for a more equal and socially just society through educational mobility and meritocracy be redeemed in the future? This is the question that persists across the generations. There is an argument that a new engagement agenda for universities and indeed for all post-school education is required which puts critical thinking and learning and research at the leading edge of change. A new 'ecology of learning' is needed which puts the social purposes and the meaning of community back into the strategic objectives of university development (Brink 2018; Davies 2021; Davies and Nyland 2022 a; Grant 2021).

As educators these issues test our humanity and our democratic engagement in both education and civic society. Education is a vital part of the social capital of a community; it cannot be right to equate it with the notion of making education yield profits from learning. Although the growth of a marketised educational system appeared to insulate universities from the disastrous effects of the longest, deepest and most sustained period of cuts to public services in modern British history, in reality this period became what Toynbee and Walker (2020) call 'The Lost Decade'. Between 2010 and 2020 NHS funding per head fell as never before, public health expenditure was decimated, social care was stripped, school spending per pupil cut by 8% and local councils weakened by cuts of up to 40%. A million public sector jobs in Britain were lost. In the context of the re-emergence of dire and distressing levels of poverty and deprivation and the entrenchment of highly unequal wealth and income inequality, and in learning the lessons of the failure of a market model, a society should surely find the ethical way of doing things. This will surely involve investing in and with communities as well as for financial stability and income generation for the capital and financial markets. It will necessarily involve building social and community capital as well as the professional capital of degrees as key objectives for all higher education. This is the context in which a new view of Access is needed; one which has the capacity and potential to transform the way we think about education and the way we use it to transform our lives for the better.

## An alternative is needed

There is an alternative model to the neoliberal model outlined previously in this book. The shareholders or stakeholders of a university are not simply the university governors or the university managers. The nation itself and the state have an interest since they provide most of the finance, through one means or another and through student loans for fees. The rhetoric of delivering a diverse and regional system with real choice needs to be made a reality so that universities are seen as the custodians of that wealth. A university represents a type of social capital and communitarian wealth, paid for ultimately by the tax payers and the common people, something not widely understood. It is not a business with commercial shareholders taking risks in a market. The purpose of a university is not to generate shareholder value and profits. The other stakeholders are the staff, the students (past, present and future) and the communities that surround and sustain the institution. These are varied and include industry and commerce in all its guises as well as local authorities which unfortunately have been enfeebled and marginalised by the national governments of the last twenty years. The alternative model must be rooted in a financial plan that protects the public realm and what are essentially public services. Higher education was not and is not a private commodity but is a social and public investment. A healthy economy and society depends on having a plurality of social forms and activities. If the United Kingdom is just one player or competitor in a free-for-all global market and our social purposes are driven by financial interests, then the basis for a just and fair society ceases to exist. On the other hand, if the basis of society is shared values and ethics, then market exchange and cost benefit analysis can never become the chief driver in the organisation of social and communal services, including higher education. A better framework and a re-imagined idea of engagement for education is needed.

## Rethinking university engagement in the light of Access

The reality of university life is complex and diverse. Universities are often huge civic and commercial institutions which impact massively on social and economic life. They are far beyond being places where scholars simply search for truth and knowledge and they are ubiquitous. Almost everywhere on the planet young people view university education as the passport to a better life. Universities are foundational to modern economy and culture. Everywhere they claim to be good at research, teaching, learning, knowledge transference and income generation. As Chris Brink (ibid 2018) has argued, they are often very 'good at' something: it is less certain that they are in general 'good for' something. Excellence, for example in research, is not enough if we are to have education which is good for the people.

This argument foregrounds the 'educational function' of universities. This can be contentious because it suggests that if every university wishes to be a 'world-class research centre' then this is a serious distraction from the educational function in which universities can be good for communities, for social solidarity and for social and ecological justice and fairness.

Finding solutions to an appropriate balance in nations which have a 'mixed economy' where market-led solutions enable choice for those with money, and welfare-led provision such as education and health for those without, is difficult. The poor never achieve the best outcomes. In these circumstances university engagement practitioners are searching for the fair and just balance between competing priorities. Individuals, employers and the society and communities in which we all live are all stake holders here but present arrangements do not provide a fair and just balance between the three parties. Players in national governments, managers of universities and the dominant culture of universities are not pre-disposed to simply shifting the balance away from financially advantageous and prestige-based rankings towards a needs-based university whose core educational functions may not yield the most prestigious or financially rewarding activities.

Universities may once have been ivory towers, their cloisters and libraries seen as bastions of knowledge and scholarship safeguarding a culture and values which, though separate from the wider society, were essential to its sense of being 'civilised'. This is no longer the case. In an accelerating capitalistic world (Noys 2014) universities have long ago joined the competition which characterizes the digital era. It is now clear, for example, following the 2019-2022 global Corona Virus pandemic that distance learning is here to stay for everyone. This case was already proven following the success of the Open University in the UK which showed that the teaching function of a university can be achieved to a large extent through distance learning (DL). Similarly the social function of higher education can be partly replicated online. There can be no refusal of the digital realities as we move onwards and these will likewise impact on all the forms of university engagement currently used. However, if by simple definition and logic every university cannot be a world-beating leader, yet aspires to be unique and distinctive in some way, there can be no doubt that all higher education is being shaped by common forces which demand conformism. Resisting these demands for conformity, many of which have at their root the workings of the global obsession with neoliberal market solutions to the world's problems, may be the best way to a richly diverse university sector- one which can respond to an authentically diverse student population rather than one selected, sorted out and differentiated via wealth and social privilege.

Furthermore and hearkening back to the Robbins Report of 1963, if the objective is to help create a society in which all those who can benefit from higher education and who wish it could participate and study the discipline of their choice, then we will need to look beyond top-down actions by universities. More attention is needed on the question of how knowledge and learning is organized and for which purposes a curriculum is devised. Whose curriculum is it and how is it taught? These questions were of course at the heart of some of the issues that the Access movement attended to, many of which had an intensely local and place-based focus in actual existing communities.

No simple and easy answers are available and never have been. However, if we assume that one of the keys to unlocking the power of universities is through the application of critical thinking perhaps we can shift the paradigm towards the educational function in a decisive and progressive way? Frameworks of thinking are just ways of ordering our experiences and our knowledge but good ideas can help change the world. For example, it has become ever more clear that knowledge which is classified as universally valid and true, whether emanating from a theology or from a particular conception of science, must also be subject to the claims of criticality. It must seek to explain its own origins within rational, critical analysis and subject itself to the burdens of proof and scientific skepticism. We can no longer assume that western rationalism and science confers a superior understanding of our environments and lives, simply because its origins were in the European Enlightenment, powerful though such origins were for the development of democratic norms and values. There are, for example, different 'frameworks' of knowledge and understanding such as the notion of 'indigenous knowledge' to which we must give proper attention (Pearson 2009; Davies 2022). These matters are under active consideration and are 'contested', as when Seidman (1998) brilliantly argued that modern social theory must be connected to public intellectual life and its moral and social concerns. However, such attempts to re-formulate our ideas about what constitutes knowledge and a knowledgeable person are not new and certainly need revisiting in every generation (Polanyi 1974). Beyond this we need to renew and reconstruct our public institutions in each generation as the commercial and technical imperatives of modernity are forced upon us. There is always a need to ask if our frameworks and paradigms are still fit for purpose and to test them against reality. The Access movement of the 1970s and 1980s, it has been suggested, was a fulcrum and testbed for new ways of thinking and organising educational opportunity and hence social change from the bottom up- from where learning actually was done and experienced. Communities of practice were made real in many different types of institutions and places across the United Kingdom. The constituent elements of Access practice were always present in the courses themselves, but they were generally untheorized and the use of frameworks may enable us to bring some theoretical understanding to Access itself.

We have seen that Access was a form of education that frequently involved learning and teaching for adult learners within an awareness of the 'wicked issues' that framed people's experience and aspirations, including the lack of opportunities for progression in higher education. Many key social issues such as poverty, deprivation, women's social role and oppressions, unemployment, social displacement, environmental degradation and social justice matters found a place in Access courses of one kind or another. In practice these issues helped shape the curriculum alongside an emphasis on literacy and numeracy needed for higher levels of study. Unfortunately this did not usually persist once students were entered into their higher learning phases where the pervasive growth of neoliberalism served to consolidate an individualistic and competitive ideology at the centre of university policy (Brown 2019; Chun and Feagin 2022).

The Access movement was effectively incorporated and co-apted by the established educational institutions for an agenda of growth and development. The existing institutional HE structure adapted itself to Access and in so doing it ensured that Access was adapted in turn to its requirements. The radical and transformative potential of Access was diminished as mass higher education evolved into a marketised and differentiated hierarchy of universities and colleges. The elite institutions wanted little of Access as a radical approach to learning and the 'mass institutions', that is to say the newer 'municipal' universities and former polytechnics, focused on the need to apply the market disciplines in order to compete on costs and fees. This approach did not allow for the diversity and difference fostered in the Access movement itself. Uniformity and conformism became the norm as institutions competed in the performance league tables which were deemed necessary to protect 'quality' and 'excellence' in the delivery of higher education. The growth of student numbers overall continued as the system expanded and this allowed greater numbers of poorer students and ethnic minorities to attend university. However, participation in higher education continued to be distorted by the impact of previous wealth and privilege. Racial and ethnic minorities succeeded in getting a few of their brightest and most able students selected into elite universities but the overall disparities and inequalities remained in place. The capacity of the elite universities to deliver a socially just outcome was severely limited by their own ideologies justifying their unfair selections of students.

## Neo-liberalising an already elitist system

The Access agenda though successful beyond the wildest dreams of its Victorian forebears had not broken through the carapace of discrimination and injustice that elite university education continues to support into the third decade of the 21$^{st}$ century. The mixed ability principle which had driven the Labour governments of the twentieth century and especially in the 1970s to militate for comprehensive schools (Ball 2002; Benn 2011) had not infiltrated the universities. In spite of the diversity and sheer size of the knowledge economy and the significance of learning and education in modern society, there had been no great meritocratic breakthrough to a more equal society and to a greater system of social justice.

This book has suggested that the fundamental impulse driving Access was one of striving for equity and opportunity by those who had been refused education and the benefits derived from it (Davies and Davies 2021). This was a long historical struggle with many different facets- but it was not a singular or linear narrative even though common 'threads through time' would appear in the story. There can be little doubt that the development of 'human capital' theories help explain the extent and penetration of skilled labour and expertise required in modern capitalism, just as theories of neoliberalism offer us an understanding of how universities have been thought about and managed in the modern era. Neoliberalism usefully highlights how market mechanisms have contributed to the solutions that universities sought when faced with precarious balance sheets. The vocabularies of managerialism and enterprise, narrowly defined, were used uncritically to keep institutions up with the competition in relation to student recruitment and consumer satisfaction. This was the neoliberalisation of higher education where in theory individuals had choices of where they might study and what they might elect to pay for it. The realities were quite different, however, and students were not independent customers paying for their own education. The state was the controlling interest and for most students it controlled the system through a combination of interest and salary repayment. It was no free market. An inefficient capital market always required government intervention to finance the country's student debt and huge subsidies were needed to sustain the production of socially necessary 'vocational' subjects such as medicine, dentistry and engineering. It has been argued that only a minority of neoliberal arguments were ever appropriated by politicians in the United Kingdom anyway and that British governments always viewed universities' primary functions as engines of growth (Freeman 2018). In this scenario government existed to intervene to produce top-down modernisation and to subsidise big business and technology projects.

These were a part of the generic economic and political contexts in which Access programmes and courses were developed, mediated by the particular circumstances of the time. These in turn included the specific cultural and social concerns of the day such as racial and ethnic perceptions of peoples' lives and

203

experiences. The wicked issues of the day ensured that struggles for social justice were often high on the political agenda and education was crucial to many of these. The old frameworks and ways of thinking about education proved inadequate by the 1970s and the dash for growth and the globalisation of economic and social life with all of its disruptions, fostered a new phase which incorporated Access within an expanded institutional hierarchy that itself was profoundly unequal. The 21$^{st}$ century has generated a need for new and radical re-thinking of the frameworks within which to conceptualise and practice learning and teaching. This book has suggested that the theme of critical engagement might be fruitful in exploring new frameworks.

## Frameworks for engaged learning and teaching

Three potential frameworks are suggested initially here as a basis for reflection and exploration. Within these frameworks we can identify points of departure which can direct our thinking to the crucial issues and themes. Frameworks can help us understand and conceptualise our taken-for-granted assumptions. Frameworks are themselves metaphors for the different paradigms that inform knowledge acquisition. The first framework focusses on the dominant capacity of industrial and scientific growth to sustain our social and communal lives. It is often assumed that our western scientific knowledge corresponds to the world out there and to the superiority of western knowledge and in particular to applied science and technology. How else could our western values have been implemented and our standards of life and needs for security be guaranteed? To state that this may be the dominant way of thinking is not to dismiss the fact that it may be contested in all sorts of ways. Nevertheless, western rationalism can surely be said to be exercise a certain hegemony within the advanced industrial nations as globalisation and industrialisation proceeds and places its demands on local and more people-centred communities which may have alternative knowledge systems. This particular framework has dominated the development and expansion of universities world-wide in the last 50 years.

The second framework employs what has been called by a notable indigenous Australian educationalist Noel Pearson, a 'peoplehood' concept (Pearson 2009). It focusses on people, communities and society. We can contrast close-knit units such as family or kinship groups such as tribe or 'mob' with the wider groups which form people's identity such as ethnic or religious affiliation or the universalism of global communities or cosmopolitans (Skrbis and Woodward 2013). These frameworks of understanding can shape our understanding of ourselves and our own history. The importance of personal learning and personal growth and the existence of a 'biographical epistemology' where a lived and personal life can be recognized should not be underestimated. It was the sociologist Anthony Giddens who suggested that the 'self' had become for many people a reflexive and personal project in which individuals 'invested', including through education (Giddens 1991, 2010).

## Frameworks

| Industrial/scientific growth | People-centred/indigenous knowledge systems (IKS) |
|---|---|
| • Knowledge is formal and recorded with limited access to it | • The earth's resources are finite and there are limits to how people can enhance them |
| • Knowledge belongs to those with qualifications | • Those who control resources also control power |
| • Almost all products can be bought and sold in the market | • The needs of the poor and communities are recognised |
| • Sustainability is about ever-increasing growth of economic capacities | • Inclusive and socially just communities are essential to an inclusive global system |
| • Economic and social interests drive progress and development | • Security and identity are vital for families and communities |
| • The earth's physical resources are inexhaustible | • Culture is performed and is vital to communities |
| • Western science and industry will provide ever new possibilities for growth | • Oral traditions are valued |
| • Waste and destruction can be absorbed indefinitely | • Knowledge of the environment is key to producing a livelihood |
| • Consumerist norms rule our desires – poverty is only inadequate growth | • Control over resources is done locally |
| • The liberal market economy can drive growth and living standards | • Economic interests and identities are reconciled |

The third framework (below) represents an attempt to specify the '**foundational**' educational function of the university (Williams 2021). This focusses upon the question of what the university is 'good for' and attempts to scale up the focus from individual and group experience at the 'people-centred' level to how education could contribute to social and economic welfare. Foundational education could address such services as health care, carbon clearance, food production and distribution, urban farming and social housing projects and places where there is a mosaic of incomes which vary according to location, housing type and community orientation. This approach assumes that a university and its communities could support projects at volume which could benefit the engaged stakeholders.

A possible Foundational Educational framework might look something like this:

| A framework for being good for something |
|---|
| • Knowledge must have a social purpose. It must also focus on critical social teaching and those who are yet to speak |
| • The community of learners and the places they inhabit are major strengths for the curriculum. Universities are foundational to local and regional economies; they can invest and directly support a zone of the economy focussed on productive enterprises and social capital |
| • A critical literacy is surely needed for those facing a precarious economic future. A truly democratic participation would be 95%; the 50% rate currently is pathetic |
| • There is no dispensing with the disciplines but creativity is a key to progressive education. Where is the critical curriculum which investigates our social lives? When does creative art, music and literature interact with science to define and expand our future possibilities? |
| • The borders we have erected around faith, ethnicity, race, social class and culture must be recognised and crossed. How can we be vigilant for tolerance whilst expressing a distinctive vision through education? |
| • The ecological precariousness of our planet must now be the object of our critical awareness. The United Nations' Sustainable Development Goals (SDGs) could/should be central to all HE curriculum planning |
| • The ecological crisis is accompanied by a crisis of digital life which is accelerating at exponential speeds. Our lives in the public spaces of the internet are commodities. Information explodes into availability and all emotional and social life can be commercially exploited through an addictive technology |
| • A curriculum has always to be chosen, it cannot evolve spontaneously: whose curriculum is chosen and in whose interests is it selected? |

These frameworks are of course not a concrete 'reality' and do not exist in a specific place or time. They are a device to help us select those features of educational provision we wish to identify as relevant and which we may wish to explore further. Real historical and contemporary universities and colleges will almost certainly have taken elements from more than one framework to construct the lived reality of learning and teaching and all of the associated functions needed to offer an education. In our attempt to understand and explain the Access movement they can help us analyse the meaning and significance of the societies in which we live and how transformative learning and teaching seeks to shape a different future. The argument here is that Access, both past and present, can be better understood therefore through the prisms of these three frameworks. They can offer us in turn *points of departure* to grasp some of the meaning if not definitive accounts of historical and social movements.

## Points of departure: the lessons of Access for a new framework:

## Learning should change futures

Progressive learning has always been about the social purposes of knowledge. The roots of social justice lie in the belief in rational and objective knowledge developed firstly in the European Enlightenment and then within the western scientific tradition. This tradition informs the social and political progress we have made and which benefits those who live in advanced industrial and democratic societies. Whatever the oppressive and alienating conditions in which people have lived, they have been compelled to struggle for a better life and to control their own existence (Davies and Nyland 2022b). We shall always need history to reveal the actual lived experience of social change and mobility and to reveal the forces of oppression as they have impacted on our lives. The importance of education for both personal and community well-being is demonstrated in the work of thinkers and reformers who have assessed the value of the university as a public educator and the idea of freedom being gained through higher education (Nyland et al 2022). The idea of freedom through education has been tarnished but not defeated and there are those still to speak who will shape the eventual outcome of the struggle for a better life and improved social outcomes through critical and transformative learning.

# Places and communities are vital to learning

In seeking our points of departure in order to better understand Access as a social movement, we need to affirm the part played by *places* in the cultures of learners and, to do this we need to re-imagine the community of learners and recognise its significance within a renewed curriculum. There is always a question of pedagogy where learning is concerned and yet we continue to ignore the positive impact of diverse cultures, students' own concerns with language and identity and the power of affective learning. The role of places and spaces is of great emotional significance and shows the potential that a treasured environment may have on personal and social understanding. This suggests a rich but often ignored resource for a more critical understanding and a new approach to the curriculum. We need to extract the experience of people in specific communities at certain times in the history of their communities, and through social interaction in the classroom and beyond it, create new learning involving objective knowledge and thought and feeling (Shor 1992). What these geographical locations tell us is that passion for the place is a marvelous resource and that we need to harness this so it becomes in turn a passion for learning. The brief example taken earlier in this chapter was that of indigenous knowledge (Davies ibid 2022) but it represents only a single instance of a more general phenomenon. The implication is clear – we need to re-define the subject matter of what we learn and teach and the ways in which people in communities can become central to learning. The critical appreciation of the layers of reality and feeling, seen for example in many rural communities, yet so often ignored, can be viewed as an example of an alternative resource to the long encounter with conventional, organised and structured knowledge which is on offer in conventional learning (Pearson ibid 2009). The social authority and constraints which accompany conventional knowledge systems have often been experienced as oppressive and alienating and change in this is on the wider agenda for change in education.

# Really useful knowledge of the wicked issues

The really useful knowledge of one generation can serve as a guide to later generations but it must be re-constructed always in the light of current challenges. The knowledge a society possesses is encoded in its culture and when it is used to select a minority for preference and privilege in life and work it becomes a negative and conservative force, not for good but for ill. Knowledge in a culture should be a process of inquiry not an affirmation of unequal and exploitative oppression, even if legitimated by false notions of meritocracy and the myths of social mobility (Wooldridge 2021; Todd 2021). This is why each generation finds itself in struggle to question the received wisdom of its elders and to find the 'really useful knowledge' its own generation needs. In the 1960s and 1970s, for example, many young people, including the campus activists, assumed they were part of an upward trajectory towards greater freedom, liberty and opportunity but experience showed that the boundaries of possibility could be re-drawn and diminished. The current generation of graduates faces a future of precarious work, low public investment in social services, a devalued and privatised degree factory system which forces huge debts on many, a housing market out of the reach of many ordinary people and the persistence of poverty and social exclusion on a truly disturbing scale. If the earlier knowledges thought to be part of a continuing liberation were partly an illusion, they at least ensured a rising participation rate and a general raising of the educational level of the people. This was secured at least partially through education. The struggles of young people and students also prepared the way for a greater consciousness of the pressing issues of 21st century whose destructive potential threatens everything.

The failure to recognise and address the wicked issues of the day is more serious than just the sin of omission. Climate change, world poverty and degradation, war and social dislocation on an unimaginable scale and environmental destruction are the great evils of the time. They are the existential issues which will make or break our way of life and they impact the whole globe and all who live on it. Our handling of these things will determine the future of our planet and species. Every individual has a stake in this matter and it transcends the burning issues of the day such as inequality, race, ethnicity, faith and injustice. Whilst we cannot and should not invite people to consider deep suffering and deprivation as a learning opportunity, these serious issues should be at the very heart of our learning and be the basis of a critical literacy relevant to all learners. These matters are surely relevant to the question of – what are universities good for? (Brink 2018; Ashwin 2020).

What dominates our conventional learning and schooling, however, is the deficit model of education. Children and students are to be filled with facts and 'knowledge' which is encoded in the official textbooks. Knowledge is bestowed from above rather than being created in interaction and dialogue; we inherit and continue to reproduce therefore a divisive culture which abandons critical literacy in favour of subject specialisms and a pre-formed and often constricted curriculum. Although we cannot abolish the academic disciplines which retain their power we have discovered that a critical and universal literacy is required to empower those whose access to knowledge has been restricted and who have been denied as a result historical and social justice (Hall 1983).

What is needed is something that resembles a critical community-based learning culture which investigates and supports the communities in which educators actually live and work. What is implied here is in fact learning beyond the classroom where the problems and challenges facing communities become the source and inspiration for learning. Instead what we have seen grow and expand in recent decades in the United Kingdom is a political climate which has seen regressive budget cuts for education and social welfare and more bureaucratic, less egalitarian and less experimental educational policy. The progressive type of participatory research and development done with community participation shows what community action could achieve with long term commitment and engagement with a progressive educational vision (Teare 2018). Financial austerity and authoritarian control from the centralised top- down managerial models of university life can only signal the demise of open education and mass participation designed for widening participation and achievement.

## Creativity as a source of knowledge

Our sources of knowledge are limited by the academic and school-based disciplines which dominate our learning. Creativity is needed which breaks out of the artificial constraints of the past. Language and literature, for example, are key sources of social knowledge which offer us an alternative way of seeing. Literature, for example, is a way of understanding reality which is distinctive; it liberates the imagination and can give us insights and pleasures available nowhere else. Literature is not to be seen as a justification of the contemporary world, though some of it may do precisely that. Through its emotional and affective impact literature along with the arts and humanities can change the way we think and act. When it does this it is part of the critical paradigm of social thinking because it reflects the real world of history, of how humans have created their own societies and their own nature. Imaginative literature allows us to ask whether the story or text has *moved* the reader to think and act beyond what is already given and experienced. Literature and art appeal to feelings and this is also a matter of social thinking which could enhance both more individualized and collective creative approaches to education. Creative thinking and creative education can teach us fresh ways of asking perhaps the most fundamental question, *what is education for*? (Robinson 2016).

Access and creativity: the arts can change the way we think, learn and act.

# The value of crossing borders

Our points of departure for rethinking our approach to education should consider the borders we erect around racial, ethnic, faith and cultural matters. These must surely be recognized and crossed so that a more tolerant and genuinely multicultural life becomes possible for all. Oppressive and intolerant laws must be contested and reversed. We must be militant for freedoms and democracy. The significance of language and culture, often hidden beneath a horizon of indifference or ignorance can never be over-estimated. Where ethnic, linguistic and national identities are played out in the inheritance of the imperialistic and nationalistic states and ideologies there must be challenges and alternatives proposed. Where we are not vigilant for tolerance we are exposed to regressive values which can easily become oppressive (Malik 2023).

# The ecology of learning

The discovery and recognition in practice of the laws of nature and of the ecological precariousness of our planet must be the object of our critical awareness and thus of our education. This awareness of the ecology of learning is not restricted to the geographical and physical environment, though it is connected to it (Barnett 2017; Davies and Nyland 2022 (a) ibid). Ecological life includes also the ways in which we live our lives in a mass culture of consumption and the acceleration of everything including our 'attentionality' (Crawford 2015). Life is lived at speed – fast cars, fast food, fast music and instant gratification and delivery of what we want if we can pay for it now. Everything is speeded up and our perception of the environment is changed as we are bombarded with advertisements in every possible shape and form and size and every public and private space becomes a venue for the sale of something. The mass data harvested in its millions and trillions of clicks per minute across the whole world harvested by the monopoly digital conglomerates multiplies exponentially. Information explodes into availability across the internet. High levels of stimulation are of course intrinsic to high levels of consumption in our mass culture. The lessons to be learned, often in settings that are beyond the classroom, are that it is possible to decelerate so that complex social and emotional processes can be identified in the places we live and work.

More participation and a negotiated curriculum which focusses on the key issues of the time plus a decelerated learning and teaching (a pedagogy for dialogue) would provide us with better tools to fashion our future. It would perhaps help learners to develop a critical commentary on public life and reality, because the systems of mass communication we have currently leave many of them immobilised, unable to understand the causes of their confusion and alienation and unable to act on them. For young people in particular this is important since they are the future and they have the most to gain or lose.

## The importance of sustainable development

Climate change, a loss of trust in institutions, the growth of public and private anxiety and the failure of economies devoted to a narrow focus on growth, regardless of its true cost, are the challenges facing us in the third decade of the 21ˢᵗ century. What cannot be easily denied is the fact that a great transformation is needed if we are to avoid climate change and ecological catastrophe on a truly global scale. The United Nations sustainable development goals shown below were adopted by world leaders in 2015 and are key parts of what we must all learn to secure a just and viable future.

The points of departure outlined above address some of the themes and concerns developed by the Access movement and critical thinkers and teachers of earlier generations who sought to expand the horizons of their students whilst literally opening the doors of their institutions to people who had been unjustly excluded. Without necessarily knowing it, they were developing *frameworks* within which a more critical and transformative education could be conceived.

# References

Ashwin, P. (2020) *Transforming University Education: A Manifesto*, London: Bloomsbury Academic.

Ball, S.J. (2002) *Class Strategies and the Education Market: The Middle Classes and Social Advantage*, London: Routledge.

Barnett, R. (2017) *The Ecological University: A Feasible Utopia*, London: Routledge.

Benn, M. (2011) *School Wars: The Battle for Britain's Education*, London/New York: Verso.

Brink, C. (2018) *The Soul of a University: Why excellence is not enough*, Bristol: University of Bristol.

Brown, W. (2019) *In the Ruins of Neoliberalism: The Rise of Antidemocratic Politics in the West*, New York and Chichester West Sussex: Columbia University Press.

Chun, E. B. and Feagin, J.R. (2022) *Who Killed Higher Education?: Maintaining White Dominance in a Desegregating Era*, New York and London: Routledge.

Crawford, M. (2015) *The World Beyond Your Head: How to Flourish in an Age of Distraction*, UK: Viking/Penguin.

Davies, D. (2021) 'Towards an ecology of learning' ch 9 in Davies, D. and Davies, E. (2021) *A Fair Go: Learning in Critical Times and Places*, UK: Amazon.

Davies, D. (2022) 'Indigenous Knowledge in Australia: Imagining a Different Society', ch 8 in Nyland, J. and Davies, D. (2022) *Curriculum Challenges for Universities: Agenda for Change*, Singapore: Springer Press.

Davies, D. and Davies, E. (2021) 'The Working Class Goes to College', ch 1 in *A Fair Go: Learning in Critical Times and Places* (2021) UK: Amazon.

Davies, D. and Nyland, J. (2022 a) 'Ways of Knowing: Towards an Ecology of Learning and Community' ch 10 in Nyland, J. and Davies, D. (eds) (2022) *Curriculum Challenges for Universities: Agenda for Change,* Singapore: Springer Press.

Davies, D. and Nyland, J. (2022 b) 'Freedom Through Education: A Promise Postponed', ch 5, and 'Academic and Scholarly Freedom: Towards a 'Disputing' University with Critically Engaged Students', ch 6 in Nyland, J. and Davies, D. (2022) *Curriculum Challenges for Universities: Agenda for Change*, Singapore: Springer Press.

Freeman, J. (2018) 'The not-so-neoliberal university' in *Renewal: A journal of social democracy,* Vol 26 no 2, 2018. UK: Lawrence and Wishart.

Giddens, A. (1991 and 2010) *Modernity and Self-Identity: Self and Society in the Late Modern Age,* Cambridge: Polity Press.

Grant, J. (2021) *The New Power University: The social purpose of higher education in the 21st century*, Harlow, England: Pearson.

Hall, S. (1983) 'Education in Crisis' ch 1 in Wolpe, AnnMarie and Donald, J. (eds) (1983) *Is there anyone here from education?* London: Pluto Press.

Malik, K. (2023) *Not So Black and White: A History of Race from White Supremacy to Identity Politics*, UK: Hurst & Co Ltd.

Noys, B. (2014) *Malign Velocities: Accelerationism and Capitalism,* Winchester, UK/Washington, USA: Zero Books.

Nyland, J., Davies, D. and Davies, E. (2022) 'The University as a Public Educator: Learning and Teaching for Engagement' ch 3 in Nyland, J. and Davies, D. (2022) *Curriculum Challenges for Universities: Agenda for Change,* Singapore: Springer Press.

Pearson, N. (2009) *Up From the Mission: Selected Writings,* Melbourne: Black Inc.

Polanyi, M. (1974) *Personal Knowledge: Towards a post-critical philosophy*, Chicago: Chicago University Press.

Robinson, K. (2016) *Creative Schools*, UK: Penguin Books.

Seidman, S. (1998) (2nd ed) *Contested Knowledge: Social Theory in the Postmodern Era,* Oxford: Blackwell.

Shor, I. (1992) *Empowering Education*, University of Chicago Press.

Skrbis, Z. and Woodward, M. (2013) *Cosmopolitanism: Uses of the Idea*, London: Sage Publications Ltd.

Teare, R. (2018) *Lifelong Action Learning: A journey of discovery and celebration at work and in the community,* Amazon Kindle pub.

Todd, S. (2021) *Snakes and Ladders: The Great British Social Mobility Myth*, London: Chatto & Windus.

Toynbee, P. and Walker, D. (2020*) The Lost Decade 2010-2020 and What Lies Ahead for Britain,* London: Guardian Books.

Williams, K. (2021) 'How and why the idea of the foundational economy is radical' in *Renewal: A journal of social democracy,* Vol 29 no 2, 2021. UK: Lawrence and Wishart.

Wooldridge, A. (2021) *The Aristocracy of Talent: How Meritocracy Made the Modern World*, UK: Allen Lane/Penguin.

A UNIVERSITY LECTURE, EARLY FIFTEENTH CENTURY
BRIT. MUS. MS. ROYAL 17 E. III. f. 209

'…it has often been asserted that by Wykeham's poor and needy scholars was meant poor children of the working classes or the gutter poor. This is quite untenable. The labouring classes were then serfs… passing on the sale of an estate to the purchasers….It was customary to fine, and fine heavily, those villeins or natives who sent their sons to school without leave from the lord…

the 'poor and needy ' scholars were scions from the first of the noble classes and the country gentry, relations of judges and civil servants and well-to-do people; and the labouring classes were expressly made ineligible by the proviso that no villein *nativus* or illegitimate was to be admitted'. ( A.F. Leach 'The Schools of Medieval England' 1916)

# Chapter 9

# Educating the Masses:
# Privileging the Elites

## From elites to a mass system

Institutions committed to Access were, as we have seen, more various, more complex and more resistant to classification than might be imagined. The relevance of both a long history of adult learning and contemporary struggles for access to education which preceded and contributed to the Access movement should not be denied. There can be little doubt though that the modern breakthrough to Britain's version of mass higher education, and by implication the opportunities for Access, came initially through the Robbins Report in 1963. Lionel Robbins, an LSE academic and notable authority on social policy research inaugurated Great Britain's version of mass participation. His report made clear the need for a larger and fairer system of access in general to higher education. Mass participation meant *widening* participation as assumptions were made that the traditional class divisions and inequalities could be modified and ameliorated through expanding educational opportunities in higher education. Robbins though did not specifically address the complexities of race, ethnicity and gender; issues that would play a far greater role in the 21st century.

In 1963 there were 118,400 university students, including postgraduates whilst in 1980 it had risen to 560,000 (Barr 2014). By 2010 there were over 2 million enrolled. In 2022 it was reported that 667,000 applicants had applied for undergraduate entry to British universities (Guardian (a) 2022). The total number of higher education students in Britain in 2021 was 2,912,380, 57 per cent of whom were female (HESA 2022). Such a staggering growth of learning activity within a working lifetime had implications for many aspects of life and was not confined to education alone. An educational transition which was concurrently a social transition was underway which has by no means run its full course.

Following a notable contribution to the critical analysis of higher education knowledge (Barnett and Griffin 1997), this book has tried to raise the issue of whose knowledge was involved in this transition and whether it brought about epistemological uncertainty and a crisis of higher education knowledge? At the end of the 20th century there certainly appeared to be an expanding universe of knowledge, especially as the technologies of communication widened. Mass participation brought with it, however, only a certain kind of access, and it came with caveats. There was to be no universal definition of a 'university education', but rather a differentiated hierarchy of universities and colleges was created where some degrees were of more value than others. Following government policies driven themselves by ideological commitments to neoliberal economic theories, market forces were to shape higher education as students became customers and the state became increasingly engaged in defining the purposes of education (Barnett 1997). The league tables of university 'quality' came to represent performativity, displacing for many the beliefs that should underpin a university such as reason, knowledge, progress and enlightenment for the public good and for improved outcomes for the marginalised and disadvantaged. This book suggests that these are the core elements of a universal curriculum that the Access movement in microcosm tried to emulate in its attempt to provide an alternative for the educationally dispossessed. Access was a human project and not a social policy or economic intervention in the labour market. Market forces and the needs of the labour market hardly explained the critical and potentially oppositional quality of the curriculum content of Access courses or the characteristics of the students themselves which were very different from classical school leavers about to become undergraduates.

Robbins had stated that all applicants with appropriate qualifications should have places (Robbins 1963: 265) and this statement illuminated what was common knowledge: university education had been and remained restricted to the economically and social advantaged classes in Britain. In 1963 only some 3 per cent of the children of manual, semi-skilled and skilled workers went on to any form of full-time higher and further education and only one girl in a hundred would go to university. The fifty-odd years since Robbins saw a complete transformation in the size and shape and meaning of higher education; a movement that went far beyond the boundaries of Britain (Cantwell et al 2018). The model for the development of a mass higher education system in the United Kingdom was, however, far from that envisaged by Robbins. The university model as it had developed up to the 1960s did indeed expand with new universities constructed on green field sites and the creation of universities from existing advanced technology colleges. But the growth of the public sector polytechnics by the 1980s saw the majority of higher education students located in the new sector (Fowler and Wyke 1993). The creation of the polytechnics was a vital stage in the creation of a mass higher education system in Britain. This was the wider context in which Access developed its distinctive contribution to the struggle for educational equity and opportunity.

Mass higher education becomes 'universal' according to David Watson (2014: 34) when participation rates rise above 50 per cent and as he noted, there was a strong sense of civilisation being abandoned when that occurred. In 2013 the UK rate was stuck at 49 per cent but Scotland had reached 55 per cent and across the UK female participation was ten points higher than for males. After 1995 and up to 2013 a majority of students had not been on full-time first degrees and the UK had become for a time a ... 'lifelong learning friendly system' with more than half of the then current registrations on other modes and levels of study than the full-time undergraduate degree ( Watson ibid: 37). However, as the decade progressed the numbers of part-time students who were mature, that is over 20 years old on entry, fell and part-time undergraduates fell by 40 per cent (Watson ibid: 47).

Robbins had argued for expansion from the principle of equality of opportunity- not on the basis of equality of outcomes. This was the view that persisted throughout the expansion period and was compatible with the ideology of meritocracy which itself favoured the elites of British society. It is clear that the middle classes benefitted most from the Robbins era growth and that a more egalitarian society did not result. As inequality of income increased inequality in higher education tracked it (Barr ibid: 72). Robbins certainly initiated growth and change in higher education itself and may have encouraged the school system to respond to what was perceived to be an opening up of opportunities for university study. What was not conceived nor intended by Robbins and the academy in general was the possibility of transformations in social justice and equality through the widening of access to universities. The purposes of higher education itself were not being considered for fundamental revision.

Throughout the period following Robbins there was no single 'big system' of higher education in Great Britain and no consistent policy or principles were laid out for its development. Wild lurches between expansion and contraction took place; radical changes of mind about the institutional status of universities occurred; debate took place on what a university is; and moral panics over dumbing down were aired in the public media. No single direction could be detected where ideas of 'excellence' and being 'world class' contradicted the social purposes and even the economic goals being set by national and regional strategies for education. By the time of the new century it was clear that the differences of mission between vastly different types of institutions had been reduced as each one conformed to the government's requirement of competitive and supposedly free-market driven funding. No such free market in university places emerged and central government control over funding and maximum fee levels remained. A managed market and a partially privatised student loans scheme was invented to ensure universities received student tuition fees. A majority of undergraduates went into serious levels of debt for their tuition, repaid through tax deductions once they had started work. Hierarchies of selectivity, research production and funding emerged as diversity diminished. Almost all universities adopted the highest levels of fees they could charge, whilst offering discounts to the different categories of students they wanted to attract. There was now less clarity or agreement on what an authentic university education was across such a large number of higher education providers. There was epistemological uncertainty as Barnett (1997 ibid) put it about the forms and types of knowledge needed in such changing and uncertain times. As inequalities in the wider society were increasing they were mirrored by those between universities in an unjustifiable hierarchy of elite institutions. The hierarchies were demonstrated by performance in league tables which, not surprisingly, reflected existing and historical differences and inequalities in wealth and cultural capital accumulated by the so-called elite institutions who came out on top in the competition.

## Unequal discourses

The hierarchy was unjustifiable because new forms of inequality and unfairness were constructed with overt collusion by the very institutions which were supposedly dedicated to providing opportunities and wider participation to those previously excluded. Widening participation certainly was happening on a massive scale over the period under review but it was simultaneously creating opportunities to be unequal. Widening participation became part of the dominant discourse along with 'equal opportunities' and the merits of meritocratic achievement within markets for education. Some discourses are, however, saturated with power, as Barnett reminds us (Barnett ibid: 169) and come loaded, as it were, with intentions and material and ideological interests that are not always clear and transparent. The education consumer had in fact little power in the market and state funding of further and higher education always comes with a political agenda. For the political interests governing Britain that agenda did not include a significant challenge to the fundamentally unequal state of British economy, society and culture. The dominant discourse was that reforms and modifications might be achieved through the creation of more consumer choice and by climbing the meritocratic ladder of opportunity through education, which was also to be thought of as a market where one might purchase or invest in one's future.

Markets were also sites of power where existing wealth and inequalities could be reproduced and could be legitimated. A rising tide floats all boats and the trickle down of wealth from the very rich to the poor and less wealthy benefits everybody were amongst arguments used to justify the reality of rising inequality. The un-achieving and poorer sections of the working class were encouraged to raise their aspirations as the way to fully participate in the modern consumer society. Through education their children might aspire to the glittering prizes by climbing the ladder of opportunity. Social mobility was in fact in decline and inequality was growing between the 1990s and the 2010s, whilst the richest 5 per cent of people in Britain grew richer (Todd 2021: 300). The rhetoric of social mobility and equal opportunity, including that of widening participation, was used to justify the unequal state of the nation and its unequal wealth and access to opportunities. Excellence, which was the result of merit, would be rewarded. The social mobility industry was created whose job was to sell the idea that upward mobility was available to everyone. The newly emerging hierarchies of universities and schools within the marketised yet managed system of education adopted much of the same rhetoric of equal opportunities *and* the discourse of excellence and social mobility. The reality was, however, opportunities to be *more unequal* became embedded in the widened and extended higher education system.

## Mass participation in the knowledge economy: turning workers into students

Following Robbins, the growth and impact of mass higher education in British society (and on a global scale) cannot be denied. The education boom of the 1960s was geared to a low literacy population and led to the growth of second chance education along with an expansion of secondary schooling and universities. By the 1970s there was talk of 'education permanente' (Faure 1972), and this became in English terms 'lifelong learning' viewed as an affirmative stage of development which encouraged the emergence of Access courses and programmes. By the end of the century a mass higher education system had evolved along with an expanded further education sector. There was a coming together of the enrolment of an increasingly diverse cohort of students in universities and colleges with efforts by government to diminish public funding for public higher education. All of this was accompanied by an ideological assumption; that Britain's educational system was capable of delivering democratic goals including that of equality of access, and greater educational opportunity. Equal opportunities were taken as proxy for actual achievements and substantive and structural inequalities remained and took new forms as new generations emerged. The need for equity and access was often affirmed but it came in the guise of individual self-development and advancement through meritocracy. The narrow focus of a curriculum in support of free market capitalism and neoliberal conservative goals and values was predominant in the governance of further and higher education. However, many teachers and learners thought differently and at the chalk face in many schools and adult centres, in the burgeoning information technology centres, in many community centres where learning was encouraged and in further education colleges and universities, potential alternatives and challenges were available (Ball 2015). This was the seed bed for the growth of the Access movement.

The dominant thinking of policy developers emphasised the importance of education for the economy of the country and human capital theory was widely used to explain the need for investment in people and work. The primary qualifications such as the undergraduate degree became 'commodities' for which it was thought an appropriate market could be organised based on consumer choice and capacity to pay (if necessary for the majority by a government-backed loan). This was not just a world built for young people. There were over 1.5 million undergraduates in the English universities and colleges in 2019 and over 30 per cent of them were mature students. Almost all postgraduate students were mature, some 480,000 or 99.2 per cent of the total. In 2021 mature applicants from the UK to universities had risen by 34 per cent to 93,390. Online teaching and learning had been catalysed by the Covid 19 pandemic (Nyland and Davies 2022) and part-time entrant numbers to the Open University had stopped falling (OfS 2021). Mass higher education and the knowledge economy was the reality and destiny for many, as an evolving labour market adapted to a changing economy where low-skilled teenage labour was no longer allowed or required. Following the decade-long increase in the proportion of school leavers opting for higher education in Britain, some 320,000 sixth formers applied for university places in 2022, more than 50,000 more than at the same stage in 2019 (Guardian (b) 2022). This was the learning society in terms of its volume numbers- a burgeoning sector of the labour market where over 50 per cent of each school leaving cohort intended to go to university. Fewer resources were devoted to the other 50 per cent of the school population, some of whom went on to do apprenticeships or into the labour market which was low paid and becoming ever more precarious for unqualified people.

This picture confirms an optimistic view that British universities offer a promise of higher education to a mass population. Furthermore, individuals at any age have a chance to learn and to open up new opportunities for themselves. For mature students, over the age of 21, university or college can be a genuine second chance to learn. Higher education is now a major industry driving the knowledge economy forward and contributing immensely to national wealth and well-being. Research and development in almost every major field of enterprise is powered by universities. The universities pension scheme is amongst the largest in the UK. For many people higher education represents the most tangible and viable route for social mobility and self-improvement.

There is a mindset that suggests the sheer extent of higher education and especially its centrality to the futures of a majority of young people in society, means we have reached a point of sufficiency. There is a university place for each person who wants one if s/he is suitably qualified and if they are sufficiently motivated and work hard. Even those who have failed or been failed by the conventional schooling system can find Access courses and Foundation courses at local universities which offer a second chance to succeed. The ladders of opportunity and mobility are there to be climbed and it could be argued the promise of Robbins has been delivered. Governments now subscribe to the idea that they have a responsibility to improve opportunity and choice for students of all ages and that there is a particular remit... 'to ensure access, success and progression for underrepresented and disadvantaged groups of students' (OfS ibid). The pioneers of Access and adult learning would surely have celebrated such evidence of progress towards a better social result through learning. Has the Access agenda then been successfully delivered now that study opportunities exist for the many? Were prospects and lives transformed by the events and processes described in this book? Can we see the lineaments of a transformation in educational and life opportunities? Has the existence of a university education for masses of people helped produce both a theory of change and the actual changes needed to bring about a fairer and more socially just and equitable society? These are the questions that still underpin why we debate and argue about the purposes and meanings of university education. These are some of the questions that have for generations informed the search for knowledge of how education and learning can both conserve and transform our culture, apparently at the same time (Bourdieu and Passeron 1990; Barnett 2017) and how educational and social capital are key to understanding how social reproduction and transition occurs (Bourdieu 1993).

# Access and widening participation as social transformation?

The answer to the question of whether the growth of access and widening participation education was transformational must be equivocal since a contradiction sits at the heart of the British education system, and has specific resonance for England. And it is this: mass higher education like mass schooling has produced a stratified and highly unequal system. Whereas by the 1970s most secondary schools had switched from a selective system to a comprehensive one, no such attempt was made with universities. The mixed-ability principle was never adopted by higher education and what was an elitist system evolved into a mass system, but one that is highly stratified. The glittering prize is a place in a handful of elite universities but is only available for a selected minority. The majority are asked to be satisfied with second or third place in the hierarchy of institutions. Though schools policy claimed to seek a less divided and fairer society in which people from different class and ethnic backgrounds were expected to mix, as the higher education sector expanded the elite universities clung to their hierarchies and unjust selection methods. These methods were effectively a form of social exclusion, often in the guise of academic selection, in which the more affluent populations took up a disproportionate share of places. Universities, especially elite ones were in the business of 'sorting them out' – that is to say, choosing those who would be admitted and those who would be rejected. Those who were successful had social class origins and backgrounds which correlated highly with the possession of family wealth and higher incomes. Private schools and selective state-supported grammar schools had a disproportionately large share of the places at elite universities. This is hardly surprising since the misnamed 'public schools' and private schools spend far in excess per pupil than state schools and some have links with Oxbridge going back centuries. In almost every way imaginable these schools have resources and forms of social, cultural and professional capital to out-compete comparatively poorly funded state schools. In 2022 the British Chancellor of the Exchequer and later Prime Minister Rishi Sunak donated £100,000 himself to his old public school, Winchester College. Even though some state sixth form providers have had striking successes, there is no level playing field in this game and this has hardly changed in the last century. Notwithstanding the growth of state school pupils entering the elite universities there are only a handful of underprivileged teenagers getting their hands on one of these golden tickets (Guardian (c) 2022).

The fact that comprehensive schooling had been established across the United Kingdom by the 1970s should not lead us to believe that this was an egalitarian system. Leaving aside that most of the children of the rich and powerful do not attend state schools, the state education system maintained a formal system of selective secondary schooling that had negative effects that reached further than the number of such schools might have suggested. They were in a minority but the doctrine of 'parental choice' ensured that all schools existed in a market- driven hierarchy in which the least desirable children from the least desirable backgrounds and communities were concentrated in the least desirable schools. Children from low income neighbourhoods tended to go to those local schools located in the low income estates and suburbs. The reverse was true for the middle classes and the affluent populations who managed to get their children into the higher status schools with better academic outcomes. The English national obsession with status and wealth hierarchies shaped and structured an hierarchical education system from top to bottom (Todd 2021). The prosperous elites were allowed to use schooling and higher education to promote inequality by effectively monopolising the selective routes to learning and higher education which were themselves part of the divisive class and elite-based social system. A nominally democratic system, subjected to market conditions and the illusory ideologies of *freedom of choice*, undermined the sense of national cohesion that an authentic, universal schooling and higher education might have brought about. The evidence seems to suggest that the elite system of hierarchies of schools and universities subverts the goals of critical thinking and progressive social action which we need to sustain a pluralistic and participatory democracy. Success for some, the relatively few, means lack of success for the many where membership of the elite is by definition always limited. However, the real freedoms which education confers allow us to think differently and to ask for success for the many by asking different questions whose answers can equip us with comprehensive literacy and critical thinking skills needed for the challenge of change facing us (Davies 2022; Nyland and Davies 2022).

## University expansion and widening participation- who benefited?

In the early years of the 21st century there was a consensus that university expansion was unquestionably a benefit for individuals and for the wider civic society. Governments of all persuasions sought to remove caps on higher education enrolments. There were specific and targeted interventions to increase participation in which it was assumed that these would capture other aspects of deprivation and exclusion. There was, however, no generic assumption that higher education was the solution to all social ills. By the third decade some of the assumptions of consensus were being questioned by conservative politicians in particular and a growing feeling could be discerned that some students should not be at university at all. A growing uncertainty was brought to bear against the belief that widening participation taps a resource of talent and ability and allows those who would not have otherwise have considered university as a route out of deprivation. Much of the argument revolved around who 'benefits' when some graduates in relatively low status subjects from low ranking universities entered the labour market and were unable to secure well paid jobs. Some of the debate centred on the idea of a 'good university' and education as a scarce commodity. The approach of the third decade of the century saw debate emerge yet again about the need to limit and cap university courses and to drive demand towards vocational training as an alternative (Augur 2019). There was debate and concern about the measurement of educational quality and elitist conservative policy makers focussed on the unproven assertion that 'more means worse' and pointed to the creation of new types of degrees and new subjects , most famously media studies in the newer universities, which received great disparagement. That the quality of degree programmes varies within a single institution was ignored (Ashwin 2020). The opponents of elitism argued the case that 'more means different' but what was less enthusiastically endorsed was the reality that the mass system had evolved into a highly differentiated and stratified set of hierarchies which embodied wholesale inequalities. A degree from the higher elite universities had in general terms far greater value and currency than one from a much lower ranked institution. All degrees, though notionally subject to the same quality control and procedures, were not the same. The place from which you received your degree mattered more than the objective content or quality of the qualification.

The reality behind these sentiments is that British working class children and teenagers have been offered second-best routes to education and training for over a century. And who then wants to be second best in life? In the era of mass higher education the routes to university and professional qualifications have been skewed to privilege those with private education and/or access to highly selective state schools. It is true that working class pupils have been increasing in numbers at university and indeed some middle class pupils undertake apprenticeships. However, in the real world the division between the academic and the practical falls between the different social classes where background and wealth shape experience and outcomes. An apprenticeship is unfortunately the second class prize in the lottery of life and opportunity (Hutton 2022). The quality and standards of what is offered rarely matches that of an academic education. Vocational education spending was significantly reduced in real terms in the ten years up to 2022, thereby limiting choice for working class young people. Despite the introduction of a levy on employers, apprenticeships for those under 25 years of age fell steadily. The demand-led nature of university admissions was retained but with government determined to ensure graduates pay more of the debt they incur through higher taxation. The effects of this seem to have been designed to discourage students with lower qualifications from applying to university. This in the light of what we know is the case –that secondary level attainment, student outcomes and choice all interact with social disadvantage and can further limit the opportunities in higher education for the socially deprived groups in our society.

The relation between the academic university system and the vocational further education system is highly unequal in terms both of finance and status and continues to underscore the need for fair access and participation in learning. Underpinning this concern lies a long history of debate and scholarship on the need for lifelong learning which takes us far beyond the single-minded concern with training for vocations or skill, important though they are. This focus on the need for learning throughout life, and as a basis for a good life and a life well-lived, can be said to be one of the foundation stones of the Access movement as well as being an important part of the subject matter of this book (Smith 1996, 2001; Davies 2021). The progressive version of lifelong learning was an underpinning of Access but was not universally shared across the general scope and reach of widening participation policy and practice, much of which was concerned with the vocational outcomes of higher and further education.

## Mature students as a proxy for Access

If the promise made to younger people of success through higher education for all has proved to be a mixed blessing, if not a false prospectus, do the achievements of the Access movement enable mature people to acquire new skills and open up new opportunities? The decision to go into higher education is often a more challenging one for them to make, and the consequences of it can be greater than those for young students. Mature students, defined as those who enter HE at the age of 21 or over, are still often overlooked. In 2018-19 there were 478,000 mature students studying at undergraduate level at English higher education providers (30.2 per cent of the total number of undergraduates) but after 2010-11 the number of UK domiciled undergraduate mature students up to 2021 declined by nearly 20 per cent, a reduction of some 47,000 students (OfS ibid: 2).

Many of the same social and economic issues that bedevilled earlier Access students still remain and they still have different motivations and needs from young students. They are less likely to live on campus, more likely to own their own home and more likely to commute. More than twice as many mature students (26.6 per cent) live in the most deprived areas of the country as in the least deprived 13.1

per cent (OfS ibid). Overcoming deprivation is still a vital element for the learning of many adults. Over the first two decades of the 21$^{st}$ century the number of mature students entering higher education dropped significantly. Around a fifth of the adult population in Britain does not have upper secondary education and less than half have university level education. The high levels of illiteracy and innumeracy that persist in British society testify to the continuing failure of education to meet the needs of large numbers of people.

Just what kind of education is thought to be appropriate to this situation where large numbers of mature students are in the conventional higher education system but where part-time opportunities and community-based provision have dramatically declined? The official and policy focus is on utilitarian and work-related skills, including new skills that can be useful to the national economy, filling gaps in sectors such as those for information and digital technology and in the National Health Service. Among those in prison, entering higher education can reduce re-offending and for some disadvantaged groups such as care-experienced students and adult refugees, higher education can be transformational. Marketing and management and top- up degrees for further education students can all help match employment and skills needs in specific areas (OfS ibid: 3). However, the decline in part-time degree students reflected the reduction of government loans for living costs for students studying for a qualification equivalent to or lower than the one they held. The increase in undergraduate student fees to £9,000 in 2012 had a negative impact on opportunities in universities for those taking care of children and families. Neither can the impact of a decade of 'austerity' after 2010, pay freezes and the growth of job precariousness and insecurity be under-estimated as disincentives for studying in higher education. For many, the reduction of part-time study options meant the loss of their chance to enter higher education at all. In the third decade of the 21$^{st}$ century for many who might have wanted or continue to seek part-time education, the Access agenda has stalled.

Regional inequalities can also disadvantage mature students who cannot afford to travel for higher education. Rural and coastal areas in the UK suffer in this regard. What is remarkable, though well known, is the fact that mature students are more likely to attend specialist providers and less selective universities than younger students. In 2020 more than a third of mature students went to universities with low average tariff scores (which often reflect lower entry requirements) whilst for younger students only 21.9 per cent did so. The elite institutions with higher tariff scores took a declining number of mature students in the period 2010- 2020 whilst FE colleges nearly doubled their intake of such students (OfS ibid: 5). The now historic working relationships between FE and HE forged in the Access growth years had laid the basis for this style of educational partnership (Farmer 2017), though the more radical and community-based versions had lost their funding and in many cases their reason to be.

There can be no doubt that mass higher education has brought with it a vast expansion of student places and courses, the sheer existence of which offer expanded study opportunities. This must lead to an improvement in life chances for many who otherwise would have been left behind. The knowledge economy and the learning society would be impossible without such developments and life in modernity incorporates the need for learning throughout life, even though this benefit is unevenly distributed. But this reality is tempered by the fact that inequality and unfairness are built in to the system. In their access and wider participation plans submitted to the Office for Students in 2020 only 40 out of 230 providers of higher education included targets related to mature students. The choices open to such students have been narrowing and they have not been prioritised by government and universities outside of certain vocational subjects (OfS ibid: 8). Part-time study has been hollowed out and so for many higher education is still not a viable option.

Across the scope of Britain's version of mass higher education we can observe that the Access agenda has not been fully met. Its purposes were much broader and deeper than that of augmenting or modifying an elite selection process. Access had the capacity and potential to benefit society as a whole by providing a model and alternative to the social engineering of the British governing elites and the self-serving supporters of meritocratic ideology. This is still needed because while 85 per cent of 17 year olds in England are in full-time education less than half of 16-18 year olds study for A–levels, the route to higher education for most. The majority of any age cohort will not attend university, at least during their late adolescent phase. Any attempts to reduce inequality must surely provide routes to further study for the future so that skills and further training can be part of an opportunity culture. However, the British Government's proposals for addressing the startling inequalities in British life in 2020s included boosting the chances of underprivileged children by creating *more* elite and super-selective state sixth forms (Guardian (b) ibid). Once again increased selection was viewed as a solution to lack of opportunity and who would deny bright sixth formers in in poor areas their right to aim high? However, the selection of an elite implies failure for some, and most probably for the majority. Selective sixth forms may in fact show that far from diminishing inequality overall, the result may be to cream off the most capable and best supported members of a cohort, leaving things for the remainder much the same. It is as if the answer to the problems of elitism and selectivity in education can be solved by creating slightly more access to that elite for a select few from disadvantaged groups. This approach leaves the majority where they were, which for elitists is preferable to removing elitism as the cause of the problem. Such an argument can be boosted by a belief in meritocracy which assures those who succeed that they have done so on merit and worth and disavows any suggestion this might be unjust or unfair.

Instead of investing in local institutions and in work-related and community-related education and in a properly funded and supported lifelong learning culture, a promise is made for a few more ladders to top universities. The wicked and genuine social issues such as social injustice, inequality and poverty, racism and unjustified discrimination against minorities are by-passed. The institutions and organisations, the curriculums, the pedagogies and the cultures of disavowel (Mercer 2017; Hall 2017: 73) within educational discourse fail too often to address such matters. The need for an Access agenda persists and the promise it offered has not been fulfilled.

## The crisis and the curriculum

This book has ostensibly been about the Access to HE movement but its sub-text has been concerned with the idea that Access was also a form of progressive curriculum, or at least pointed the way towards a challenge to university orthodoxies and hierarchies. Between the 1960s and 1980s new approaches to the curriculum were possible and some took root, especially as the new digital technologies became widely available. Inter-disciplinary studies and degrees were on offer, modular learning created new routes to degrees, student-centred and independent learning became available and in some places the authority of traditional disciplines could be challenged and new ones brought into being. Knowledge became more publicly contested as did social theory which in some respects became more closely connected to public intellectual life through studies and social thinking on race, ethnicity, identity and feminism (Seidman 1998). In the later 'neo-liberal' 1980s and 1990s, as the new managerialism and 'performativity' took over leadership thinking in universities, much of this progressivism was to be dismantled (Holmwood 2011; Scott 2021: 16) and the development of human capital and support for economic growth became the dominant functions for universities. By the late 1990s some academics were predicting the end of knowledge as we had known it in higher education (Barnett and Griffin 1997). Scholarship and research became increasingly industrialised and neither the high elitism of Oxbridge nor the mass growth of universities both in the number of institutions and their size could provide a viable alternative. Many of those who led and managed these institutions had no interest in such alternatives and indeed they were amongst its most rewarded beneficiaries as they became 'chief executives' and 'presidents' of their management and governing boards and able to ensure salaries and rewards for themselves as if they were 'captains of industry', developing and creating in their own minds the wealth of the nation and society. In reality it was of course public funding and civic society which sustained almost all university expansion and not the privatised, so-called 'free market' in education as a private consumer good. The myth was, however, pervasive and perniciously influential as the neoliberal globalized economy powered ahead in the 21$^{st}$ century.

In the third decade of the century it appears that the world-wide economic trends have stalled and the 'evil issues' of mass poverty, climate crisis, ecological destruction and the threats of pandemics and war have produced widespread disenchantment and even disillusion with democracy itself (Eatwell and Goodwin 2018). The threats deriving from populist politics and anti-democratic tendencies have brought into question many of the taken-for-granted assumptions we make about the stability and 'normality' of our societies. This is part of the crisis of our times and it presents educationalists with their own existential crisis. How has the expanded mass system of higher education responded and has critical and transformative thinking occurred which might hold out hope for solutions to the crises of our times? It seems clear that universities, which were themselves a significant part of economic growth in many countries, hold few if any potential solutions if we are to judge them from their own strategic purposes which focus on maintaining or improving their positions in the hierarchy of performances and league tables which generate their student-led cash income and research funding.

## Solutions to the crisis of higher education?

Solutions are dependent partly on how and on which questions and agendas are taken to be of central importance in defining the question to be asked. There can be no single solution to the questions which have been outlined here but perhaps there can be what have been called points of departure for future and current debate so that our focus and concerns more properly reflect the great issues of the day and the challenges which face each one of us.

We need a universal higher education system where the old divisions and hierarchies which discriminate against so many people are abolished. Such a system would, I believe, require a critical and open curriculum which focusses knowledge and scholarship and research on the existential issues facing all of us. A participation rate of around 80 per cent for a universal system would be advisable and necessary, even if our ambitions for future generations were only to match those of nations such as South Korea. The historic divisions between vocational and academic knowledge must be rescinded and arbitrary distinctions between graduate and non-graduate jobs must disappear as we respond to changing labour markets and social needs.

As a greatly expanded HE system develops the issue of fair access and greater equality of outcomes will come to the fore yet again. The mass access system produced in the UK and elsewhere between 1960 and 2020 was highly divisive and unfair. An elite of universities was consolidated whilst the mass of 'convenience' or service universities strove to differentiate themselves and gain market share of students and resources. The Access Movement had shown what might be possible with different approaches and concerns but this was eventually restricted to the margins of the university system in spite of widening participation having been the declared goal of substantial parts of the same system. Diversity was said to be one of the aims and characteristics of the mass system, but there was no consensus on what diversity should mean or how it might be achieved. The elite universities failed to challenge those inequalities which inhibited diversity. The core mission of elites was to preserve the elite and the tension between excellence and equality was not resolved in spite of brave attempts to encourage change (Kettley and Murphy 2021). The knowledge claims of universities remained rooted in traditional and conservative disciplines, with notable exceptions (Barnett 2017 ibid) and the opportunity to build on the Access tradition was refused. Only limited initiatives took place across the HE sector to develop a curricular space for reflexively engaged learning and teaching with world issues which were existentially vital to all our futures.

In the UK the question of who pays tuition fees remains to be resolved. If higher education is a public and social good, why is it not free and funded from general taxation? Most Access students did not personally pay tuition fees and there is widespread belief in the idea that ability to pay fees should play no part in determining who has access to higher education. Fees in a neoliberal system become part of the 'market' mechanism but are still hugely contentious, especially in their impact on socially disadvantaged groups where the notion of fairness has great importance. Undoubtedly we have a widened system but is it fairer? In the elite universities everywhere a disproportionately large number of students continue to be recruited from the most socially advantaged groups.

Fair and equitable access requires a thorough revision of the ways in which academic and quality standards are shaped and manipulated so that an unfair and disproportionate number of students from affluent backgrounds cannot continue to get access to the elite universities and consequently to the most desired and often most economically rewarding graduate job markets. The argument here is not about these manifestly unfair selection processes which discriminate against socially disadvantaged groups, serious though this problem is. Rather, the argument should be that the educational role of the university needs re-thinking. Such a point of departure takes us beyond the idea that we should modify a widening participation approach which re-shapes the deficient student so s/he better fits the institution and can be shaped to conform to existing conceptions of success. This is essentially the deficit model of access and widening participation and, as this book has argued, it has been found wanting in that the transformations expected of higher education could not materialize. What was missing was the required emphasis on the educational role of university education and in particular the need for critical curriculum change and reform. The purpose of a university has to contain an educational function which goes beyond measurements of quality and performance so there is an engagement with intent and concern to change life for the better. Paul Ashwin expressed this in the following way… 'the educational purpose of a university education is not to prepare someone for their role in the future workforce. Rather … (it) is to bring students into a transformational relationship to knowledge that changes their sense of who they are and what they can do in the world ' (Ashwin 2020: 3). This is also the authentic meaning of Access and widening participation as argued in this book. The Access movement gave space for the claims of popular and useful knowledge to be part of the university curriculum with intent to change both who could study in higher education and what could be studied.

the rationale of literary elitism.....

*In any period it is upon a very small minority that the discerning appreciation of art and literature depends: it is (apart from cases of the simple and familiar) only a few who are capable of unprompted first-hand judgment. They are still a small minority, though a larger one, who are capable of endorsing such judgment by genuine personal response ... The minority capable not only of appreciating Dante, Shakespeare, Baudelaire, Conrad (to take major instances) but of recognising their latest successors constitute the consciousness of the race (or a branch of it) at a given time.... Upon this minority depends our power of profiting by the finest human experience of the past; they keep alive the subtlest and most perishable parts of tradition. Upon them depend the implicit standards that order the finer living of an age...In keeping...is the language, the changing idiom, upon which fine living depends..*

"no one concerned with English teaching can fail to respond with excitement to this sort of thing"
D. Steager, 1972

F.R. Leavis, 1930

The purposes and meanings of a university education are questions which inform the search for knowledge.

# References

Ashwin, P. (2020) *Transforming University Education: A Manifesto*, London: Bloomsbury Academic.

Augur Report (2019) *Review of Post-18 Education and Funding: Advisory Panel Report,* https://assets.publishing.service.gov.uk.

Ball, S.J. (2015) 'Living the Neo-liberal University' in *European Journal of Education*, Vol 50, No 3, 2015.

Barnett, R. (1997) A Knowledge Strategy for Universities, ch 13 in Barnett, R. and Griffin, A. (eds) (1997) *The End of Knowledge in Higher Education*, London: Cassell.

Barnett, R. (2017) *The Ecological University: A Feasible Utopia,* London: Routledge.

Barnett, R. and Griffin, A. (1997) *The End of Knowledge in Higher Education*, London: Cassell.

Barr, N. (ed) (2014*) Shaping higher education: 50 years after Robbins*, London: LSE.

Bourdieu, P. (1993) *The Field of Cultural Production: Essays on Art and Literature,* Cambridge: Polity Press.

Bourdieu, P. and Passeron, J-C. (1990) *Reproduction in Education, Society and Culture,* London: Sage.

Cantwell, B., Marginson, S. and Smolentseva, A. (2018) *High-Participation Systems of Higher Education,* Oxford: Oxford University Press.

Davies, D. (2021) The Working Class Goes to College, ch1 in Davies, D. and Davies, E. (2021) *A Fair Go: Learning in Critical Times and Places,* UK: Amazon.

Davies, D. (2022) Critical Thinking for an Engaged University, ch 1 in Nyland, J. and Davies, D. (2022) *Curriculum Challenges for Universities: Agenda for Change,* Singapore: Springer Press.

Eatwell, R. and Goodwin, M. (2018) *National Populism: The Revolt Against Liberal Democracy,* UK: Pelican Books.

Farmer, J. (2017) 'Mature access: the contribution of the Access to Higher Education Diploma', *Perspectives: Policy and Practice in Higher Education*, 2017, Vol 21: 63-72, Taylor and Francis Online.

Faure, E. (1972) *Learning to Be/Education Permanente,* Report, Paris: UNESCO.

Fowler, A. and Wyke, T. (1993) *Many Arts Many Skills: The origins of The Manchester Metropolitan University*, Manchester: the Manchester Metropolitan University Press.

Guardian (a) 16 June 2022: 21 'Leading universities' offer rate declines after surge in applications', London.

Guardian (b) 17 February 2022: 15, London and UCAS (University Central Admissions Service).

Guardian (c) *Journal editorial* 21 February 2022, London.

Hall, S. (2017) *Familiar Stranger: A Life Between Two Islands*, UK: Allen Lane, see ch 4.

HESA (2022) – (Higher Education Statistics Agency)- Statistical Bulletin SB 262 January 2022, London: government agency.

Holmwood, P. (ed) (2011) *A Manifesto for the Public University*, London: Bloomsbury Academic

Hutton, W. (2022) Comment & Analysis: There's a class lottery for resources, London: The Observer 27.02.22.

Kettley, N. and Murphy, C. (2021) Augmenting excellence, promoting diversity? Preliminary design of a foundation year for the University of Cambridge, *British Journal of Sociology of Education*, 2021, Vol 42, No 3, 419-434.

Mercer, K. (ed) (2017) *Stuart Hall-The Fateful Triangle: Race, Ethnicity, Nation,* Cambridge, Mass and London: Harvard University Press, see page 21.

Nyland, J. and Davies, D. (2022) 'The New Normal After Coronavirus: Is There Anyone Here from Education?' ch 11 in Nyland, J. and Davies, D. (2022) *Curriculum Challenges for Universities: Agenda for Change*, Singapore: Springer Press.

OfS- Office for Students- (2021) Insight 9, May 2021, London: Office for Students-government agency.

Robbins Report (1963) Report of the Committee on Higher Education appointed by the Prime Minister under the Chairmanship of Lord Robbins, 1961-63, London: HMSO Cmnd 2154.

Scott, P. (2021) *Retreat or Resolution? Tackling the Crisis of Mass Higher Education,* Bristol University Press: Polity Press.

Seidman, P. (1998) *Contested Knowledge*, Oxford: Blackwell Publishers Ltd.

Smith, M. K. (1996, 2001) *Lifelong Learning, The encyclopedia of pedagogy and informal education*, https://infed.org.mobi/lifelong learning.

Todd, S. (2021) *Snakes and Ladders: The Great British Social Mobility Myth,* London: Chatto & Windus.

Watson, D. (2014) 'What happened later? The British road to mass higher education', ch 3 in Barr, N. (ed) (2014) *Shaping higher education: 50 years after Robbins,* London: LSE.

# Chapter 10

# Access and the Social Purposes of Education

## The positive lesson of Access

The Access agenda in the United Kingdom in the 1970s had no clear, unilinear and concise conception of how the structures of an unequal society interacted with the contingencies of life lived in difficult circumstances for many learners. In this sense there was no single or coherent agenda for Access. There was a multiplicity of courses and an explosion of demand and provision for learning across multiple communities and places. This diversity had elements of democratic involvement and control as local communities articulated their own demands and needs for education. Students and teachers generally gave actual and symbolic recognition to the places and communities from which they came and to which they would return to use the learning they had acquired. The life course of students became a part of the curriculum for many and Access recognised their lives and personal identities (Huttunen 2007). The rights and achievements of a mature person could be recognised through credit accumulation and the accreditation of prior learning and experience in ways and volumes simply beyond the capacity of conventional undergraduate study. The growth of self-confidence, self-respect and self-esteem accompanied the acquisition of critical literacy and the study skills needed for advanced study. The building blocks for social capital were constructed from the functional resources of family, community and the workplace as individuals demonstrated their learning achievements and entered universities in their thousands.

Wherever Access students and teachers emerged in universities the meaning of higher education was expanded because universities were forced to deal with something other than their instrumental purposes. They were confronted with demands to advance common purposes, to consider the nature of a common culture of learning and to debate what might be common capacities for citizenship. All of this required an engagement with open enquiry, scientific enterprise for public-welfare outcomes and engaged learning and teaching. Some of this no doubt derived from the socially just and liberating messages of the authors of the Robbins Report itself in 1963 (Barr 2014) and the inheritors who 50 years later asserted that universities have to be active in making sure that our collective life is democratic and socially just (Todd 2021; Scott 2021; Davies and Nyland 2022).

## Prospects opened: transformations delayed

When people begin to grasp the idea that there is a deep psychological need for belonging and recognition across communities, and that culture and education are deeply embedded in this, we may get progress towards the society we desire. In this perspective, learning and especially lifelong learning opportunities are as vital as economic investment. In many ways they are coterminous and one is only possible when the other exists alongside. Education and employment together are essential for a thriving community; they are essential to the creation of a shared public understanding of what reality is and can be. A narrow and vocationalist, skills-led approach to learning cannot address the challenges of the 2020s and beyond. Neither can future education prospects be forever rooted in elite university systems which consolidate existing class divisions and exclude the wider public from debate and participation.

There are doubts about the significance and meaning of mass higher education, however, and many are not convinced that mass higher education can promote democratic access that can challenge and overcome the hierarchies of inequality and unfairness which persist not only in Britain but across the globe. Some argue that mass expansion of HE has actually served to consolidate rather than erode social differences (Scott ibid: 12) or at the very least reconstructed them in different and less obvious but no less divisive ways. Danny Dorling of Oxford University has argued that …'We have an educational system that is designed to polarise people- one that creates an elite who can easily come to have little respect for the majority of the population; who think that they should earn extraordinarily more than everyone else; and defines the jobs of others as so low skilled that it apparently justifies many living in relative poverty' (Dorling 2018: 228).

Yet mass access has increased participation and the acquisition of knowledge and skills must lead to better outcomes than those which rest on exclusion and ignorance. The general level of education has been raised enormously through mass access and perhaps a claim can be made for a commensurate increase in civilised behaviour and progressive values, though such a claim is no doubt contestable. In Britain educational achievement is still correlated highly with social class (Savage 2015; Todd 2021 ibid), which though true, does not deny the significance of shifting social class indicators and of other demarcations such as gender and ethnicity. Nor does it counter the importance of intersectional factors when we state that the graduate class of people is still very much a middle class, even though its constituent parts are now composed of a greater variety of ethnic and social groups.

There is an argument that the highly stratified and variable graduate population which has emerged from the hierarchical higher education system has benefitted from the legitimating ideology of meritocracy. Many believe they have succeeded because they deserved to do so without ever examining the manner in which our social elites are formed and reproduced and the way in which inequalities are embedded in economic, social and cultural life. There is much to do in devising a universal literacy and a critically informed graduate class who should be aware of such social forces and ideologies. Widening participation enabled millions more people to study and acquire degree qualifications though it became clear that the graded snobberies of the elite institutions would also be refashioned for new generations to impose inequalities and to continue to privilege the wealthy. The realities are that mass participation may also have helped restrict access to the more highly stratified labour market by limiting job opportunities to only those possessing a degree. Older, apprentice-based routes to occupational progression have diminished and opportunities for non-graduates have been restricted.

Culturally it may be the case that burgeoning metropolitan universities have created new urbanised communities centred on regional and urban hubs. Wholesale districts and 'quarters' have been built in cities around student and graduate life, stressing the 'cosmopolitan' lifestyle on offer and the advanced and technologically based employment and entrepreneurial opportunities available. To a degree this type of development may have highlighted the diminishing attractions of the older, industrially-based communities and impoverished rural communities which have been starved of investment and 'left behind' as the digitally-based revolution in employment and consumption has proceeded. The corporate university has emerged as the dominant form of university at the 'hub' of regional educational activity but at the other end of the spoke, at the edge of the wheel, there may be disenfranchised communities whose colleges and campuses have been shut down in the interests of managerial efficiency (Davies 2021). The persistent and egregious problems of poverty and inequality have not disappeared from advanced capitalist societies and they continue to disfigure the lives of many for whom the promise of educational opportunity remains just that – but a promise unfulfilled (Toynbee and Walker 2020).

The promise of educational achievement has been delayed, if not denied but there exists a possible future where education, including higher education, will depend on there being a plurality of stakeholder types, instead of a single type of HE institution which monopolises everything within a managerial and controlling culture. New types of social enterprise are emerging, building on a tradition of social action and co-operativism which at its core creates social capital through creating access to people and education (Teare 2018). Innovative businesses, mutual trusts, co-operatives, public benefit companies, not-for-profit businesses are all different forms of social enterprise which support social and community relationships. They can intentionally foster and support re-enfranchising a group or place so that the well-being of a community is the measure of success instead of perhaps the financial balance sheet of an institution. Barnett (2017) has called for an 'ecological philosophy' where universities can be involved in a range of ecologies- social , cultural, political and environmental- and where intentions and values can infuse and interpenetrate learning and teaching about the world issues which face us. The thread or Leitmotif running through a critical account of university learning is therefore that real understanding comes when we grasp the relation of one thing with another: when there is a connection, understanding grows. We need to better understand the relation of university education, engagement and learning to our communities and we need to be clear about the social purposes of higher education.

## Is there transformational learning?

Many of those who commit to a working life in education argue that that we need practical and transformative learning and a positive prospect or manifesto to bring about desired change (Teare ibid; Ashwin 2020). However, when we reflect, as we must, we need theory to make the connections clear and to test ideas against experience. We may in fact need to theorise a type of universal literacy which equips learners with the critical thinking skills and tools as advocated by notable critical thinkers and theorists who adopt a sociological approach to these issues (Habermas 1972; Hall 1983, 1990; Shor 1992, 1996; Ashwin 2020). Yet there is no single theory of education nor is there a single 'framework' to explain the meaning of the different themes, issues and problematics of our times which impact on learning and community engagement in and for universities. A single and unifying narrative can surely never be the intention yet we clearly need the insights that a developed and argued conscience for higher education might deliver, if it were rooted in critical and transformative thinking. An openness to experience and critical reflection on the many different and contrasting sources of knowledge can be recognized (Smith 1996, 2001; Seidman 1998; Davies 2022). If we are to have a vital framework for access and engagement the evidence suggests there must be a diversity of topics and themes and approaches, which reflects the fact that we do not live a linear life, yet we share common origins and our destiny is likely to be shared by all as the existential issues impact on everyone.

In the search for a transformative education we must surely acknowledge the contradiction we have already encountered in this narrative of Access. Educational systems such the mass participation version we have in Britain can be both transformative *and* conservative (Desjardins 2015). They can both change our realities and prospects and prevent a new prospect from ever emerging into the light of day. It is not just education itself but the social, cultural and political contexts in which learning takes place that matter for transformations of society. This book has argued that it is through 'really useful' knowledge' that change can be brought about. Using critical thinking we can find ways of learning and teaching that are commensurate with social justice. How this happens is not a straightforward process as social science has consistently demonstrated over successive generations (Bourdieu and Passeron 1990). The different kinds of capital that exist in the world (Bourdieu 1986; Picketty 2014) and the acceleration of capitalist production as a destructive force as well as for wealth creation should alert us to the real contexts in which our education systems exist- accelerating and negative forces which threaten us with destabilisation and precarity (Noys 2014). We must understand these and grasp the alternatives through critical thinking and analysis as elements of social action.

The great global inequalities which are shaping our lives and futures are experienced and refracted through the lived experiences of people at the local level- where people actually live out their lives in communities and neighbourhoods, and where they work and learn. Yet the focus cannot simply be on the local which is necessarily narrow. Education must account for the wider public policy frameworks and the institutional frameworks in which learning is embedded (Kerslake 2019). Access was an innovation which promised some of the elements for a transformation in educational opportunity. Its limitations were demonstrated by its restricted capacity to address some deep and extensive social, cultural and economic realities which lay far beyond its reach. Its success was to shine a light on what could be achieved and to open up prospects in spite of and in recognition of the limitations. Access created new meanings and identified possibilities for those it served. Those possibilities may yet serve as a promise delayed, but not yet denied.

## Goodbye Mr Chips- the unloved mass university

Peter Scott, in his influential analysis of the crisis of mass higher education (Scott ibid: 14) refers to the 'normative coherence possessed by earlier, and smaller universities'. The Oxbridge colleges have historically provided an idealised model of the collegial university in which academics shared the democratic governance of their institutions and where endowments provided economic security over generations and students had often a familial connection with the college , again sometimes over generations. Such 'ideal types' could never probably have existed in reality but they represented an imagined and desired community of learning which could exercise a hold over its graduates throughout their lives. They provided havens for some of the great minds to develop and for scholars to educate and socialize the coming generations who would populate the elite positions in British society and its empire. They were not and did not claim to be institutions for the creation of equity and fairness, yet they did in some cases uphold values of freedom of speech and enlightened thought. They did become key centres of science and rational debate. They inculcated a deep sentimental attachment in their students who, with exceptions obviously, felt known, recognized and valued.

In the 1936 film version of Goodbye Mr Chips we see an English 'collegial' school in its conservative setting where Mr Chips, teacher of Latin, knows each student personally and probably their fathers and even grandfathers. It is an all male school (naturally) where women, when not invisible, are positioned as the carers and ultimately servants of men and where each individual is known and is humanely valued; even a German teacher who is killed in the central social/political event of the film, the First World War. Not even the unprecedented catastrophe of World War with its awful and needless deaths and industrial-scale carnage can shake the foundations of the institution and the comradeship and belonging the students feel for their alma mater. Indeed it is the school which transmits the sentiment that it is a glorious thing to serve the nation in its hour of need and if necessary to die for it. The sheer bloodiness and human butchery and its scale is obscured by the Hollywood production values used by the film, but this cannot obviate the impact that this conflict still had less than a decade after it ceased. There is little or no social ' critique' in this film but there is a statement I believe about the importance of the values of tolerance, decency, commitment, constancy and the love of learning and teaching which few popular films have ever been able to capture. This collegial spirit has lived on in the popular imagination of what an educational institution might be, though realities often proved to be different and the graduates of this imagined education have been less than beneficial as they have governed an increasingly divided and unequal society characterized by crises and wicked issues discussed in this volume (Dorling ibid; Verkaik 2019).

If the Oxbridge College was revered and possessed a normative coherence, the modern corporate university, Scott suggests, is unloved. It has emerged in the era of mass expansion of higher education and it can be argued has failed to challenge the social inequalities and hierarchies as something like near-universal participation has evolved. Elites and hierarchies dominate the higher education scene with new and old divisions and status distinctions ensuring that the middle and upper classes have benefitted most. Meritocracy is the distorting ideology of choice and the old elites still dominate the entry to the 'best' universities. The graduate job market is highly stratified, favouring the older, higher elite institutions and privileging their graduates over all others. The universities in the UK and elsewhere are increasingly corporate, financially complex and driven by national government policy rather than academic communities. The question of what universities are actually *for* has been raised again (Brink 2018; Ashwin ibid; Scott ibid) and who they serve so that there is a gathering crisis of higher education in the third decade of the 21st century which replicates in part and extends the crisis of learning and knowledge experienced at the start of the new millennium by those who thought modernity, vocational utilitarianism and postmodernism might threaten the basis of university thinking itself (Barnett and Griffin 1997).

# References

Ashwin, P. (2020) *Transforming University Education: A Manifesto*, London: Bloomsbury Academic.

Barnett, R. (2017) *The Ecological University: A Feasible Utopia*, London: Routledge.

Barnett, R. and Griffin, A. (1997) *The End of Knowledge in Higher Education*, London: Cassell.

Barr, N. (ed) (2014*) Shaping higher education: 50 years after Robbins*, London: LSE.

Bourdieu, P. (1986) 'Forms of Capital' in Richardson, J. (ed) *Handbook of Theory and Research for the Sociology of Education* (pp 241-258), Westport, CT: Greenwood.

Bourdieu, P. and Passeron, J-C. (1990) *Reproduction in Education, Society and Culture,* London: Sage.

Brink, C. (2018) *The Soul of a University: Why Excellence is Not Enough*, Bristol: Policy Press.

Davies, D. (2021) We once built a University in Buxton, ch 8 in Davies, D. and Davies, E. (2021) *A Fair Go: Learning in Critical Times and Places*, Amazon pubs.

Davies, D. (2022) Critical Thinking for an Engaged University, ch 1 in Nyland, J. and Davies, D. (2022) *Curriculum Challenges for Universities: Agenda for Change,* Singapore: Springer Press.

Davies, D. and Nyland, J. (2022) Freedom through education: a promise postponed, ch 5 in Nyland, J. and Davies D. (2022*) Engagement Matters: Curriculum Challenges for Universities,* Drayton North, Queensland: Engagement Australia Ltd.

Desjardins, R. (2015) 'Education and Social Transformation', *European Journal of Education,* Vol 50, No 3, 2015.

Dorling, D. (2018) *Peak Inequality: Britain's Ticking Time Bomb*, University of Bristol: Policy Press.

Habermas, J. (1972) *Knowledge and Human Interests,* London: Heinemann.

Hall, S. (1983) Education in crisis, part one: The politics of education, Wolpe, AM. and Donald, J. ( eds) *Is there anyone here from education?* London: Pluto Press.

Hall, S. (1990) Cultural identity and diaspora, in Rutherford, J. (ed) *Identity, community, culture, difference,* London: Lawrence & Wishart.

Huttunen, R. (2007) 'Critical adult education and the political-philosophical debate between Nancy Fraser and Alex Honneth', *Education Theory*, 57 (4) 423-433.

Kerslake Report( 2019) *Truly Civic: Strengthening the Connection between Universities and their Places*, Final Report of the UPP Foundation Civic University Commission, London: UPP Foundation.

Noys, B. (2014) *Malign Velocities: Accelerationism and Capitalism*, Winchester UK/Washington USA: Zero Books.

Nyland, J. and Davies, D. (2022) 'The New Normal After Coronavirus: Is There Anyone Here from Education?' ch 11 in Nyland, J. and Davies, D. (2022) *Curriculum Challenges for Universities: Agenda for Change*, Singapore: Springer Press.

Picketty, T. (2014) *Capital in the 21st Century*, Cambridge, Mass/London, England: The Belknap Press of Harvard University.

Savage, M. et al (2015*) Social Class in the 21st Century*, UK: Pelican/Penguin Books.

Scott, P. (2021) *Retreat or Resolution? Tackling the Crisis of Mass Higher Education,* Bristol University Press: Polity Press.

Seidman, P. (1998) *Contested Knowledge*, Oxford: Blackwell Publishers Ltd.

Shor, I. (1992) *Empowering Education: Critical Teaching for Social Change*, Chicago: University of Chicago Press.

Shor, I. (1996) *When Students Have Power: Negotiating Authority in a Critical Pedagogy*, Chicago: University of Chicago Press.

Smith, M.K. (1996, 2001) *Lifelong Learning, The encyclopedia of pedagogy and informal education*, https://infed.org.mobi/lifelong learning.

Teare, R. (2018) *Lifelong Action Learning: A journey of discovery and celebration at work and in the community*, UK: Amazon.

Todd, S. (2021) *Snakes and Ladders: The Great British Social Mobility Myth,* London: Chatto & Windus.

Toynbee, P. and Walker, D. (2020) *The Lost decade 2010-2020 and What Lies Ahead for Britain,* London: Guardian Books.

Verkaik, R. (2019) *Posh Boys: How English Public Schools Ruin Britain*, London: Oneworld Publications Ltd.

# Getting to the top of the distant peaks of Access

Cartoon by Sarah Ormrod- Access and accreditation at the University
of Cambridge (see Credit Where It's Due 1995)

# Conclusion

## Really useful knowledge in a changing world

Because the higher education system is so large and diverse and because many of its institutions have been transformed into a 'multiversities' with myriad functions and vast and complex operations, some of which involve extensive corporate property empires and global digital presences across continents, its core purposes are hard to identify This 'system' is now an infinitely complex network and web of human activity and endeavour and is part of the global knowledge economy as well as being a cultural phenomenon which impacts on every technologically advanced economic community. There is no single purpose that binds different universities to a commonly shared vision and thus there can be no single solution to the problems encountered even in a single nation state (with its different national identities) such as the United Kingdom. In spite of this, many if not all universities view themselves as having 'civic responsibilities' and many suggest they are committed to serving their local and regional communities (Kerslake 2019). In general the notion of 'engagement' has been predominant and university engagement, both with civic concerns and the welfare and progress of students, has become a significant and diverse enterprise in its own right in many different cultures and societies (Nyland 2017, 2019; Bell 2019; Advance HE 2022; TASO 2022).

There is, however, another dimension we should consider; that universities are a part of what we know and understand as a 'free society'. A democratic and open society enables freedom of thought and its expression to flourish. Dissent and differences of view and the clash of values are part of the expected discourse and dialogue of a free society. The freedom to teach and publish controversial opinions and scholarship carries a high value for a civilized society. These values and the practices that sustain them are not 'private goods' to be bought and sold in a market place; they are not part of a corporate learning experience designed to enhance profitability and enterprise. A university education should allow people to change themselves if they so wish and to change the world around themselves and in doing so facilitate the possibility of authentic transformations. It is the acquisition of knowledge, really useful knowledge, which makes this possible. Universities remain as keystones within the free and democratic societies and must recreate and renew this in each generation of students so that a university education is an education for democratic life and engagement (Davies 2022). Yet we live in a world where realities often speak another language.

## We live in a world where...

We live in a world dangerously divided along racial, ethnic, class, religious and generational lines (Cox et al 2022). We live in an increasingly divisive society where communities live separate and distinctive lives. We live in a world where democracy is failing its greatest tests; where liberal democratic values are assaulted by racism and where authoritarian regimes suppress dissent and persecute their opponents. We live in a world where war is used to annihilate innocent people and drive them from their homes. We live in a world where we cannot ignore the growing gaps in wealth and the regional disparities which impoverish so many. We live in a world in which change is perhaps the only constant and where modern capitalism injects accelerating insecurity and uncertainty into many lives (Noys 2014). We live also in a world where traditionally liberal democracies placed value on individual freedom and choice and there was a widespread belief that education was the engine of change and of social mobility and progress. Yet we live in a world where neoliberalism has posed great threats to our democratic values and way of life (Brown 2019).

These wicked issues and the seminal challenges they present are the actual real-life context in which the demand for mass higher education has evolved. The creation of the Access movement was part of a process which, it has been argued, paradoxically held out the hope for social change through individual and collective struggle for knowledge and learning, yet which also re-asserted the unequal and divisive links between social and economic capital, educational connection and social class. These links in the past had suppressed the legitimate social democratic demands of working people for generations and continued to support the distinctions between university educated elites and everyone else in modern times. Mass higher education changed the game but new conventions and rules were invented to exclude those who had a deficit of wealth and 'culture'. A hierarchy of elites and elite institutions emerged to monopolise the opportunities and places on the ladder of opportunity.

A university education was and is still a powerful cultural symbol of aspiration and opportunity. Access opened up the possibility of change and a better life for the excluded and it offered us a view of a more healthy democratic future which is inseparable from an open and democratic education system. This was a promise which must work for everyone and belongs to all. The primary purpose of a university education is educative. Beyond the provision of access to the labour market and the satisfying of the need for a certain type and volume of graduate skills, all of which have an importance, and beyond the need to simply raise the education levels of populations who have been denied access to learning, there exist economic, social and psychological forces which shape our lives and futures. These forces are now *existential* in that our planetary future can only be assured if we adapt and change our behaviour to combat world-wide social inequity, poverty, climate change, ecological destruction and the threat of nuclear annihilation. This is surely the truly educative role of universities and models are needed to bring about the changes in thinking which this demands of us. Perhaps the Access movement and the waves of widening participation of which it was a part can be an indicator of the kind of new learning that will be needed.

## Lessons learned for a future postponed- not denied

There is an argument that globalisation and the marketisation of so much of our social life has somehow run its course. The Covid-19 pandemic which broke out in 2019 has often been cited as signalling the end of an era and the need for a 'new normal' (Nyland and Davies 2022). This came at the end of a period in which austerity was the major public policy driving down expenditure and investment in public services of all kinds including net per capita expenditure on education and health, allied to an explosion of market-driven and debt-based consumption. The net effect was to create new forms of poverty and deprivation so that differences in life chances between the rich and poor are virtually as great as they were one hundred years ago. This disfigures British society and makes inequality an abiding and familiar feature of our lives (Toynbee and Walker 2020). What is to come next, it is said, must be better and fairer than what went before. A new sense of common purpose can perhaps be generated which can re-instate a more socially just society in which poverty, deprivation and social exclusion can be challenged and overcome. The inequalities are unsustainable for the future. A sense of something needing to be done to atone for the failures of the last decade is palpable in the wider society. The lessons learned from the first decades of the 21st century and the last decade of the 20th century must surely equip us with a greater understanding of how education is both the solution to our problems yet co-existentially part of the problem as long as massive and persistent inequalities exist. The radical relevance of Access remains on the agenda since it points the way to potential solutions.

These could include recognition of the need for a universal higher education system where old and new divisions and hierarchies which discriminate against so many people are abolished. We need a critical curriculum which focusses knowledge on the key existential issues; a curriculum which is based on forms of academic knowledge which allow true access to opportunity for all not the privileged elite. Really useful knowledge for the majority is required. It is clear that, for example, 80 per cent plus participation is advisable and necessary, if only to catch up with the leading nations in post-school education. We need a curriculum which does not discriminate between vocational and academic knowledge because these divisions are disappearing as the nature of work and labour markets themselves change. We need a curriculum which acknowledges and recognises the need for dialogue and discovery wherever it is found- in schools and universities, and in communities and workplaces where education can help transform lives and futures and where even the poorest can have inclusive access for structured, recognised lifelong learning (Teare 2018).

## Radical change to overcome elitism

The story of Access, this book has suggested, is the story of a struggle for educational opportunity and against disadvantage whilst simultaneously charting the growth of a socially stratified education system. This system ensures that those born to privilege and wealth are educated into the highest earning and status jobs whilst at the same time holding back those born to parents who had no such opportunities. Just some 7 per cent of children attend private schools in Britain but make up almost one in three undergraduates at the country's most prestigious universities (Observer 2022). The ranks of the higher civil service, the judiciary, diplomats and the senior editors in the media as well as those in cabinet levels of government are dominated by this privately educated elite. This result is not a product of their ability but of the vast resources that are invested in their education and the social and cultural capital created and used to secure their futures.

There are social harms and dysfunctions as a result, which shut out other, more able young people who do not possess these advantages. The legitimacy of this system is upheld by a widespread belief that Britain is a meritocratic society where on the whole people are fairly rewarded for their talent and efforts. This is plainly not the case. Even where meritocracy can be shown to be working, it does not produce equality and fairness. What characterises the education system is tangible inequality. It seems clear that wherever it takes place, selective schooling privileges children from more advantaged backgrounds. At the university level, it is clear that a ridiculously stratified system has emerged. The institution a young person attends stands proxy for their employment potential and prospects, rather than the quality of degree they have earned. Oxford and Cambridge represent the pinnacle of this self-serving and unaccountable system. Only a radical change to overcome this elitism is likely to produce benefits for everyone. The Access agenda represents one possible point of departure for this change and in the face of a conservative culture retains its radical charge and potential for the future.

## Finding meanings

There is something vital in looking beyond appearances so we can get to understand the real and *essential meanings* of things. Things are not always what they seem at first sight and the connections and the *relation of things* is crucial. Aubrey Black, the moving spirit, leader and activist for the Manchester Open College taught me English as an 11 year old at Ducie High School, Manchester and guided those of us who stayed the course through A Level English Literature seven years later (where the first famous Hollywood actor to play Mr Chips on film, Robert Donat, was also a pupil). We learned to study critically and creatively the works of John Donne, Dryden, Wordsworth, Shakespeare and the marvelous Emily Bronte and make the connections between the imagination and critical social issues. Dialogue and critique was always encouraged. The best of teachers always make these connections clearer and show us a way beyond our taken-for-granted knowledge and sometimes our illusions. If our thinking is clear and reflexively critical, our values and commitments can be true and authentic and then education can deliver its promise of transformational thinking and social progress. Authentic education builds a bond of reciprocal obligations and benefits and these can be built from new if we build universities and colleges committed to a better social result and a fairer society.

The Access movement gave us insight into some of these vital issues by constructing courses and learning experiences which addressed them. In doing so the creators of learning and the learners themselves showed us a possibility for doing things differently and this possibility remains as a legacy to be used for good. Access was both real and an idea; the two aspects intersected each other. There were (are) actual courses with students and there were values and engagements with ideas that were radical and critical. The curriculum of Access was based in reason which was seeking spaces to refocus the way universities saw their students and might see their future students, who would be different. Reflexively engaged, we have no viable alternative but to learn from our past. Access showed us that we should favour changing the world around us, rather than adapting to it. Perhaps this is the essential and true meaning of Access?

In finding meanings for Access and for learning in its generic significance for humankind, we cannot ignore the fact that the demands of the human animal in the third decade of the 21$^{st}$ century are driving mass extinction on the planet. The biosphere is unable to absorb greenhouse gasses, there is an ecological disaster threatening much of the world's population as the planet becomes less inhabitable and climate change destroys our capacity to exist. There are limits to growth and technological invention may not save us from ecological collapse and the resource wars and conflicts that will inevitably result, if change does not come. These are wicked issues that dwarf all previous social problems in their scale, their reach and severity. Human communities must now adopt environmental stability as the key priority for human survival and this is the primary learning agenda for ALL. Co-ordination and co-operation of human energy and resources, which is educational and social in its deepest meaning, is surely the reason why we must learn and continue to learn.

# References

Advance HE (2022) *Access, retention, attainment: an integrative review of demonstrable impact on student outcomes*, UK, York: AdvanceHE.

Bell, S. (2019) Re-imagining the university as an anchor institution, in *Transform: The Journal of Engaged Scholarship*, No 1, 2019, publ. Queensland: Engagement Australia.

Brown, W. (2019) *In the Ruins of Neoliberalism: The Rise of Antidemocratic Politics in the West,* New York/Chichester, West Sussex: Columbia University Press.

Cox, B., Goodhart, D., Kaufman, E. and Webber, R. (2022) *Whatever happened to integration?* Westminster, London: Policy Exchange.

Davies, D. (2022) Critical Thinking for an Engaged University, ch 1 in Nyland, J. and Davies, D. (2022) *Curriculum Challenges for Universities: Agenda for Change,* Singapore: Springer Press.

Kerslake Report (2019) *Truly Civic: Strengthening the Connection between Universities and their Places*, Final Report of the UPP Foundation Civic University Commission, London: UPP Foundation.

Noys, B. (2014) *Malign Velocities: Accelerationism and Capitalism*, Winchester UK/Washington USA: Zero Books.

Nyland, J. (2017) Re-imagining the Engaged University, published in *Transform-The Journal of Engaged Scholarship,* No 2, 2017, Queensland: Engagement Australia.

Nyland, J. (2019) The university's social and civic role: A way forward for an engaged university? in *Transform: The Journal of Engaged Scholarship,* No 1, 2019, Queensland: Engagement Australia.

Nyland, J. and Davies, D. (2022) 'The New Normal After Coronavirus: Is There Anyone Here From Education?' ch 11 in Nyland, J. and Davies, D. (2022) *Curriculum Challenges for Universities: Agenda for Change*, Singapore: Springer Press.

Observer (2022) 'Our schools need radical change to overcome elitism', 04.12.2022, London.

TASO (Transforming Access and Student Outcomes in Higher Education) (2022) London: TASO- https://taso.org.uk

Teare, R. (2018) *Lifelong Action Learning: A journey of discovery and celebration at work and in the community*, UK: Amazon.

Toynbee, P. and Walker, D. (2020) *The Lost decade 2010-2020 and What Lies Ahead for Britain,* London: Guardian Books.

Printed in Great Britain by Amazon

Acknowledgements are due to Engagement Australia Ltd, Queensland, Australia for photographs from *Engagement Matters: Curriculum Challenges for Universities,* 2020, (pp 34, 54,116 and 136)- Authors and editors: James Nyland and David Davies; and to Judy Keiner for the illustration on page 236.

Printed in Great Britain
by Amazon

22447635R00152